W9-CKI-627

DATE DUE

Allegories of War

Allegories of War

*Language and Violence in
Old English Poetry*

John P. Hermann

Ann Arbor
THE UNIVERSITY OF MICHIGAN PRESS

Copyright © by The University of Michigan 1989
All rights reserved
Published in the United States of America by
The University of Michigan Press
Manufactured in the United States of America

1992 1991 1990 1989   4 3 2 1

Library of Congress Cataloging-in-Publication Data

Hermann, John P., 1947–
  Allegories of war : language and violence in Old English poetry /
John P. Hermann.
    p.   cm.
  Includes bibliographical references.
  ISBN 0-472-10147-1 (alk. paper)
  1. English poetry—Old English, ca. 450–1100—History and
criticism.   2. Christian poetry, English (Old)—History and
criticism.   3. Prudentius, b. 348. Psychomachia.   4. Spiritual life
in literature.   5. Good and evil in literature.   6. Violence in
literature.   7. Battles in literature.   8. War in literature.
9. Allegory.   I. Title.
PR203.H47   1989
821'.1009353—dc20   89-39966
                                                                    CIP

Preface

Allegories of War was written over a fifteen-year period. It began as a dissertation at the University of Illinois in 1973, later revised as a series of articles appearing in *American Benedictine Review, Annuale Mediaevale, Papers on Language and Literature,* and *Philological Quarterly.* More scholarly than critical, these early pieces attempted to reflect the workings of the text, but not to account for its allegorical processes. *Allegories of War* is, in part, an autocritique: its arguments undercut the assertions, methods, and conclusions of my earlier scholarship. As a result, some fellow Anglo-Saxonists have accused me of lusting after strange gods. But others have welcomed my attempts at organizing a conjuncture between critical theory and the powerful and entrenched philological tradition that has nurtured—and stunted—Old English studies over the last two decades.

I first glimpsed the direction my subsequent work in Old English studies would have to take in 1978 while editing a volume of studies in literary iconography. Composing the introduction to *Signs and Symbols in Chaucer's Poetry* led me to investigate semiotics, structuralism, and post-structuralism, and this in turn led to disturbing questions about the theoretical bases of Exegetics and iconography. I tried to think through the problems involved in attempts to limit the signifier to a monovalent signified, especially when such attempts relied on the authority of paraliterary texts. While exploring the limits of iconographic practice, I came across Jacques Derrida's critique of the sign, and was nonplussed. For ten years, as a graduate student and assistant professor, I had looked upon literary criticism from what I took to be the superior standpoint of philological tradition: I could determine the literary and historical context of a work through the study of sources, analogues, topoi, iconography, and biblical exegesis, and in so doing contribute to knowledge. But the literary criticism of medieval texts seemed to be full of the merely anachronistic opinions of twentieth-century writers. Like most medievalists, my theoretical speculation was conservative, devoted to resisting assaults on the presuppositions of the field. I had been working within foundationalist limits, and reacted defensively to the antifoundationalist tendency in the strange theory my colleagues in English and French departments had taken up.[1] Although I did not recognize it at the time, my practice as an Anglo-Saxonist had already determined my allegiances in the recurrent conflict between literary history and theory that has characterized English studies since the late nineteenth century, when the power of Classical studies was contested by the study (and invention) of a classical literature of the English nation.

While reading Nietzsche's *The Use and Abuse of History*, I first realized that my instinctive historicism was itself worthy of reflection, and that my attempts to mirror the past had been ignoring the role of the present. Nietzsche helped me understand that all history is contemporary.[2] I investigated the historical and social forces that affected the student of medievalia,[3] and I began to read literary studies in terms of the institutionalized limits within which Anglo-Saxonists were operating. At this time I discovered the work of Reginald Horsman and Stanley Hauer on the history of Anglo-Saxon study in the United States.[4] And I learned of Daniel Calder's plea for openness to theory at the 1982 Modern Language Association meeting.[5] I wanted to find out why Old English was defended and taught, why its study had taken the forms it did, why the field had once flourished, and why it was now in decline.

---

1. "Foundationalist" is a term taken from Stanley Fish, "Pragmatism and Literary Theory, I: Consequences," *Critical Inquiry* 11 (1985): 433–58.
2. Friedrich Nietzsche, *The Use and Abuse of History*, trans. Adrian Collins (New York, 1949).
3. Those interested in pursuing this line of inquiry should consult the work of Hayden White, *Metahistory: The Historical Imagination in Nineteenth-Century Europe* (Baltimore, 1973); Lee Patterson, *Negotiating the Past: The Historical Understanding of Medieval Literature* (Madison, 1987); and Allen J. Frantzen and Charles L. Venegoni, "The Desire for Origins: An Archaeology of Anglo-Saxon Studies," *Style* 20 (1986): 142–56.
4. Reginald Horsman, *Race and Manifest Destiny: The Origins of American Racial Anglo-Saxonism* (Cambridge, Mass., 1981); Stanley R. Hauer, "Thomas Jefferson and the Anglo-Saxon Language," *PMLA* 98 (1983): 879–98.
5. Daniel Calder, "The Isolation of Old English Studies: Past, Present, and Future," paper presented at the Modern Language Association meeting, Los Angeles, 1982.

E. G. Stanley's *The Search for Anglo-Saxon Paganism* proved quite helpful in answering these questions.[6]

I studied Derrida intensively in a faculty theory colloquium that began in 1981 and still meets regularly. My readings in deconstruction were accompanied by a growing interest in the nature of metaphor in Freud, Marx, and the Bible. My first attempt at a post-structuralist reading of an Old English literary work focused on *Juliana*. A revised version appears in *Allegories of War*, which is a systematic development of the critical model broached in that piece.

Writing about Old English poetry in terms of recent developments in critical theory has often made me feel as if I were treading *enge anpaðas, uncuþ gelad*. I would like to thank all those who helped me along the way, especially Jack Campbell, Joe Trahern, Tom Cable, Jim Marchand, John Hurt Fisher, Joe Hornsby, Tom Hill, Charlie Wright, and Matthew Marino, who contributed ideas about Anglo-Saxon literature; members past and present of the Critical Theory Group at the University of Alabama, especially Greg de Rocher, Liz Meese, Richard Rand, Greg Jay, Bill Ulmer, and David Miller; the students in my Old English and Critical Theory courses at the University of Alabama; my department chair, Claudia Johnson, who generously provided me with word processing equipment and released time; the Research Grants Committee of the University of Alabama, which supported this project at an early stage; Sara Davis of the College of Arts and Sciences and Bill Macmillan of the Graduate School, who offered help with manuscript preparation; and LeAnn Fields and Christina Milton of the University of Michigan Press, whose editorial ministrations have been intelligent and tactful. Finally, I would like to acknowledge the following journals, which have allowed me to make use of work that previously appeared in their pages: *American Benedictine Review* and *Neuphilologische Mitteilungen* (chap. 1), *Annuale Mediaevale* and *English Language Notes* (chap. 2), *Papers on Language and Literature* (chap. 4), *Texas Studies in Literature and Language* (chap. 6), and *Philological Quarterly* (chap. 7).

---

6. E. G. Stanley, *The Search for Anglo-Saxon Paganism* (Cambridge, 1975).

Contents

Introduction

Allegories of War explores the relationship between violence and spirituality in Old English poetry. It examines the theme of spiritual warfare by focusing on the rhetorical borders separating good from evil, *Ecclesia* (Church) from *Diabolus* (Devil), soul from body, and spirit from letter. Attention to such fundamental oppositions can help readers make sense of the ways Old English Christian texts are constructed, and can tell us much about the construction of psyche and society in Anglo-Saxon England as well.

The book is organized about two axes—one formal, the other critical. First, a formal partition of the literature of spiritual warfare divides it into the allegorical modes of personification and exegetical allegory, which are treated in Parts 1 and 2 respectively. Second, a variety of critical and metacritical approaches to the study of Old English literature—from philology, through the old New Criticism and typological readings, to what has come to be known as "critical theory"—intersect with this formal axis. The reader can look forward to a study of the two allegorical modes of spiritual warfare as well as a critique of traditional strategies for reading Old English poetry.

Part 1 of *Allegories of War* treats the psychomachia theme—that is, the representation of the life of the spirit as a battle. Chapter 1, "Psychomachia Allegory," discusses historical, psychological, and social aspects of personification allegory as an artistic mode for representing inner conflict in Old English poetry. A survey of the Prudentian and Cassianic traditions of spiritual combat leads to consideration of their reception in Anglo-Saxon England. Chapter 2, "Recurrent Motifs of Spiritual Warfare," offers microreadings of major elements in this personification allegory of war. It sets the stage for the argument that the Old English representation of spiritual life as a violent conflict is complicitous with social violence. These two chapters introduce the fundamental theoretical preoccupations developed in the course of the book.

Part 1 offers backgrounds to the literary and theoretical argumentation in Part 2, which shifts its focus from personification allegory to the allegoresis of war—that is, to allegory as a hermeneutic mode for uncovering the spiritual significance of battle narratives.[1] It also shifts critical strategies, especially those based upon traditional reflection of the language of the text. Allegorical commentaries have left their traces on the composition of Old English poems, according to Exegetics, one of the most influential strains of criticism in medieval studies. Exegetical critics have made it possible to conceptualize the allegoresis of war, a well-defined field for the analysis of psychosocial violence in Old English literature.

Readers who are more interested in this book's negotiations with Derridean, Lacanian, and Marxian theory may find Part 1 too traditional. These chapters have been designed to prepare the way for readings of *Exodus, Elene, Andreas, Juliana,* and *Judith.* Yet even in Part 2, such readers will find the preliminary scholarly treatment of allegorical dimensions of these poems to be both philological and historical. It is the deconstructive, psychological, and sociological approaches taken to allegorical practice in these poems—and to the tradition of modern commentary grown up around them—that open alternatives to traditional ways of interpreting Old English poetry and culture. In other words, *Allegories of War* consists in a discussion of the reception of psychomachia traditions in England; a gradual encounter with critical approaches to the recurrent motifs of spiritual warfare; and a set of Derridean, Marxian, and Lacanian arguments about the construction of society and psyche in Anglo-Saxon England.

A brief mise-en-scène of the latter chapters may prove helpful. Chapter 3 examines the Exegetical claim that *Exodus* shows traces of an allegorical conflict between *Ecclesia* and *Diabolus.* Exegetics, in league with New Criticism, has informed the reading of the poem in numerous ways, allowing us to make sense of notorious cruces like the Red Sea crossing. After a survey of the allegoresis of war in *Exodus,* however, a dialectical reversal takes place: the chapter goes on to explore the limits of the reading techniques upon which it had relied. Particular attention

---

1. For an explanation of the four allegorical levels, see the Introduction to Pt. 2.

is given to the Exegetical critic's positioning as a reader, especially in terms of the allegorical sublation of worldly power into spiritual. Sublation, one of those concepts central to the book that may prove difficult for the reader, is the translation I have chosen for Hegel's *Aufhebung*: in sublation, one concept subsumes another by both negating and conserving it.[2] The counter-reading advanced in the remainder of the chapter examines historical effects in *Exodus* that are resistant to allegorical sublation. This argument is deconstructive—meaning, in a local sense, that the hierarchical opposition between *Ecclesia* and *Diabolus* is scrutinized in order to determine whether the margin dividing these concepts is as firm as it might appear. The text already embodies this work of deconstruction to the extent that it displays a less than complete subsumption of worldly power into spiritual.

In chapter 4, Exegetics and New Criticism are cast as disabling enablers of reading. Source study of *Elene* highlights the importance of the conflict of the *milites Dei* with *Diabolus*; this allegorical opposition is then submitted to a deconstructive reading that focuses on textual resistance to the harmonious sublation of *Synagoga* in *Ecclesia*. The remainder of the argument, a critical examination of influential interpretations of the poem, seeks to historicize the poetics of terror in *Elene*.

The pattern established in the preceding chapters is disrupted in chapter 5, largely because of the bizarre ideological affiliations of hagiographic practice in *Andreas*. A deconstructive reading broached at the outset of the chapter focuses on the construction of the category of the foreigner, as well as homologies between cannibalism and the sublated cannibalism of the Eucharist. Later in the chapter, attention is given to the politics of cultural change and ideological violence in the early Middle Ages.

Chapter 6 argues that *Juliana* conspicuously defers engagement with the very typological elements that Exegetics has sought to foreground. Deconstruction of the categories of Church/State, saint/devil, and soul/body in the poem leads to consideration of social and psychological context, particularly the extent to which internal necessities of monasticism leave their traces on textual operations.

Chapter 7 will disturb some readers, I expect, but *Judith* itself is a disturbing poem. An examination of the conflict of allegorical and tropological levels in the work leads to the consideration of psy-

---

2. A fuller definition of the term appears in the Introduction to Pt. 2.

chopolitics in the early Middle Ages. The Lacanian argument concluding this chapter is followed by an Afterword that takes up the role of theory in Anglo-Saxon studies.

This book's claim to significance can be simply stated: in the course of engaging the Old English allegories of war, it attempts to deflect the force of reigning models for the criticism of Old English literature. It does so by gradually unfolding its theoretical approaches, in order to appeal to Anglo-Saxonists unfamiliar with them. Those who wish to take a more precipitous approach may want to turn ahead to the Afterword, although the value of its claims depends upon the shape of the argument preceding it. *Allegories of War* has been designed as a tactical intervention within a discipline that typically downgrades mere interpretation in favor of new facts and hard data. Hence, the double organization of the work, allowing the modal pattern to be crossed by critical approaches ranging from traditional philological negotiations, to New Criticism, to Exegetics—and eventually to post-structuralist registers that will seem rather strange to many Anglo-Saxonists. But for many of us the traditional is not always a source of consolation, nor is the strange always cause for discomfiture.

Part 1
Personification Allegory

This first part of *Allegories of War* is concerned with the varieties of psychomachia in Old English—that is, with literature based on the premise of personified abstractions in combat. Chapter 1, Psychomachia Allegory, examines the Anglo-Saxon reception of Prudentian and Cassianic traditions of spiritual combat, tracing their influence on the *Vita Oswaldi*, Aldhelm's *De Virginitate*, Alcuin's *Liber de Virtutibus et Vitiis*, Aelfric's *Homily on Midlent Sunday*, and *Solomon and Saturn*. Chapter 2, Recurrent Motifs of Spiritual Warfare, focuses on the fragmentary personification allegory of war most commonly found in Old English poetry: for example, the motifs of the *hostis antiquus*, the arrows of the devil, and the soul as a besieged fortress. The varieties of psychomachia examined in Part 1 are treated from a predominantly philological perspective, although the reader will also find discussions of important psychological and sociological aspects of spiritual violence. These discussions are in the nature of brief sketches, however, in order to avoid interrupting a broad overview of psychomachia in Old English.

If Part 1 tends to read spiritual warfare from the standpoint of critical reflection, Part 2 tends to subvert just such an approach. Spiritual violence, the argument runs, is complicitous with social violence, but this complicity can be read from the right or the left. *Allegories of War* tries to do both. And in that order.

Chapter 1

Psychomachia Allegory

As E. G. Stanley has pointed out, Old English scholarship traditionally "exalts whatever in the Germanic literature of the Dark Ages is primitive (that is, pagan), and belittles or even fails to understand whatever in it is civilized, learned, and cosmopolitan (that is, inspired by Christianity)."[1] In part, this bias can be traced to the Romantic origins of modern Anglo-Saxon scholarship. The resurgence of German nationalism following the defeat of Prussia at Jena in 1806 led scholars to search the pagan, Germanic past for inspiration. The impetus for modern Anglo-Saxon studies, then, comes from the need to reappropriate the past for specific political and social objectives. Perhaps because this origin remains influential, Old English scholarship has traditionally shown more interest in literal descriptions of battle than in the Christian allegorical conflict that occurs so frequently. But the varieties of psychomachia in Old English are also deserving of study.

By psychomachia, I mean an allegorical description of battle like the spiritual warfare St. Paul writes about in Ephesians:

Induite vos armaturam Dei, ut possitis stare adversus insidias diaboli: quoniam non est nobis colluctatio adversus carnem et sanguinem: sed adversus principes, et potestates, adversus mundi rectores tenebrarum harum, contra spiritualia nequitiae, in caelestibus. Propterea accipite armaturam Dei, ut possitis resistere in die malo, et in omnibus perfecti stare. State ergo succincti lumbos vestros in veritate, et induti loricam iustitiae, et calceati pedes in praeparatione Evangelii pacis: in omnibus sumentes scutum fidei, in quo possitis omnia tela nequissimi ignea extinguere: et galeam salutis assumite: et gladium spiritus (quod est verbum Dei) . . . .

---

1. Stanley, *The Search for Anglo-Saxon Paganism* (Cambridge, 1975), 1.

[Put on the armor of God, so you may be able to withstand the deceits of the devil. For our struggle is not against flesh and blood, but against principalities and powers, against rulers of the world of darkness, against spirits of wickedness in high places. Therefore, put on the armor of God, so you can remain firm in the evil day, and stand perfect in all things. Stand, therefore, your loins girded with truth, wearing the breastplate of justice, your feet shod in the readiness of the gospel of peace, always using the shield of faith, so you may be able to resist all the fiery darts of the evil one. Wear the helmet of salvation, and the sword of the spirit (which is the word of God). . . .][2]

The military apparel of Roman legionaries is here symbolically transformed into spiritual qualities associated with the fight of the *miles Christi* (soldier of Christ) against sin and temptation. An Anglo-Saxon, even one who had pored over Isidore's *Etymologies*, might not have been familiar with all the military trappings of Empire, but the armor of God, the breastplate of righteousness, the helmet of salvation, and the sword of the spirit would still have made sense. There are, however, important differences between spiritual militancy at the beginning and end of the first millennium, and this book attempts to inaugurate the process of historicizing allegories of war. For present purposes, it is enough to notice Paul's strategy of re-presentation of the self figurally, distancing it in order to make its processes more accessible. The detour of such metaphorical structures is a linguistic act of spiritual construction as well as one of psychic definition.

The most valuable background to the subtleties of spiritual conflict in Old English poetry is the *Psychomachia* of Prudentius, which elaborates Paul's premise at great length. The first poem of its kind, it served as the model for the personification allegory of war, influencing painting, sculpture, and literature throughout the Middle Ages. Personifying virtues and vices was not original with Prudentius, and the idea of the life of the soul as a warfare was well established before he took it up. But credit for combining these two notions into a full-fledged allegorical epic must go to the fourth-century Spaniard.

The *Psychomachia* treats the struggle of virtues and vices for the possession of the human soul in an especially violent way. If the death of

---

2. Eph. 6.11–17. Unless otherwise indicated, all translations are my own. All references to the Bible, unless otherwise indicated, are to the *Biblia Sacra iuxta Vulgatem Clementinam*, ed. R. P. Alberto Colunga and Laurentio Turrado (Madrid, 1953). But quotations from this convenient edition of the Vulgate have been checked against Pierre Sabatier, ed., *Bibliorum Sacrorum Latinae Versiones Antiquae*, 3 vols. (Paris, 1775).

epic is the birth of allegory, the *Psychomachia* occurs at just such a historic juncture. Prudentian allegory interiorizes epic, a project that constitutes the modern moment of Old English poetry as well, if Anglo-Saxon modernity is to be located in the dismantling of Germanic epic through internalization.[3] I will try to indicate by summary its curious blend of sanctity and violence.

I

The *Psychomachia*'s brief preface of sixty-eight lines uses allegoresis in the service of allegory. Abraham, who "pugnare nosmet cum profanis gentibus / suasit" (*Prefatio* 9–10) [advised us to fight against the ungodly peoples], arms 318 servants to rescue his kinsman Lot, who has been taken captive.[4] Prudentius sublates this political conflict in an allegory of the Church: 318, represented by the letters TIH in Greek, is symbolic of Christ (IHSOUS) on the Cross (T). Tropologically, this conflict represents the psychomachia itself, a battle of vices and virtues which tells how "strage multa bellicosus spiritus / portenta cordis seruientis uicerit" (*Prefatio* 13–14) [the warlike spirit has conquered, with great slaughter, the monsters in the enslaved heart]. Textual violence is overdetermined in allegoresis of this exemplum, and its tropological level is marked by a linguistic extravagance characteristic of early Christian and early medieval spiritual conflict. These events from Genesis 14, suitably interpreted, become a model for life, and for the poem that follows:

> Haec ad figuram praenotata est linea
> quam nostra recto uita resculpat pede:
> uigilandum in armis pectorum fidelium
> omnemque nostri portionem corporis
> quae capta foedae seruiat libidini
> domi coactis liberandam uiribus . . . .

> (*Prefatio* 50–55)

---

3. The notion of modernity here is Paul de Man's, that of the modern as a panchronic stage rather than a literary period. Like Wordsworth's *Prelude*, Shelley's *Prometheus Unbound*, or Joyce's *Ulysses*, Old English poetry displaces the violence of epic heritage in a characteristically modern gesture.

4. All quotations from the *Psychomachia* are taken from Maurice P. Cunningham, ed., *Aurelii Prudentii Clementis Carmina, Corpus Christianorum, Series Latina* 126 (Turnhout, 1966), which has been checked against corrigenda found in the appendix to Cunningham's "The Problem of Interpolation in the Textual Tradition of Prudentius," *Transactions and Proceedings of the American Philological Association* 99 (1968): 119–41.

[This sketch has been drawn beforehand as a model for our life to retrace with true measure, showing that we must watch in the armor of faithful hearts, and that every part of our body that is captive and enslaved to filthy desire must be freed by gathering our forces at home . . . .]

Vigilance is to be achieved through the memorial services of the poem: attending to the encounters of virtues and vices should help us to recognize, even constitute, ourselves. Reading becomes not only constative, but performative, as a mimesis of psychic description becomes a mimesis of psychic production as well. Reading becomes writing. Prudentius's emphasis on psychic reorganization rather than societal restraint is historically significant, according to Macklin Smith, completing "a tendency only sporadically felt from St. Paul to the post-Nicene period: the relocation of the moral life in the psyche."[5]

The poem proper begins with an address to Christ, who occupies the epic slot traditionally held by one of the pagan divinities. Christ, seen as a trinitarian unity with difference, is asked to name the force within the soul that enables it to expel sins. The reference is to the virtues, which only become themselves through the encounter with the vices—that is, with the difference human unity bears within itself. Vice is paradoxically essential for virtue, according to a curious writing operation within the soul. Neither exists independently.[6]

The prayer of petition to Christ is followed by what Maurice Lavarenne has called an "assez gauche" bridge:

Vincendi praesens ratio est, si comminus ipsas
virtutum facies et conluctantia contra
uiribus infestis liceat portenta notare.

(18–20)

[A plan of victory is now present, if we can mark the very features of the Virtues and the monsters struggling violently together in close combat.]

---

5. Macklin Smith, *Prudentius' Psychomachia: A Reexamination* (Princeton, N.J., 1976), 139.

6. According to Macklin Smith, vice is prior to virtue: "The virtues and vices are not permanent faculties of the soul like memory and will and intellect. The soul may be said to contain virtue but not the virtues, Original Sin but not the vices. The vices are particular, occasional, temporary manifestations of sin; the virtues are manifestations of a particular, occasioned counterattack against the vices" (156). On such economies of difference, see Jacques Derrida, "Différance," in *Margins of Philosophy*, trans. Alan Bass (Chicago, 1982), 3–27.

Spiritual victory is once again associated with notation—not only the writing of the poem, but the act of re-marking by the reader as well. The first encounter, between *Fides* (Faith) and *Veterum Cultura Deorum* (Worship-of-the-Old-Gods), follows (21–39). The appearance of the virtue is presented, then its significance. *Fides'* bare arms, untrimmed hair, and unstylish dress represent the ardor of her holy ambition. She is weaponless, seemingly defenseless against pagan gods and goddesses. But such literal vulnerability is tribute to Faith's power, which is made evident when *Veterum Cultura Deorum* bites the dust:

> . . . pede calcat
> elisos in morte oculos animamque malignam
> fracta intercepti commercia gutturis artant;
> difficilemque obitum suspiria longa fatigant.
>
> (32–35)

> [{*Fides*} tramples her eyes underfoot, crushing them to bits in death. Blocking the windpipe, she chokes off the scant breath in her throat; long gasps for air lead to slow and difficult death.]

In this example of the textual excess promised by the *Prefatio*, *Fides* makes her enemy suffer an agonizing death by suffocation. Perhaps more surprising than this graphic violence, as in the surreal detail of eyeballs popped from their sockets and ground underfoot, is the reaction of the other virtues, who *exultant* (leap for joy). The *concupiscentia oculorum* (concupiscence of the eyes), equated with the desire for knowledge in exegetical tradition, requires violent suppression; this suppression, in turn, leads to a form of psychosocial joy.

Next, *Sodomita Libido* (Lust the Sodomite) falls upon *Pudicitia* (Chastity, 40–108). The vice's pinewood torch underscores her fiery nature, a traditional attribute of lust. When *Pudicitia* strikes her opponent's hand with a stone, the fiery torch no longer blinds with its smoke, so the vice can be vanquished:

> Tunc exarmatae iugulum meretricis adacto
> transfigit gladio. Calidos uomit illa uapores
> sanguine concretos caenoso, spiritus inde
> sordidus exhalans uicinas polluit auras.
>
> (49–52)

[Then, with a sword stroke, she pierces the throat of the disarmed whore, who vomits hot vapors congealed in filthy blood; exhaling her sordid breath, she pollutes the surrounding air.]

This gruesome description is a touchstone of Prudentian style, a violent rhetoric elaborating a violent subject matter. Revulsion at the corruption and filth of lust surfaces textually in the loathsome issue of blood and fumes. The triumphant speech of *Pudicitia* that follows (53–97) allegorizes the story of Judith and Holofernes: a tropological interpretation mentions each Christian's power to sever the head of the vice. This speech is replete with curses ("Abde caput tristi . . . abysso; occide . . . manes pete, claudere Auerno . . . Te uoluant subter uada flammea" (91–95) ["Bury your head in the abyss! Die! . . . May you be shut up in hell with the spirits of the dead! . . . May the rivers roll you beneath waves of fire!"], incantatory pleas for a suppression that cannot be complete. Hence, the lush rhetoric of verbal performatives that are meant to produce, by a kind of linguistic magic, an impossible effect. After such violent discourse celebrating such a violent series of battles, the short description of *Pudicitia's* purifying her sword in the river Jordan—*spiritualiter* (in a spiritual sense), the sacrament of Baptism—comes as a relief. Emphasis is placed on the cleanliness of the sword, which will shine with corruscating radiance, a light metaphor founded upon the violent imagery preceding it.

In the third battle, between *Patientia* (Patience) and *Ira* (Anger, 109–77), traditional motifs delineate the vice, who bares her teeth, foams at the mouth, and darts her bloodshot eyes to and fro. Unperturbed, *Patientia* waits for *Ira* to slay herself. The scene becomes increasingly comic, and the proper reader response is indicated by that of the internal audience, when Job smiles at the Virtue's victory. If *Patientia's* encounter offers relief from the extreme violence of the work, it remains true that this relief is predicated upon a violence so successful that it can avoid direct conflict between the two antagonists.

In the central battle, between *Superbia* (Pride) and *Mens Humilis* (Humility, 178–309), the vice rides about on an unbridled horse covered with the fell of a lion. Pride's fearsome speech promises hard going, until the vice falls into a pit *Fraus* (Deceit) had dug to trap the advancing ranks of Virtues. *Spes* (Hope) then offers *Mens Humilis* the *ultorem gladium* (sword of vengeance) with which *Superbia's* head is severed:

Illa cruentatum correptis crinibus hostem
protrahit et faciem laeua reuocante supinat.
Tunc caput orantis flexa ceruice resectum
eripit ac madido suspendit colla capillo.

(280–83)

[Holding her bloodied enemy by the hair that she has seized, she drags her forward, then turns her face upward with her left hand. Although the vice is begging for mercy, she severs the bowed neck, then lifts up the head, holding it by the hair that is dripping with gore.]

Decapitation takes place while the victim pleads for her life. After alluding to the story of David and Goliath, *Spes* flies away. That is: Hope can inspire Christians to action, but cannot itself perform such actions. Although occasional foretastes of heaven are granted, life is a continual *bella terrena* (earthly combat). The hope in question is one aimed at this powerful inner violence. The poem is a blueprint for reconstruction of the psyche that necessarily involves destruction, a wounding of the self by the self.

The defeat of *Superbia* is the turning point. No longer will the Vices attempt to conquer by military prowess. The subsequent battle between *Sobrietas* (Soberness) and *Luxuria* (Indulgence, 310–453) involves less clearly defined threats of debauchery and ease. *Luxuria*, which incorporates the concepts of *gula* (gluttony) and *acedia* (sloth) as well as lechery, is seen as coming *occiduis mundi de finibus* (from the western boundaries of the world, 310), with perfumed hair, shifty eyes, and a languid voice. Although sensuality has frequently been associated with the Orient, in the Middle Ages the West was symbolically evil, as it was for the laconic Anglo-Saxon monk who glossed this passage: *quia in occidentalibus: hominibus: maxima luxuria regnat* (because in Western peoples, the greatest dissipation prevails, British Library Additional MS. 24199). Although previously seen as unsteady of stride and belching, the vice nevertheless captivates her opponents while riding by in a gorgeous chariot. When the virtues lay down their spears in admiration, *Sobrietas* encourages them to stand firm, citing David, Samuel, and Jonathan as examples, then holds up a crucifix, frightening her opponent's horses. *Luxuria* is mangled in the chariot wheels, her face is smashed with a stone, and she finally vomits chunks of her own flesh, bone, and blood. The poem is quite explicit about this violence: when the vice's face is beaten, the mangled lips and tongue fill her mouth, causing her to gulp it all down on a queasy stomach. All this is capped by a passage in which *Sobrietas* tells her to drink up her vomit, since her diet had been overloaded with wine and gourmet food. Even (or especially) when spiritualized, this violence is troubling; as literal description, it is sadistic. Hence the problem for the modern reader, who cannot become a fourth-century Christian, in trying to think through a violence that, finally, can only be applauded with moral difficulty.

Plunder from this savage encounter is picked over by *Avaritia* (Avarice) and her retinue (454–631). The stories of Judas Iscariot and Achar are recalled by the opponent of *Operatio* (Good Works), who disguises herself as *Frugi* (Thrift), a stratagem that succeeds until *Operatio* strangles, then stabs her. *Avaritia*'s disguise consists of snaky tresses like Medusa's or Bellona's, but it is *Operatio* who acts as a Medusa, paralyzing the *mendax Bellona*. After this triumph of the will, *Operatio*'s violence is described: the virtue puts a hammerlock upon the vice, crushing her throat, her pulse throbbing in the throes of an agonizing death by strangulation, which is elaborately described. The graphic violence of Prudentius's descriptions reaches its peak in dealing with *Luxuria* and *Avaritia*. When *Operatio* strangles *Avaritia* with *uincla lacertorum* (arms like iron fetters, 592), the description resembles a scene in a martial arts movie offering the obscenity of violence for the delectation of viewers. As the vice struggles in her death throes, *Operatio* kneels upon her, stabs her between the ribs, then despoils the corpse of the wealth kept inside her body.

The critical problem in reading such scenes is how to make sense of spiritualized brutality in an influential Christian text. As H. J. Thomson pointed out back in the days when racial generalizations were permitted in polite company, "The zeal with which Prudentius (perhaps owing to his Spanish blood) dwells on the gruesome details of slaughter often obscures the fact that the poem has a religious purpose."[7] If the explanation may be wrongheaded, the observation isn't. Violence increases at this stage in the poem, as episodes lengthen. This is so not only because *Luxuria* and *Avaritia* present a more difficult heuristic problem, but because the writing machinery of the text is itself triggered by violence.

---

7. H. J. Thomson, "The *Psychomachia* of Prudentius," *Classical Review* 44 (1930): 109.

Next, *Pax* (Peace) and *Concordia* (Concord), thinking the war has ended, return to camp singing psalms, like the people of Israel after the Red Sea crossing (631–64). But the army of the virtues has not counted upon the danger of *Discordia-Heresis* (Discord-Heresy), the only vice that attacks in time of peace. *Concordia* receives a skin wound from *Discordia*, who is portrayed with a torn outer garment. The vice leaves her snake whip behind on the battlefield in order to pass as one of the virtues (665–725). After *Fides* immobilizes her opponent in the appropriate manner—by shoving a javelin through her tongue—the army of virtues wreaks horrible vengeance: bits of her body are ripped off, then tossed to dogs, crows, sea-monsters. Adolf Katzenellenbogen has noted how the threat of *Discordia*, the only vice that comes in time of peace, parallels the opening conflict with *Veterum Cultura Deorum*.[8] But such formal symmetry is founded on the violence of the *sparagmos*, symbolic retribution for *Discordia*'s dismemberment of the body of Christ. This lush violence on the part of the virtues, who take pleasure in a cruelty discountenanced in the vices, creates happiness and peace within the poem by allowing security for the *pacificos sensus* (peaceful feelings, 729).

After this abrupt transition from war to peace, *Fides* and *Concordia* advise the immediate construction of a temple (726–822). *Concordia* recommends abolition of any dissonance or discordance within the soul, and the creation of unity and peace without difference. On the other hand, heresy is represented as wolflike, an indication that theological difference is conceived as an external threat rather than a creative force within *Ecclesia*. The *purgati corporis urbs* (city of the cleansed body, 818) requires building, an artificial biblical image emblematic of the self constructed through psychomachia. A work of social production, such self-constitution can also be found in the religious and literary text.

Details from the biblical description of the heavenly Jerusalem are added to the primary meaning of the temple within the believer's soul (823–87). *Sapientia* (Wisdom) lays out the temple with her scepter, a living rod that blooms, yet needs no contact with the ground. The theological notion of the rod of Aaron, which silenced dissension

---

8. Adolf Katzenellenbogen, *Allegories of the Virtues and Vices in Mediaeval Art* (New York, 1964), 2.

among the Israelites, leads to this image bridging the worlds of nature and human artifice, a naturalizing metaphor for the artifice of psychic construction.

A prayer of thanksgiving (888–915) recapitulates Prudentius's vision of life as psychomachia. This warfare is one between the flesh—*not* merely a term for the non-spiritual part of man—and the spirit, between light and darkness in traditional visual metaphorics, with victory never secure until Christ helps. Spirit, associated with the breath of God, dwells within *nigrantis carcere cordis* (the dark prison of the heart, 906), where it refuses the *sordes* (filth, 907) of the body. For Prudentius as well as Yeats, Love has pitched his mansion in the place of excrement. The graphic violence of the *Psychomachia* develops, almost imperceptibly, into a vision of the peace that is the goal of spiritual warfare. Imagery of light and darkness serves as a static emblem for complex processes of psychic reformation.

To execute his original conception of an allegorical epic, Prudentius had to reappropriate pagan literary models, most obviously the *Aeneid* of Virgil, less evidently the *Eclogues* and *Georgics*, Ovid's *Metamorphoses*, Lucan's *Pharsalia*, and the *Thebaid* of Statius. He is fond of using the standard epithet for Jupiter, *tonans* (the Thunderer), to refer to the Christian God, and his vices are often associated with the Furies of classical mythyology.[9] In Prudentius's writings, Christianity represents not jarring discontinuity with Roman civilization, but its fulfillment. Such pragmatic appropriation of the literary heritage of Empire resembles the appropriation of the Germanic epic poetic by the Anglo-Saxons. And their works are haunted by a similar question—just what Ingeld might have to do with Christ. If the Israelites' plundering of Egyptian gold does not serve as an exact parallel, it is because the problem is that of utilizing one's own cultural history.

In his discussion of the reappropriation of traditional epic language in the *Psychomachia*, Macklin Smith reads its allegorization as a reaction to late Imperial culture, which mounted a conservative defense

---

9. For the influence of Latin poetry on Prudentius, see *Aurelii Prudentii Clementis Carmina*, ed. Cunningham, 418–22; *Aurelii Prudentii Clementis Carmina*, ed. Ioannes Bergman, *Corpus Scriptorum Ecclesiasticorum Latinorum*, 61 (Vienna, 1926), 455–69; Albertus Mahoney, *Vergil in the Works of Prudentius* (Washington, 1934); Christian Schwen, *Vergil bei Prudentius* (Bern, 1937); and J. P. Hermann, "*Psychomachia* 423–26 and *Aeneid* 5.468–70," *The Classical Bulletin* 54 (1978): 88–89.

against Christianity by deifying Virgil, the sacred poet of *Romanitas*. The Christian poetry of spiritual conflict emerges from the fragments of a discredited mythos of secular conflict. Old English poetry has similar origins—if "origins" were not precisely what is put into question in such cases. Like late classical Christianity, Anglo-Saxon Christianity is formed in opposition to the past and shows traces of its repressed other. There is room for more than one mythos in the *Psychomachia*: the image of *Sapientia*'s temple, new construction founded upon the destruction of the old city, condenses the literary genealogy of the poem itself.

Old English literature reenacts this scene of violent literary appropriation several centuries later; its reveling in violence cannot be written off as an unfortunate inheritance from pagan forms, any more than it can in the *Psychomachia*. After all, the opposition of Christian charity to pagan violence is also mutual dependence, since the temple of Christian poetry is erected upon the ruins of a pagan system. The very ideological violence of Christianity helped dismantle the former civilization, and the rubble of the old forms was used to construct new ones. Early medieval Christian poetry is a complex psychosocial deflection of desire which is marked by an alien other. This trace, which can be detected in Christian self and text, underwrites the recurrent literary violence of early medieval spirituality.

II

In what specific ways did the *Psychomachia* influence Anglo-Saxon culture? We can begin to answer this question with manuscript evidence, which indicates that the *Psychomachia* was one of the most popular works in early medieval England. Johan Bergman's research into manuscript provenance, which has been supplemented by the work of Neil Ker, Helmut Gneuss, and Gernot Wieland, suggests the high esteem in which it was held.[10] The number of *Psychomachia* manuscripts written in England at this time, and of glossed manuscripts serving a wider reading public, offers testimony to the place of honor accorded the poem.

---

10. Johan Bergman, *De Codicibus Prudentianis* (Stockholm, 1910); Neil R. Ker, *Catalogue of Manuscripts Containing Anglo-Saxon* (Oxford, 1957); Helmut Gneuss, "A Preliminary List of Manuscripts Written or Owned in England up to 1100," *Anglo-Saxon England* 9 (1981): 1–60; Gernot R. Wieland, "The Anglo-Saxon Manuscripts of Prudentius's *Psychomachia*," *Anglo-Saxon England* 16 (1987): 213–31.

J. D. A. Ogilvy mentions several instances of the use of the *Psychomachia* by Anglo-Saxons.[11] He points out that Bede quotes from it several times in his *De Arte Metrica* (On the Art of Metrics), and mentions its use in the anonymous *Vita Oswaldi* (Life of Oswald). The latter work illustrates the importance of Prudentius's poem in Anglo-Saxon spirituality. When Ælfsin insults the deceased Odo, the anonymous author of the *Vita Oswaldi* uses the *Psychomachia* to characterize the Archbishop's vainglory:

> Post obitum viri Dei successit ei in regno sacri principatus nomine Ælfsinus, qui propter prosperitatem fallentis saeculi inflatus, contra famulum Dei surrexit post obitum, quem autumabat esse defunctum; sed Ille, Qui *est vita, veritas, et via* Sanctorum, demonstravit caelitus quod Suus cum Eo viveret episcopus. Detraxit mortuum vivus contra praeceptum Davitici regis, dicentis, *detrahentem secreto proximo suo* persequitur Deus. Quadam die dum staret supra sepulcrum viri Dei, sic ad eum exorsus est, dicens, "Episcope, ecce prostratus jaces, et ego fruar jura triumphi. Te vivente non merui, te obeunte percepi." Sic eripuit, et de episcopatu semetipsum exaltavit, virgaque quam manu gestabat tumbam indigniter tetigit et recessit, oblitus penitus quod scriptura ait,
> *Magna cadunt, inflata crepant, tumefacta premuntur,*
> *Disce supercilium deponere, disce cavere*
> *Ante pedes foveam, quisquis sublime minaris.*
> Et infra,
> *Pervulgata viget nostri sententia Christi,*
> *Scandere celsa humiles, et ad ima redire feroces.*[12]

[After the death of the man of God, one by the name of Ælfsinus followed him in the reign of holy preeminence. Inspired by the prosperity of the deceitful world, he rose up against the servant of God after his death—at least after what was said to be death. But He who is life, truth, and the way of the saints, showed clearly that his heavenly bishop dwelled with Him. The living one slandered the dead man, going against the precept of King David, who said that God punished the slanderer in his most private moments of solitude. One day, while he was standing above the tomb of

---

11. For much of the following information, I have relied upon J. D. A. Ogilvy, *Books Known to the English, 597–1066* (Cambridge, Mass., 1967), 230–32. An example of the need for caution in using this groundbreaking work, which is currently being revised, may be found in its assertion that "*Psychomachia* appears as *Sigomachia* in the Worcester book-list" (232). It actually appears as *Sychomagia*.

12. James Raine, ed., *The Historians of the Church of York and Its Archbishops*, *Rerum Britannicarum Medii Aevi Scriptores* (London, 1879), 71.1.408.

the man of God, he began speaking to him, saying, "Bishop, behold how you lie here cast down, and I enjoy the rights of victory. What I could not obtain while you were living, I took when you were dead." In this manner he had snatched away and exalted himself to the episcopacy, and he shamefully struck the tomb with the staff that he bore in his hand. Then he withdrew, defiled inwardly, on which account the literary work says: "The great fall, the pompous crumble, those swollen with pride are crushed. / Learn to put away arrogance, learn to beware / The pit at your feet, all you who are haughty." And later on it says: "Well known is the saying of our Christ, / That the humble ascend to high places and the arrogant are brought down to the depths."]

These quotations, from the speech made by *Spes* while holding *Superbia*'s severed head, thematize a violent ecclesiastical contestation of forces, marking the distance between the Old English period and the late classical. To compare the *Vita Oswaldi*'s use of the *Psychomachia* to Prudentius's use of Virgil is to understand how different Old English religious contexts are from those of the fourth century. That it occurred to the author of the *Vita Oswaldi* to cite these verses suggests the esteem in which the *Psychomachia* was held by learned Anglo-Saxons, and illustrates a prevalent tendency, nurtured in large part by the *Psychomachia* itself, to see in historical events the working out of the abstract pattern of the war between the virtues and vices. But in this case, the war is within the walls of *Ecclesia*, Christian joined against Christian in a power struggle that extends past the grave.[13]

---

13. When our author describes the character of his revered Oswald, he again cites the *Psychomachia*:

> Erat enim, ut sanctis et veris amicis Dei usuale est, binis fulcitus columnis, id est dilectione Dei et proximi, cui erant quinque sagaciter adjunctae, quae firmiter domum suam sustentabant ne a vento quassaretur, velut mutabunda quae in paludibus stare cognoscitur. Habebat enim pacem cum proximo, cujus in corde non erat malum, recordans spirituali intelligentia illud Scholastici dicentis:
>
> Pax plenum virtutis opus, pax summa laborum,
> Pax belli exacti pretium est, pretiumque pericli,
> Sidera pace vigent, consistunt terrea pace.
>
> Et, infra, ipse idem.
> Offerat in primis pacem, nulla hostia Christo
> Dulcior . . . (Ibid., 416)

[Truly, as is common among true and holy friends of God, he was upheld by twofold columns—i.e., the love of God and neighbor—in addition to which, wisely, there were five adjuncts which firmly supported his house so it would not be shaken by the wind, like the reed which is known to stand in marshes. Truly, he kept peace with his neighbor in whose heart there was no evil, remembering that which the

One final form of the *Psychomachia* testifies to its popularity in England—the illustrated manuscripts: Cambridge, Corpus Christi College MS. 23, British Library Additional MS. 24199, British Library Cotton MS. Cleopatra C. viii, and Munich Staatsbibliothek MS. Clm. 29031b were executed in England during the Anglo-Saxon period.[14] Such illuminated manuscripts greatly influenced later medieval art and sculpture.[15]

But it is to consideration of literary influence that we must now turn. The *Psychomachia*'s original conception of the full-fledged allegorical epic influenced Aldhelm's *De Virginitate* (On Virginity) and the *Pater Noster* (Our Father) battle sequence in *Solomon and Saturn*. Aldhelm's *De Octo Principalibus Vitiis* (On the Eight Chief Vices), originally intended to serve as a conclusion to the poetic *De Virginitate*, was frequently and wrongly considered a separate work.[16] Max Manitius, following the correct practice of Ehwald, wrote:

> Die poetische Paraphrase, die sich eng an den Prosatext hält, aber leichter verständlich ist als dieser, schließt mit Vs. 2445, doch hat A[ldhelm] noch eine Fortsetzung gedichtet, die in den Drucken fälschlich als eigenes Gedicht De octo principalibus vitiis erscheint. Daß es sich nur um eine

---

Scholastic said with spiritual knowledge: "Peace is the completion of the work of a virtue, peace the perfection of her labors, / Peace the reward of the war that has ended, and the reward for danger. / The stars live in peace, earthly things stand firm in peace." And later on, by the same writer: "Above all, one should offer peace. No sacrifice is sweeter to Christ . . ."]
Dante relies on this passage too, in the last ineffable lines of the *Paradiso*. Peace, the sweetest offering, is the result of the life of Christian warfare for him as well as for Prudentius and the Anglo-Saxon author. Such reliance upon the *Psychomachia* in the life of St. Oswald of Worcester, written by a monk of Ramsey—probably the learned Byrhtferth himself—shows the important place Prudentius's poem held in Anglo-Saxon monastic life. On the probability of Byrhtferth's authorship, see S. J. Crawford, "Byrhtferth of Ramsey and the Anonymous Life of St. Oswald," in *Speculum Religionis, Being Essays and Studies in Religion and Literature from Plato to Von Hügel* (Oxford, 1929); Michael Lapidge, "The Hermeneutic Style in Tenth-Century Anglo-Latin Literature," *Anglo-Saxon England* 4 (1975): 90–94; and Peter Baker, "The Old English Canon of Byrhtferth of Ramsey," *Speculum* 55 (1980): 22–37.
    14. On the illustrated *Psychomachia* manuscripts, see Richard Stettiner, *Die illustrierten Prudentius-Handschriften* (Berlin, 1895); *Tafelband* (Berlin, 1905); Helen Woodruff, *The Illustrated Manuscripts of Prudentius* (Cambridge, Mass., 1930).
    15. See Katzenellenbogen, *Allegories of the Virtues and Vices in Mediaeval Art*; Emile Mâle, *L'Art religieux du XIIIe siècle en France* (Paris, 1910), 124ff.; Louis Bréhier, *L'Art chrétien* (Paris, 1918), 203.
    16. As in the *Patrologia Latina* 89:281–90.

Fortsetzung handelt, geht ganz klar aus Vs. 2446 ff. und 2861–2867 hervor. . . .

[The poetic paraphrase, which sticks close to the prose version but is easier to understand, ends with line 2445; however Aldhelm had written a continuation, which in the printed versions appears incorrectly as an independent poem entitled *De Octo Principalibus Vitiis*. That what is in question is a continuation becomes quite clear from lines 2446 ff. and 2861–2867 . . .][17]

Certain *incipits* (here begins . . .) and *explicits* (here ends . . .) suggest that Anglo-Saxons themselves made the same mistake later editors did. One manuscript of the ninth or tenth century, MS Rawlinson C. 697, written at Bury St. Edmunds, not only treats the virtues-vices conflict as a separate work, but follows it with what appears to have been its literary model, the *Psychomachia*: *EXPLICIT ALDHELMI ARCHI-EPISCOPI DE OCTO UITIIS PRINCIPALIBUS: INCIPIT LIBER PSYCHOMACHIAE QUEM COMPOSUIT AURELIUS PRUDENS CLEMENS.*[18] [Here ends Archbishop Aldhelm's *De Octo Principalibus Vitiis*; here begins the book of the *Psychomachia* which Aurelius Prudens Clemens composed.] This proximity to Prudentius's poem suggests that the compiler of this manuscript found the eight-vices section in *De Virginitate* poem reminiscent of the *Psychomachia*. There is no doubt that certain passages reveal the direct dependence of *De Octo Principalibus Vitiis* upon the *Psychomachia*, although in some cases Ehwald has pointed out Prudentian echoes heard by his ears only.

While the construction of the Rawlinson manuscript suggests the influence of the *Psychomachia*, disparities between the two works are noteworthy. Aldhelm's poem is an allegorical epic of a less vivid sort than Prudentius's. Lavarenne could say of it, admittedly: "On y trouve des vers . . . qui constituent presque un plagiat de Prudence."[19] [One finds there verses . . . which are all but plagiarism of Prudentius.] Yet very little of Prudentius's delight in graphic battle description is shared by Aldhelm. The relationship between these works is at once less clearcut and more complex than Lavarenne indicates.

The poem itself falls into two parts: the virtue-vice material (2446–

---

17. Max Manitius, *Geschichte der Lateinischen Literatur des Mittelalters* (Munich, 1911), 1:139.
18. Ibid., 471.
19. Lavarenne, ed., *Psychomachie*, 26.

2761) and the concluding section (2762–2904). A brief exordium (2446–2761) serves as a bridge to Aldhelm's new focal point, shifting concentration from the merits of the virgins and fathers to the conflict of the soul against the eight vices. The passage that Lavarenne thought almost a plagiarism from Prudentius seems indeed, at first sight, to promise that Aldhelm will deliver a modified *Psychomachia*:

> Ecce catervatim glomerant ad bella falanges,
> Iustitiae comites et virtutum agmina sancta;
> His adversantur vitiorum castra maligna,
> Spissa nefandarum quae torquent spicula rerum,
> Aemula ceu pugnat populorum turma duorum,
> Dum vexilla ferunt et clangit classica salpix
> Ac stimulant Martem legionum cornua cantu.
> His, inquam, denso virtutes agmine plures
> Occurrunt vitiis: gestantes bellica signa,
> Cassida cum thoracis necnon ancile duelli
> Et macheram verbi peccati monstra necantem
> Se in spatium pariter portant ad proelia mundi;
> Virtutes quoque parmarum testudine sumpta
> Saeva profanorum contundunt tela sparorum.

(2454–67)

[Behold, bands of soldiers gather together in companies for combat, comrades of Justice and holy armies of the Virtues. The wicked encampment of Vices opposes them, hurling showers of evil arrows, as rival troops of two nations fight bearing their standards, while the trumpet of battle resounds and horns of the legions incite battle with their song. Many Virtues, I say, attack the Vices in a compacted army. Carrying banners of war, with helmet and breastplate indeed, with shield of war and the sword of the Word, killing the monsters of sin, they march to their stations in the war of the world. In a shield-wall formation, the Virtues demolish the cruel weapons of the profane nations.]

The military vehicle is more compact, a selection of choice details culled from the classical lexicon of warfare. But the mock-epic tone has been dropped, and narrative pleasure has shifted to intellectual delight at seeing this lexicon deployed so elaborately. The highly artificial, scholastic quality of this passage is typical of the poem. The reference to Mars continues the Prudentian theme of criticism of the pagans, but as an idiomatic grace note rather than a contestation with an imminent threat to Christianity. Personification of the virtues turns out to be insubstantial, and the battle figure so vividly introduced remains static and abstract, a decorative trope that never burgeons forth into the graphic violence of the *Psychomachia*.

One reason for this contrast in treatments is structural. Aldhelm adheres strictly to the Cassianic order of the eight principal vices, a scheme more appropriate for a monastic than a lay audience. Prudentius had written when there were as yet no well-organized cenobitic communities with well-developed theologies of spiritual growth. Consequently, he was able to present a relatively original conception of the battle for the soul, which concerned itself with temptations more likely to befall lay men and women than monks and nuns. Aldhelm's poem stems from monastic concerns entwined in a social text radically unlike Prudentius's.

The Cassianic order Aldhelm employed is both dramatically deficient and theologically well-developed. Cassian set forth his arrangement of vices in the *Conlationes* (Readings at Meals), a staple in the life of medieval monks. Since Cassian's authority had set a precedent, Aldhelm, who would become abbot at Malmesbury, preferred the Cassianic *ordo naturalis* (natural order) to artful disposition of his material. He brings his vices forward in *De Octo Principalibus Vitiis* precisely as the *Conlationes* does. Cassian saw each vice growing out of the preceding one, and hence presenting an increasing order of difficulty.[20] Be-

---

20. Haec igitur octo uitia licent diuersos ortus ac dissimiles efficientias habeant, sex tamen priora, id est gastrimargia, fornicatio, filargyria, ira, tristitia, acedia quadam inter se cognatione et ut ita dixerim concatenatione conexa sunt, ita ut prioris exuberantia sequenti efficiatur exordium . . . . residua uero duo, id est cenodoxia et superbia sibi quidem similiter illa qua de superioribus uitiis diximus ratione iunguntur, ita ut incrementum prioris ortus efficiatur alterius (cenodoxiae enim exuberantia superbiae fomitem parit), sed ab illis sex prioribus uitiis penitus dissident nec simili cum eis societate foederantur, siquidem non solum nullam ex illis occasionem suae generationis accipiant, sed etiam contrario mode atque ordine suscitentur. [These eight vices allow for diverse origins and have dissimilar effects; nevertheless, six come first, i.e., gluttony, lust, greed, anger, dejection, and sloth. By a certain relationship (and as I have said, a concatenation) they are connected in such a way that from the superabundance of the former comes the beginning of the one that follows . . . . There are two which remain, i.e., vainglory and pride, which are joined in the same manner as the former vices: the growth of the former is followed by the origin of the second (for the superabundance of vainglory produces the kindling-wood of pride). But they are throroughly separated from those six former vices, and are not allied in the same fellowship with them, since not only are they not generated from them, but they are also produced in a different manner and in a different order.]

cause this order is more applicable to the spiritual growth of a cenobite than of a fourth-century Christian living in pagan society, it does not reflect urgent social threats such as the challenge to faith of *Veterum Cultura Deorum* or *Discordia*. Cassian's theology of sin devotes more attention to the vices assailing contemplatives, while Prudentius's emphasis on mundane vices is largely confined to the first half of the Cassianic list. Writing at a time when the eightfold order was known to all his fellow monks, Aldhelm could rely upon his audience in a way Prudentius could not. As a result, Aldhelm does not seek to invent new forms, but to amplify old ones. The Cassianic order could have been transmuted into a dramatically effective one, but that was not Aldhelm's conception of his poem or materials.

The first vice treated, *gastrimargia* or *ingluvies ventris* (gluttony), shows Aldhelm's differing notion of allegorical epic. He relies upon Cassian for details where Prudentius would have made use of literary invention, fueled by knowledge of Scripture and the classics. He begins with the allegorical exegesis of a scriptural passage:

> Sed plebs Aegipti rubro sub gurgite mersa,
> Qui turmas flustris densas perdebat aquosis,
> Ingluviem ventris iuste signare potestur.

> (2482–84)

[But the people of Egypt, submerged under the Red Sea, which destroyed the close squadrons in the sea waters, can rightly be taken to symbolize gluttony.]

The Egyptian defeat is tropologically the defeat of *gastrimargia*. As Ehwald's notes point out, this detail, like many in the poem, finds its source in the *Conlationes* of Cassian:

> Octo esse principalia uitia quae inpugnant monachum cunctorum absoluta sententia est. quae figuraliter sub gentium uocabulo nominata idcirco nunc omnia non ponuntur, eo quod egressis iam de Ægypto et liberatis ab una gente ualidissima, id est Ægyptiorum, Moyses uel per ipsum dominus in Deuteronomio loquebatur. quae figura in nobis quoque rectissime stare

---

(Cassian, *Conlationes* V, 10, ed. Michael Petschenig, *Iohannis Cassiani Conlationes XXIIII*, *Corpus Scriptorum Ecclesiasticorum Latinorum* [Vienna, 1886], 13:129–30).

deprehenditur, qui de saeculi laqueis expediti gastrimargiae, id est uentris uel gulae uitio caruisse cognoscimur.[21]

[That there are eight principal vices among all those attacking the monk is the meaning that is being narrated. Therefore, all are not now reckoned figurally under the name of the nations that are mentioned, because Moses—or through him the Lord—spoke in Deuteronomy of those now passing out of Egypt and set free from a most powerful nation, the Egyptians. This figure is also most rightly found to apply to us. Unshackled from the snares of the world, we are known to be free from gluttony, i.e., from the vice of the stomach or throat.]

Aldhelm next describes the vices which proceed from *ingluvies ventris*, echoing Cassian's mention of *comesationes* (feastings) and *ebrietates* (drunken episodes) in the same context:

> Quam sequitur scelerata falanx luxusque ciborum
> Ebrietasque simul necnon et crapula cordis,
> Ingluviem dapibus quae semper pascit opimis . . .
>
> (2487–89)

[A phalanx of wicked soldiers follows {gluttony}: excess of foods, and at the same time drunkenness and intoxication of the heart, which always feasts gluttony on sumptuous banquets.]

But rather than develop the role of this Prudentian phalanx, Aldhelm abandons it to move on to the story of the Fall:

> Nam protoplaustus, quem rex formavit Olimpi
> Ruricolamque rudem palmis plasmaverat almis
> Pectora fecundans caelesti flamine vitae,
> Iamdudum cecidit prostratus fraude gulosa,
> Dum vetitum ligni malum decerperet ambro;
> A quo pestiferum glescebat semen in orbe,
> Unde seges spissa spurcis succrevit aristis.
>
> (2494–2500)

[For the first-created man, the young tiller of the ground, whom the king of heaven formed and molded with kind hands—fructifying his soul with

---

21. Ibid., 143–44.

the breath of heavenly life—long ago fell, cast down by the sin of gluttony when the glutton plucked the forbidden apple from the tree. From him deadly seed flourished in the world, whence the thick field grew up into impure fruits.]

Precisely the same parallel was drawn by Cassian in his discussion of *gastrimargia*.[22] For the remaining portion of his treatment of the vice, Aldhelm allows scriptural parallels and Virgilian echoes to carry the weight of his argument. Nowhere does he describe a battle between *gastrimargia* and a particular opposing virtue, preferring instead an indirect mode of narration:

> Idcirco hanc belvam studeat superare virago,
> Ne balena vorax valvas explodat Olimpi,
> Spiritus ut nequeat paradisi scandere sceptrum!
> Dura quidem iugiter virtutes bella fascessunt
> Ingluviem contra vincentem ferrea corda,
> Sed tamen integritas ieiunis viribus obstat,
> Frangantur dapibus ne propugnacula mentis.
> Nectaris idcirco contemnit pocula mulsa
> Atque opulenta fugit pro Christo fercula virgo,
> Virginitas felix queat ut servire Tonanti.

(2534–43)

[Therefore may the woman warrior strive to overcome this monster, lest that voracious whale drive away the gates of heaven, so that the spirit is unable to rise to the kingdom of heaven. Indeed, the virtues perpetually wage harsh warfare against gluttony, which conquers hard hearts. Nevertheless innocence resists with the powers of abstinence, lest the ramparts of the mind be broken by feasting. Because the virgin disdains sweet

---

22. In illis enim passionibus etiam ipse temptari debuit incorruptam imaginem dei ac similitudinem possidens, in quibus et Adam temptatus est, cum adhuc in illa inuiolata dei imagine perduraret, hoc est gastrimargia, cenodoxia, superbia, non in quibus post praeuaricationem mandati imagine dei ac similitudine uiolata suo iam uitio deuolutus inuoluitur. gastrimargia namque est qua interdicti ligni praesumit edulium . . . . [For those very passions with which Adam was tempted while he remained in that unharmed image of God, {Christ} himself—possessing the uncorrupted image and likeness of God—also had to be tempted. He was not enveloped in those passions, i.e., gluttony, vainglory, and pride, which occurred after transgression of the commandment, fallen now from the violated image and likeness of God. For it is gluttony by which {Adam} takes the fruit of the forbidden tree.] (Ibid., 124–25)

drinks of nectar and flees splendid dishes for the sake of Christ, happy virginity is able to serve God.]

Aldhelm's play with the texture of language can be found in his use of *virago* (2534) for *virgo*, a linking of "virgin" and "warrior" emblematic of the violence necessary to restrain desire—*virginitas felix* (happy Virginity) is the product of violence. But this imaginative treatment of the linguistic surface does not reach as far as the dramatic treatment of battle scenes. Where Prudentius would have portrayed the violent destruction of the vice, Aldhelm is content with asserting the perpetual warfare the virtues wage against *ingluvies ventris*. He envisions the soul as a besieged fortress as well, alluding to such recurrent motifs of spiritual warfare without developing them, and relying upon exempla culled from allegorical exegesis of the Old Testament. He devotes a greater portion of his descriptions to these than does Prudentius, who used exempla to illustrate, but never to carry the burden of his description of a vice. Aldhelm's strategy makes his miniature psychomachia less descriptive, more abstract. We find none of the vivid debates between virtues and vices which add dramatic color to Prudentius's poem: no particular opponent among the virtues is personified thoroughly enough to justify detailed description of the encounter between it and a corresponding vice.

The seven remaining encounters of *De Octo Principalibus Vitiis* also rely heavily upon Cassian's *Conlationes*, and are characterized by the same abstract mode of narration. The vices appear, not in any dramatically effective manner, but *seriatim*. While the Cassianic order is scrupulously followed, no attempt is made to develop it vividly.[23] The virtue-vice section of *De Virginitate*, despite a prologue which suggests a full-blown allegorical epic, differs markedly from the tradition inaugurated by the *Psychomachia*. In Aldhelm's poem we find no debates, few fully personified vices and virtues, and only brief mention of the mere possibility of actual battles. Although allegoresis was put to illustrative use in Prudentius's poem, in Aldhelm's it comprises a substantial portion of the treatment of the vices. These differences, which make sense in terms of differing social contexts for the works, must not

---

23. Further discussion of Aldhelm's poem can be found in J. P. Hermann, "Some Varieties of Psychomachia in Old English," *American Benedictine Review* 34 (1983): 198–202.

be erased.[24] Through the *Conlationes* of Cassian, to pick only one of several instances of the genre he would have known, Aldhelm was exposed to the tradition of the *conflictus vitiorum et virtutum* (dispute of the vices and virtues), which was based on a conception of the relationship between virtues and vices differing markedly from Prudentius's. Although I shall define the *conflictus* tradition differently than Hans Walther, his dichotomy of medieval vices-virtues poetry is useful:

> Unter den poetischen Conflictus lassen sich zwei Gruppen sondern, solche, in denen reine Parallelaufzählung von Tugenden und Lastern stattfindet, und solche, die Kampfschilderung oder seltener wirklichen Dialog mit Bezugnahme auf die Worte des Gegners bieten.[25]

> [Two distinct categories of poetic *conflictus* can be found: in one, a simple lining up of virtues and vices in parallel occurs, while the other offers the description of battle or, infrequently, actual dialogue between the combatants.]

What Walther calls the *Parallelaufzählung* group, I shall refer to as the *conflictus* tradition; what he refers to as the *Kampfschilderung* group, I shall call the psychomachia tradition.

The *conflictus* tradition was immensely popular in the early Middle Ages, eclipsing almost totally the tradition inaugurated by the *Psy-*

---

24. For these reasons, I would quarrel with the view that Aldhelm modeled his poem upon Prudentius's. Max Manitius said of *De Octo Principalibus Vitiis*: "Hier führt A[ldhelm] aus, daß die Keuschheit ohne den Kampf gegen die Hauptlaster—nach Art des Prudentius in der Psychomachie—nicht bestehen könne" [Here Aldhelm enlarges on the notion that purity can not persist without battling the capital vices—after the fashion of Prudentius in the *Psychomachia* (*Geschichte*, 1:139).] This position was more forcefully stated by Hans Walther in *Das Streitgedicht in der lateinischen Literatur des Mittelalters*: "Ganz unter dem Einfluß von Prudenz steht Aldhelm, der seinem vielgelesenen Werke *De laudibus virginum* einen langen Abschnitt *De octo principalibus viciis* anhängte, worin er zeigen wollte, daß die Keuschheit sich nur im Kampfe gegen die Laster zusammen mit den anderen Tugenden behaupten könne" [Aldhelm remains completely under the influence of Prudentius; his much-read work *De Laudibus Virginum* appends a long section entitled *De Octo Principalibus Vitiis*, in which he would show that purity can hold its own only in combat, together with the other virtues, against the vices]. (Rev. ed. in *Quellen und Untersuchungen zur lateinischen Philologie des Mittelalters* [Munich, 1920], 5, Pt. 2:112.) For a more moderate restatement of this position, see Gernot Wieland, "Aldhelm's *De Octo Vitiis Principalibus* and Prudentius' *Psychomachia*," *Medium Aevum* 55 (1986): 85–92.

25. Hans Walther, *Das Streitgedicht in der lateinischen Literatur des Mittelalters* (Munich, 1914), 90–91. (This is an earlier edition than that which appeared in *Quellen und Untersuchungen*.)

chomachia. In prose written by Anglo-Saxons, the main exemplar of the *conflictus* is Alcuin's *Liber de Virtutibus et Vitiis* (Book of the Virtues and Vices). The virtues and vices are discussed individually in the characteristically static manner. When spiritual warfare is mentioned in this work, it is treated clinically:

> Fornicatio est omnis corporalis immunditia, quae solet fieri ex incontinentia libidinis, et mollitia animae, quae consentit suae carni peccare. Nam anima domina debet esse, et imperare carni; et caro famula, et obedire dominae suae, id est, rationali animae. Quae fornicatio fit per commistionem carnis cum femina qualibet, vel etiam alia quacunque immunditia ad explendum libidinis ardorem. De qua [fornicatione] nascitur caecitas mentis, inconstantia oculorum vel totius corporis amor immoderatus; saepe periculum vitae, lascivia, joca, petulantia, et omnis incontinentia; odium mandatorum Dei, mentis enervatio, et injustae cupiditates; negligentia vitae futurae, et praesentis delectatio. Quae vincitur per castitatem et continentiam consuetam, et recordationem ignis aeterni, et timorem praesentiae sempiterni Dei.[26]

> [Fornication is all bodily impurity. It is usually done because of the incontinence of desire and weakness of the soul, which consents to sin in the flesh. For the soul ought to be the one which rules and governs the flesh; and the flesh ought to be a servant, and obey its governess (i.e., the rational soul). Fornication arises through sexual union with woman in any way, or through any other impurity by whatever means that is directed towards sating the burning of desire. From fornication is begotten blindness of the mind, inconstancy of the eyes, or unbridled love throughout the whole body; oftentimes, risk of life, lewdness, jesting, wantonness, and all inability to restrain one's impulses; hatred of God's commandments, enervation of mind, and wrongful desires; carelessness about the future life, and delight in the present. It is conquered through chastity, the practice of continence, recollection of eternal fire, and fear of the presence of the eternal God.]

Alcuin treats the other virtues and vices in this same detached manner, the manner of *De Octo Principalibus Vitiis*, which had also relied upon Cassian's contribution to the *conflictus* tradition. Monastic tradition had codified spiritual combat, rendering it less a dramatic individual confron-

---

26. *Patrologia Latina* 101:633–34. An Old English translation of this work appears in B. Assmann, "Übersetzung von Alcuin's *De Virtutibus et Vitiis Liber. Ad Widonem Comitem*," *Anglia* 11 (1889): 371–91.

tation with a rich variety of dangers than a predictable stage in the soul's growth. Such a way of textualizing the experience of temptation defused some of the irruptive force of sin. The Church at this time was no longer marginal, but had moved into a position of social dominance. Threats to its reign within the psyche did not have to be conceptualized in the emotionally charged manner of the *Psychomachia*. The vices were stripped of their former imaginative investments, suborned through processes of recodification. As a result, the stirring drama of temptation became stereotypical and predictable. Of course, in the *Psychomachia* the outcome of the struggle was known in advance, but the means were uncertain and each attack was allowed its individual menace. Such defusing of the imaginary entails the transformation of one genre of writing into another. In this case the unliterary turns out to be merely another ruse of the literary, the result of its very success in troping readers. Paradoxically, the triumph of the monastic fascination with the mapping of the soul's progress in the *Psychomachia* can be seen in the shift from a poetics to a technology of the soul. The presentational mode of the psychomachia tradition became so powerful that it could erase itself into the discursive mode of the *conflictus*.

Aelfric uses Alcuin's work in his second Midlent Sunday homily.[27] It begins with allegorical exegesis of the account of the seven nations (plus Pharaoh, so the numerical scheme will come out right) who were overcome by Joshua and the Israelites. Aelfric followed a commentary tradition which read these events *spiritualiter* as the eight capital sins. After glossing his material in this way, Aelfric paraphrased Ephesians 6.13–17 on the spiritual struggle: "Mid þisum gastlicum wæpnum we sceolon ongean ðam awyrigedum gastum þurh Godes mihte stranglice feohtan. gif we willað sigefæste to ðam behátenan earde heofenan rices becuman."[28] [With these spiritual weapons we must fight boldly against those accursed spirits through God's power, if we wish to enter victoriously into the promised land of the kingdom of heaven.] A list of the vices is then given in the Cassianic order, via Alcuin's treatise—and therefore in the *conflictus* tradition. Aelfric's comment upon this list is characteristic of his style:

---

27. On Alcuin's influence, see Max Förster, "Über die Quellen von Aelfrics Exegetischen Homiliae Catholicae," *Anglia* 16 (1894): 46–48.

28. *Aelfric's Catholic Homilies: The Second Series: Text*, ed. Malcolm Godden (Oxford, 1979), 123.

"Hit is gecweden þæt se ealda israhel oferwánn seofen ðeoda. eahteoðe wæs pharao. ac hí oferwunnon micele má þonne ðær genamode wæron. swa eac ælc ðyssera heafodleahtra hæfð micelne team. ac gif we ða modru acwellað. þonne beoð heora bearn ealle adydde."[29]

[It is written that the old Israel overcame seven tribes. The eighth was Pharaoh. But they overcame much more than were named there. Each of these capital sins also has a large progeny, but if we kill their mothers, then their children are also destroyed.]

But the vices are not personified, so the colors of rhetoric never shift from decorative trope to substantial allegory.

Only when describing remedies for the vices does Aelfric move away from Alcuin's framework, in an exhortation to take up arms against powerful opponents:

Þisum heafodleahtrum we sceolon symle on urum ðeawum wiðcweðan. and ðurh godes fultum mid gastlicum wæpnum ealle oferwinnan. gif we ðone heofenlican eard habban willað; To ðam earde we wæron gesceapene.   ac we hit forwyrhton;   Nu næbbe we hit næfre buton we hit eft gewinnon mid gastlicum gecampe ðurh godes fultum.   swa swa Israhel ðone eard gewann.   ðe abraháme ær beháten wæs.[30]

[We should always fight against these capital sins in our habits, and through God's protection overcome them all with spiritual weapons, if we wish to attain the heavenly dwelling place. We were created for this dwelling place, but we forfeited it. Now we will never have it, unless we obtain it again with spiritual warfare through God's assistance, just as Israel obtained the land promised to Abraham.]

This ritualistic injunction is the memorial invocation of a stirring drama. Necessarily belated, it depends upon the existence of another body of literature. Stemming from the list of vices and their remedies in Alcuin's *Liber de Virtutibus et Vitiis*, a typical work of the static *conflictus* tradition, this meditation is founded upon the motif of the *miles Christi* as the opponent of the vices. Aldhelm too preferred this mode of allegory, although he sometimes pays homage to the psychomachia tradition by personifying vices and virtues in an underdeveloped way. The figure of

29. Ibid., 124.
30. Ibid., 125.

the *miles Christi* was one of the characteristic forms that spiritual war-
fare took in Old English poetry, a movement away from the personifica-
tion allegory of war that began with Aldhelm's *De Octo Principalibus
Vitiis*.

For the survival of the psychomachia tradition in Old English litera-
ture we must turn to *Solomon and Saturn*. Saturn, a prince of the Chalde-
ans, is zealous in wanting to discover more about the Lord's Prayer, "se
gepalmtwigode Pater Noster" (the Pater Noster decked with palm
branches, 12). Couched within Solomon's long reply in praise of that
prayer is a series of descriptions of its efficacy in spiritual combat. Solo-
mon's encomium is fervent:

> And se ðe wile geornlice   ðone godes cwide
> singan soðlice,   and hine siemle wile
> lufian butan leahtrum,   he mæg ðone laðan gæst,
> feohtende feond,   fleonde gebrengan. . . .
>
> (84–87)

[And whoever is earnestly willing to sing the word of God truly, and
always love him without sins, may put the hateful spirit, the fighting
enemy, to flight.]

Whenever such conditions are present, the letters of the Pater Noster
will fight against the devil. Most letters of the prayer are then presented
by means of prosopopoeia, first in the runic alphabet, then in their
Roman forms.[31] Personified as courageous warriors against the devil,
their spiritual potency is suggested by vivid battle descriptions. These
descriptions are elaborate for some letters, truncated for others.

Certain letters behave in a way that suggests the influence of the
Psychomachia. In the introduction to his edition of the poem, Robert J.
Menner wrote that "the personification of the letters and the detailed
description of battles are an extraordinary feature of the poem to which
it is hard to find an exact parallel. The battles are vaguely reminiscent of
those in the *Psychomachia* of Prudentius."[32] There are several parallels
to the *Psychomachia* in the battle descriptions of the Old English poem,

---

31. Of the nineteen letters that make up the prayer, only sixteen are actually used,
some are not accompanied by their runic equivalents, and their sequence is scrambled in
places.

32. Menner, *The Poetical Dialogues of Solomon and Saturn* (New York, 1941), 42.

and the vague reminiscences Menner noted might be considered artistic transformations of its materials.

The T–rune description is a case in point:

. ↑ T. hine teswað   and hine on ða tungan sticað,
wræsteð him ðæt woddor   and him ða wongan brieceð.[33]

[T injures him and sticks him in the tongue, twists his throat and breaks his jaws.]

This description is tripartite: the letter T stabs the grim fiend's tongue, throttles him, and breaks his jaws. The first element finds an exact parallel in Prudentius's poem. After *Fides* listens to the vaunting speech of *Discordia/Heresis*, she drives the point of her javelin through the vice's tongue:

Non tulit ulterius capti blasfemia monstri
uirtutum regina Fides, sed uerba loquentis
inpedit et uocis claudit spiramina pilo
pollutam rigida transfigens cuspide linguam.

(715–18)

[Faith, queen of the virtues, no longer endured the blasphemies of the monstrous prisoner, but stopped the vice's speech and shut her voice passage with a spear, thrusting its hard point through the filthy tongue.]

This imagery is appropriate for a figure like *Discordia/Heresis*, whose heretical teachings—promulgated in language—can only be defeated by faith. I have been unable to find such imagery in any other works which might be supposed to have influenced the Anglo-Saxon poet.[34] The

---

33. *Solomon and Saturn*, 94–95. All references to Old English poetry, unless otherwise indicated, are to *The Anglo-Saxon Poetic Records*, ed. George Philip Krapp and Elliott Van Kirk Dobbie (New York, 1931–53).

34. I have been unable to discover such imagery in the Bible, or in the works of Vergil, Statius, Lucan, Juvencus, Avitus, Cyprianus Gallus, Arator, or Aldhelm. A different sort of image, in which a weapon completely severs the tongue, occurs quite frequently. It should also be noted that the similarity of the T–rune to the cross may have caused the Anglo-Saxon poet to recall the commonplace of the bait of Christ's humanity and hook of his divinity catching Leviathan at the crucifixion. For a full treatment of this figure, see Johannes Zellinger, "Der geköderte Leviathan im Hortus deliciarum der Herrad von Landsperg," *Historisches Jahrbuch* 45 (1925): 161–77.

other two elements of the description are paralleled by the *Operatio-Avaritia* encounter in the *Psychomachia*:

Inuadit trepidam Virtus fortissima duris
ulnarum nodis obliso et gutture frangit
exsanguem siccamque gulam; conpressa ligantur
uincla lacertorum sub mentum et faucibus artis
extorquent animam, nullo quae uulnere rapta
palpitat atque aditu spiraminis intercepto
inclusam patitur uenarum carcere mortem.

(589–95)

[The most powerful Virtue attacks the vice, who is filled with trepidation, with the unyielding grasp of her arms, strangling her until her throat is bloodless and dry. The tight bands of her arms are wound together under her chin, and squeeze out the life from her crushed throat. Ravished by no wound, she throbs in her death throes. Her breath stopped, it suffers its end locked up in the prison of the pulse.]

The second element of the T–rune description, throttling the vice, is present in this passage from Prudentius, and the breaking of the jaws of the devil was probably suggested by the powerful grip of *Operatio*'s arms beneath the chin of *Avaritia*, which was discussed earlier in the chapter. The S–rune is given fuller treatment than the T–rune:

Đonne •ᚻ•S. cymeð,   engla geræswa,
wuldores stæf,   wraðne gegripeð
feond be ðam fotum,   læteð foreweard hleor
on strangne stan,   stregdað toðas
geond helle heap.   Hydeð hine æghwylc
æfter sceades sciman;   sceaða bið gebisigod,
Satanes ðegn   swiðe gestilled.

(111–17)

[Then S comes, leader of angels, written character of glory; he grips the hostile enemy by the feet, smashes his cheek forward against the hard stone, strews his teeth throughout the hellish throng. Each of the fiends hides himself throughout the shadowy gloom; the warrior is afflicted, Satan's thane is silenced.]

This description is fourfold: the letter S seizes the fiend by his feet, pounds his cheek upon a stone, which results in his teeth being scattered, and causes each of the fiends to hide in darkness. The parallel passage in the *Psychomachia*, which occurs when *Sobrietas* attacks *Luxuria*, was touched upon earlier:

> Addit Sobrietas uulnus letale iacenti
> coniciens silicem rupis de parte molarem,
> hunc uexilliferae quoniam fors obtulit ictum
> spicula nulla manu sed belli insigne gerenti.
> Casus agit saxum, medii spiramen ut oris
> frangeret et recauo misceret labra palato.
> Dentibus introrsum resolutis lingua resectam
> dilaniata gulam frustis cum sanguinis inplet.

(417–24)

[Sobrietas gives the death blow as {Luxuria} lies there, by hurling a huge block of stone from the rock. Because luck has offered this weapon to the standard-bearer (since she carries no javelins in her hand, but only her emblem of battle) chance drives the stone so it breaks the air passage in the midst of the face, and mashes the lips into the roof of her mouth. The teeth inside are loosened, her throat cut, her shredded tongue fills her mouth with bloody morsels.]

The first element of the S–rune description, seizure of the fiend by his feet, is not to be found in this passage. Furthermore, there is some variation in the manner in which the gruesome imagery of the *Psychomachia* is employed, although the sequence and basic materials are identical. *Sobrietas'* smashing the stone against the face of the fiend is answered in the Old English poem by the description of the S–rune's smashing the face of the fiend against the stone. The strange image of the scattering of the fiend's teeth is a more graphic description than that of the Latin poem, where the teeth are spewed forth from *Luxuria's* mouth: "Insolitis dapibus crudescit guttur et ossa / conliquefacta uorans reuomit quas hauserat offas" (425–26) [Her gorge rises at the unaccustomed banquet; gulping down the liquified bones, she vomits back the lumps she had swallowed]. Finally, the behavior of the lesser fiends who hide themselves after the slaughter of their leader (115b–17) furnishes an exact parallel to the behavior of *Luxuria's* retinue of vices: "Caede ducis dispersa fugit trepidante pauore / nugatrix acies" (432–33) [After the slaughter of their leader, her frivolous battalion scatters, fleeing in alarm and trepidation].

With both runes, violence is associated with the mouth, the locus of speech. Fiendishness is punished there, through poetic language aimed at a vicious counter-language threatening society and psyche. The self-referential and self-canceling language of punishment of the mouth is also emblematic of the self-imposed censorship commended within the social text. Violence is appropriately directed against illegitimate speech. Saturn, who has tasted many books (*ealra hæbbe / boca onbyrged* [2b–3a]), later points out that earnest utterance of the prayer which will make the devil flee (80–84).[35] Poetic language in these two passages is focused upon the need for silencing another kind of speech. Such silencing is central to *Solomon and Saturn*, which attempts to demonstrate Christian superiority to the purported wisdom of the East. True wisdom is the destruction of all that lies outside the margins of true speech. By relying upon the language of destruction associated with Germanic epic, Old English poetry reduplicates the Prudentian strategy of turning a warlike classical epic against itself. In both cases, the violence of the previous pagan form is turned within.

Although the letters *S* and *T* become Prudentian characters in *Solomon and Saturn*, another allegory of war in the poem cannot be traced to any specific tradition. *P* is a warrior with a long golden rod who smites the fiend; *A* and *E* also help him beat the demon, along with *N* and *O*; *Q* and *U* use light spears against the demon; *R* whirls the fiend by his hair; *L* and *C* harass the devil, along with *F* and *M*, who set the fiend's hair on fire; *G*, *D*, and *H* assist in the mayhem. All this graphological allegory illustrates the unified power of the prayer, which empowers every man to put the troop of evil demons to flight *ðurh mannes muð* (through the mouth of man). Only the briefest narrative development of these conflicts takes place, faint traces of the full-fledged allegory found in the *Psychomachia*.[36]

---

35. Later, God's word is again represented as able to put the devil to flight *ðurh mannes muð* (148).

36. For further discussion, see J. P. Hermann, "The Pater Noster Battle Sequence in *Solomon and Saturn* and the *Psychomachia* of Prudentius," *Neuphilologische Mitteilungen* 77 (1976): 206–10.

Chapter 2

Recurrent Motifs of Spiritual Warfare

Sustained personification allegory was not the customary way of treating spiritual conflict in Old English poetry, which never attains Prudentian epic status. Only brief, unsustained allegories occur in Alcuin and Aelfric. Although it is important to recognize the Prudentian cast of the Pater Noster battle sequence, the graphological premise of *Solomon and Saturn* does not allow individuated description. And in Aldhelm's difficult Latin poem, confrontations between virtues and vices are not Prudentian, but Cassianic, although the poem's anticipation of a psychomachia has convinced some critics that they were actually reading one. Dominated by the formal order of Cassian's archetext, which invokes scientific objectivity rather than narrative invention, Aldhelm's conflict of virtues and vices reflects its social context: the distance between the *Psychomachia* and its Old English analogues is the distance between a late classical Christianity forming itself in opposition to the paganism of the cultured classes and a hegemonic monastic culture with a highly formalized technology of the psyche. On the level of poetics, Old English literature displaces the mock-heroic conflict of Old and New *Romanitas* in Prudentius by substituting the canonical structures of Cassian's psychology. Although Cassian has neither the psychological acuity of Augustine nor the rhetorical zest of Prudentius, his practical approach to problems of the spirit transformed the poetry of spiritual conflict.

Far more prevalent than sustained personification allegory in Old English are microallegories of war, fragments of an implicit allegorical system that does not operate the personified virtues and vices of Prudentian tradition.[1] The affiliations of these recurrent motifs of spiritual

1. I do not claim that this system of recurrent motifs was ever present in the totalized form in which I represent it. I would instead argue that the allegorical system of

warfare can be mapped out in terms of the biblical notion of the spiritual warrior. An Old English poetic version of the Pauline figure of spiritual armor can be found in *A Journey Charm*:

> Biddu ealle   bliðu mode
> þæt me beo Matheus helm,   Marcus byrne
> leoht, lifes rof,   Lucos min swurd,
> scearp and scirecg,   scyld Iohannes,
> wuldre gewlitegod   wælgar Serafhin.
>
> (26–30)

[With a happy heart, I pray to all {the angels} that Matthew will be my helmet, Mark my brilliant and bold breastplate of life, Luke my sharp and bright-edged sword, John my shield, and the glorious Seraphim my spear.]

The speaker has asked for protection through the chanting of a victory-word (*wordsige*), a victory-bringing "charm" (*sygeealdor*) that can keep him safe on his journey. In a transformation of the imagery of Ephesians 6.11–16, the Evangelists take the place of the various virtues. Now, an *ealdor* is a "charm" to the extent that it is an "incantation." But it also alludes to the power of the *lectio divina*. As metonymic invocations of the gospels, the four troped evangelists function in terms of a culture of writing and the book. More than an instance of semipagan syncretism, *A Journey Charm* can be read as a learned invocation of the fruits of monastic meditation on the Bible. Spiritual warfare in Old English typically reveals such traces of learned, Christian tradition.

A frequent way of referring to the warfare between Satan and man in Old English poetry is through a cluster of terms for the old strife. In *Elene*, when Judas and his fellow townspeople are moved to praise the Son of God, the Devil appears, furious at this threat to his power:

> "Hwæt is þis, la, manna,   þe minne eft
> þurh fyrngeflit   folgaþ wyrdeð,
> iceð ealdne nið,   æhta strudeð?
> Þis is singal sacu.   Sawla ne moton
> manfremmende   in minum leng

---

spiritual warfare exists in much the same fashion as Northrop Frye's modal paradigms—i.e., as entelechies, rather than origins.

æhtum wunigan.   Nu cwom elþeodig,
þone ic ær on firenum   fæwstne talde,
hafað mec befeafod   rihta gehwylces,
feohgestreona."

(902–10a)

["Lo, what man is this who destroys my following through this ancient strife, increasing the old war and plundering my possessions? This is perpetual battle. Evil souls no longer remain my possessions. Now a stranger has come, one whom I previously considered steadfast in sins; he has robbed me of each of my possessions and treasures."]

Satan's possessions are being destroyed in what is represented as a perpetual battle (*singal sacu*) that cannot be limited to any series of historical events. Historical instances of this *fyrngeflit*, *ærgewin*, or *eald nið* occur principally in the soul of man.[2] Of such widespread influence was Ephesians 6.11–16 that the briefest reference to *fyrngeflit* evidently could summon up an extensive chain of associations. Repetition of terms associated with the ancient strife is frequently ritualistic, with only minimal development of the figure. The old strife stems from the mythic prehistory when Satan and the rebel angels initiated the war in heaven, and its mere mention inscribes present spiritual conflict within a panoramic time span. Because it originates "outside" time, it can be represented as taking place everywhere within it, in a paradox of invagination characteristic of mythic rhetoric.[3]

The notion of the old strife minimizes idiosyncracy in the intense psychological conflict of temptation by summoning up the Christian warrior's memory of past victories. Spiritual struggle might entail an irruption of dark forces threatening to dismantle psychic structure. But equilibrium can be reestablished if temptation is resisted, making the spiritual warrior even stronger. By placing the human struggle against sin within a mythic framework, the recurrent motif of the old strife helps disarm "rulers of the world of darkness, spiritual forces of wickedness on

---

2. See also *Beowulf* 1689 (*fyrngewinn*) and *Juliana* 623 (*ealdne nið*) for further references to the old strife. *Fæhð* is used in this sense in *Andreas* 1386 and *Christ* 368, 617. See also J. P. Hermann, "*The Dream of the Rood*, 19a: *earmra ærgewin*," *English Language Notes* 15 (1978): 241–44.

3. Invagination is the term for such philosophical problems of the container and the contained: for further discussion, see chap. 3.

high." Diabolical assault is warded off by a return to the wellspring of resistance, the force of prayer, in a movement toward psychic and societal structure and away from destructive self-assertion. To the solitary experience of temptation this imagery brings recollection of membership in the Church Militant, rendering individual struggle mythic and lending grandeur to the everyday struggle with sin. The recurrent motif of the old strife also encourages the aggressive instincts, forestalling or foreclosing the lapse into passivity. The social and psychological discourses of power imbricated with the trope of the soul's combat will be explored further in Part 2.

Numerous instances of epithet and antonomasia for Satan and the rebel angels are associated with the old strife: *ealdfeond*, *ealdgeniðla*, *fyrngeflita*, and *fyrnsceaþa*. So pervasive was this way of conceiving the Devil that reference is made to *se ealda*, or more frequently, to the Devil as *feond*, *sceaða*, *andsaca*, or *gewinna*.[4] Old enemies or adversaries are normal in a military society, but the concept of the *hostis antiquus* from Christian tradition re-marks these terms. When the enemy is seen as ancient, present assaults are framed within the history of the Christian warrior, as well as mythic prehistory. This enemy, resisted successfully in the past, can be overcome once again. Satan was also seen as a murderer of souls, and as a hunter with his net ever ready to trap unwary, animal-like prey who could not fit the experience of temptation into the broader framework adduced by poets and theologians.[5] The Germanic allitera-

---

4. *ealdfeond*: *Phoenix* 401, 449; *Guthlac* 141, 203, 218, 365, 390, 475; *The Descent into Hell* 89; *altfiant* appears in *Muspilli* 44; *ealdgeniðla*: *Andreas* 1341; *fyrngeflita*: *Panther* 34; *fyrnsceaþa*: *Andreas* 1346. For Old English words for the devil and their source in Christian Latin literature, see James Walter Rankin, "A Study of the Kennings in Anglo-Saxon Poetry," *Journal of English and Germanic Philology* 9 (1910): 56–59. *Se ealda* occurs in *Homiletic Fragment I*, 32; *Christ and Satan*, 34. *Feond*: *Genesis* 306, 322, 334, 449, 453, 488, 688, 1261; *Elene* 207, 899, 953; *Christ and Satan* 76, 103, 195, 443, 461, 477; *Solomon and Saturn* 69, 174, 499; *Beowulf* 101, 2128; *Phoenix* 595; *Juliana* 317, 348, 523, 630; *Panther* 58; *Vainglory* 27, 47; *Andreas* 20, 49, 1196, 1294, 1619, 1693; *Guthlac* 326, 421, 436, 442, 566, 691, 773, 803; *Kentish Hymn* 25; *Christ* 569, 623, 733, 770, 1394, 1404, 1415, 1485, 1614, 1625; *Seafarer* 75; *sceaða*: *Genesis* 606; *Christ and Satan* 57, 72; *Christ* 775, 1395; *Solomon and Saturn* 116, 128; *Andreas* 1291; *Elene* 761; *helsceaða, Maldon* 180; *andsaca*: *Genesis* 320, 442; *Christ and Satan* 190, 268, 279, 339, 717; *Guthlac* 210, 233; *gewinna*: *Andreas* 1197; *Juliana* 243, 345, 555; *gæstgeniðla*: *Juliana* 245. See also J. P. Hermann, "The Selection of Warriors in the Old English *Exodus*, Lines 233–240a," *English Language Notes* 14 (1976): 1–5.

5. *Bana*: *Descent into Hell* 88, 97; *Beowulf* 1743; *Guthlac* 87, 429; *Christ* 264, 1393; *Andreas* 616, 1293; *Christ and Satan* 466; *Solomon and Saturn* 131; *gastbona*: *Beowulf* 177; *suslbana*: *Christ and Satan* 638; *feorgbana*: *Whale*, 41; For the devil as a hunter with net see *Andreas* 943 and C. Abbetmeyer, *Old English Poetical Motives Derived from*

tive poetic often dealt with old adversaries, but its resources were grafted to the notion of the *hostis antiquus* in a complex cultural production. Christianity itself was transformed in this scene of intertextuality, which opens up a distinctively Old English spirituality and literature. The missiles of the devil constitute a frequently recurring motif for the warfare between good and evil within the soul of man.[6] The use of this figure in *Beowulf* offers a classic example. After recounting the story of Heremod, Hroðgar mentions a hypothetical ruler who shows an analogous spiritual corruption:

> "Wunað he on wiste;   no hine wiht dweleð
> adl ne yldo,   ne him inwitsorh
> on sefan sweroceð,   ne gesacu ohwær
> ecghete eoweð,   ac him eal worold
> wendeð on willan   (he þæt wyrse ne con),
> oðþæt him on innan   oferhygda dæl
> weaxeð ond wridað.   Þonne se weard swefeð,
> sawele hyrde;   bið se slæp to fæst,
> bisgum gebunden,   bona swiðe neah,
> se þe of flanbogan   fyrenum sceoteð.
> Þonne bið on hreþre   under helm drepen
> biteran stræle   (him bebeorgan ne con),
> wom wundorbebodum   wergan gastes . . ."

(1735–47)

---

the Doctrine of Sin (Minneapolis, 1903), 36. See also J. Rivière, "Muscipula diaboli. Orìgine et sens d'une image augustinienne." *Recherches de Théologie Ancienne et Médiévale* 1 (1929): 484–96.

    6. See especially E. G. Stanley, "Old English Poetic Diction and the Interpretation of *The Wanderer, The Seafarer* and *The Penitent's Prayer,*" *Anglia* 73 (1956): 418–22; Fr. Klaeber, "Die christlichen Elemente im Beowulf," *Anglia* 35 (1911): 128–30; Arthur B. Skemp, "The Transformation of Scriptural Story, Motive and Conception in Anglo-Saxon Poetry," *Modern Philology* 4 (1907): 423–70; C. Abbetmeyer, *Old English Poetical Motives,* 35–36. In addition to material cited below, see also *Juliana* 471; *Christ II,* 756–82a; *Seasons for Fasting* 164–75; *Andreas* 1048, 1330; *Guthlac* 185, 1141b–45a, 1154, 1286; *Charms* 4.23ff.; *The Riming Poem* 61–73; *Solomon and Saturn* 84 ff., 145, 506; *Vainglory* 26–39. The most extended use of this figure in Old English literature occurs in the fourth Vercelli homily; see M. Förster, ed., *Die Vercelli-Homilien, Bibliothek der angelsächsischen Prosa,* 12 (Hamburg, 1932), 103–7. See also J. P. Hermann, "*The Riming Poem,* 45b to 47a," *The Explicator* 34 (1975): 7–9, a reading of a notorious crux contested by O. D. Macrae-Gibson, ed., *The Old English Riming Poem* (Cambridge, 1983), 48–50, but accepted by Karl Wentersdorf, "The Old English *Rhyming Poem:* A Ruler's Lament," *Studies in Philology* 82 (1985): 286. On *deofles stræl* in *Andreas* 1189, see Fred C. Robinson, "Anglo-Saxon Onomastics in the Old English *Andreas,*" *Names* 21 (1973): 133–36.

["He dwells in prosperity; nothing bothers him, not sickness or old age or sorrow that darkens the mind, nor does battle anywhere make sword hatred manifest, but the entire world turns according to his will (he does not know anything worse) until within him a portion of pride grows and flourishes. Then the guardian sleeps, the protector of the soul; that sleep is too deep, bound with cares, the slayer very close who shoots him with sins from his bow. Then he is hit with a stinging arrow in the breast underneath his helm (he is unable to protect himself), with the wicked, mysterious commands of the accursed spirit . . ."]

Beowulf is at the zenith of his success in physical combat. Hroðgar rewards him with twelve treasures, as well as with this wisdom gained through suffering: success in literal battle can lead to spiritual defeat. The plantlike growth of pride in the soul of Hroðgar's hypothetical ruler is indicated by the metaphorical verbs *weaxað* and *wridað*. This incipient tendency towards reification of spiritual states grows more explicit. Just as a literal town in danger of enemy siege has a guard, so, figurally, does the soul. As pride grows this guard sleeps, although a murderer with his bow (*flanboga*) is nearby. The arrows (*biteran stræle*) are glossed by Hroðgar as the wicked mysterious commands of the Devil (*wom wundorbebodum wergan gastes*). Ironically, this ruler who felt safe from literal strife and enmity has fallen under the onslaught of the internal arrows of the spiritual warfare.

The theological underpinnings of this figure were discovered by Klaeber, and later elaborated by Abbetmeyer: the arrows of the devil represent the first stage of the fourfold Gregorian scheme, which consists in *suggestio*, the incitement to sin; *delectatio*, the stirrings of pleasure in the flesh; *consensus*, the formal assent to sin; and *defensionis audacia*, the justification of sin brought on by pride.[7] The notion of the missiles of the devil, a translation of psychical conflict into terms associ-

---

7. Abbetmeyer, *Old English Poetical Motives*, 35; Fr. Klaeber, "Die christlichen elemente im Beowulf," *Anglia* 35 (1911): 129. Gregory argues that: "Quatuor quippe modis peccatum perpetratur in corde, quatuor consummatur in opere. In corde namque suggestione, delectatione, consensus, et defensionis audacia perpetratur. Fit enim suggestio per adversarium, delectatio per carnem, consensus per spiritum, defensionis audacia per elationem." [To be sure, sin is brought to fruition in the heart in four ways, in four ways it is brought to fulfillment in deed. For in the heart it is brought to fruition though suggestion, delight, consent, and impudence of defense {of one's wrongdoing}. Suggestion is brought about through the Adversary, delight through the flesh, consent through the spirit, and impudence of defense through self-exaltation (*Moralia in Job, Patrologia Latina* 75:661).]

ated with warfare in the external world, is a reification with both religious and literary value. Evanescent spiritual assaults are cast into a form of language—that is, into a form of life—which renders them public, not simply private. In order to prevent the motion of the soul toward *cupiditas* from running its course unchecked, this complex of imagery associates it with a stirring drama in which choices to fight or yield are reinscribed within ancient cultural patterns of self-representation. Such Old English dramaturgy offers a socially reinforced script for self-fashioning. The Christian warrior fending off the arrows of the devil is cast into the role of a heroic thane in a poem like *The Battle of Maldon*, where overtones of the spiritual combat also occur.[8] It is all the more significant that Hroðgar uses the imagery of the missiles of the devil to stir up Beowulf's courage to resist spiritual evil: if even pagans knew the preeminent importance of spiritual struggle, certainly members of the Church Militant could pass on the epic heritage by resisting arrows of temptation.

In *Juliana*, Cynewulf adds to the figure of the arrows of the devil the trope of the soul as a besieged fortress.[9] These figures do not appear in the Latin source that Cynewulf used, but stem from the metaphoric system of spiritual combat:

> "Gif ic ænige   ellenrofne
> gemete modigne   metodes cempan
> wið flanþræce,   nele feor þonan
> bugan from beaduwe,   ac he bord ongean
> hefeð hygesnottor,   haligne scyld,
> gæstlic guðreaf,   nele gode swican,
> ac he beald in gebede   bidsteal gifeð
> fæste on feðan,   ic sceal feor þonan
> heanmod hweorfan,   hroþra bidæled,
> in gleda gripe,   gehðu mænan,
> þæt ic ne meahte   mægnes cræfte
> guðe wiðgongan,   ac ic geomor sceal
> secan oþerne   ellenleasran,

---

8. In Byrhtnoth's death speech and Byrhtwold's exhortations in the face of defeat, where the movement from literal to metaphorical battle is reversed: the war in the spirit is invoked in the course of urging slaughter of historical enemies.

9. See James F. Doubleday, "The Allegory of the Soul as Fortress in Old English Poetry," *Anglia* 88 (1970): 503–8. A subversive reading of this figure appears in chap. 7.

under cumbolhagan,   cempan sænran,
þe ic onbryrdan mæge   beorman mine,
agælan æt guþe.   Þeah he godes hwæt
onginne gæstlice,   ic beo gearo sona,
þæt ic ingehygd   eal geondwlite,
hu gefæstnad sy   ferð innanweard,
wiðsteall geworht."

(382–401a)

["If I meet any soldier of the Lord who is brave in the face of a shower of
arrows and unwilling to flee from battle, but wisely lifts his shield against
me (the holy shield and spiritual armor) and will not fail God—one who,
bold in prayer, takes his stand steadfastly in the army—I must go far away,
abject in mind and deprived of pleasures, to lament my sorrows in the grip
of flames because I could not overcome him by strength in combat, but
sad-minded must seek out another less courageous soldier in the battle-
lines whom I can puff up with my leaven and hinder in the battle. Al-
though he may begin to do some good work spiritually, I immediately
scrutinize his conscience, how his mind is made fast within, how its de-
fense works are constructed."]

The quantity of military imagery in this passage is extraordinary. Satan
represents himself as powerless against the *milites Christi* or *metodes
cempan* who resist the onslaught of arrows (*flanþræce*), raise the shield
of faith (*haligne scyld*), and wear the spiritual armor (*gæstlic guðreaf*).
But against the more cowardly soldier (*cempan sænran*), he can easily
triumph. Satan deftly sizes up (*geondwlite*) his fortress-soul and, since it
is not well protected (*gefæstnad*), decides how to attack it:

"Ic þæs wealles geat
ontyne þurh teonan;   bið se torr þyrel,
ingong geopenad,   þonne ic ærest him
þurh eargfare   in onsende
in breostsefan   bitre geþoncas
þurh mislice   modes willan,
þæt him sylfum   selle þynceð
leahtras to fremman   ofer lof godes,
lices lustas."

(401b–9a)

["Through an injury, I open the gate in the wall; once the tower is opened up, I send bitter thoughts into his mind by means of an arrow volley, through various desires of the mind, so that it seems better to him to perform vices, lusts of the body, rather than the praise of God."]

Once the gate is opened, a volley of arrows (*eargfare*) is launched—the longing for sin. When bodily appetites are indulged freely and no thought is given to praising God, according to this representation of the inner life, the fortress of the soul has fallen. The arrows which defeat the *cempan sænran* are the very ones the *metodes cempan* are able to resist. The notion of a long siege highlights the communal nature of resistance to temptation by the members of the Body of Christ, in whose individual successes and failures all Christians are implicated. This reification of spiritual struggle socializes it, encoding the struggle against sin in terms of a cultural tradition that celebrates resistance to military aggression. Defensive military strategy takes on heroic attributes that might not ordinarily spring to mind when the individual Christian experiences recurrent assaults of *suggestio* and *delectatio*. The conception of the soul stormed by hostile powers makes the abstract notion of the *ealdgewinn* concrete, a strategy particularly well-suited to the resources of Anglo-Saxon poetic tradition. The remains of Anglo-Saxon fortresses that are still extant are eloquent monuments to terror, material equivalents of the barricaded self: Anglo-Saxon poetry was itself a means of self-fabrication as self-protection, a delineation of the very evils for which it offered apotropaic remedies.

Closely allied with the allegoric subsystem of the missiles of the Devil is that of the wounds of sin.[10] If the missiles are often associated with the Gregorian stage of *suggestio*, the wounds imply *consensus*, marking permanent or temporary defeat in the war against the powers of evil. The richest development of the wounds of sin is found in *The Judgement Day II*, where it is amplified by the trope of Christ as the heavenly physician:

---

10. *Juliana* 355, 710; *Elene* 514; *Almsgiving* 9; *Psalm 50*, 51, 141, 154; *Christ* 763, 770, 1313, 1321; *Judgment Day II*, 38–52; *Guthlac* 284; *Homiletic Fragment I*, 30; *Soul and Body I*, 90, 95; *Soul and Body II*, 84, 88. See also J. P. Hermann, "*Solomon and Saturn II* 339a: *niehtes wunde*," *English Language Notes* 14 (1977): 161–64. With verbs signifying wounding the figure is also found: *Homiletic Fragment I*, 22–30; *Andreas* 407; *Christ and Satan* 131, 156; *A Prayer* 3; *Dream of the Rood* 14.

Ne þær owiht   inne ne belife
on heortscræfe   heanra gylta,
þæt hit ne sy dægcuð,   þæt þæt dihle wæs,
openum wordum   eall abæred,
breostes and tungan   and flæsces swa some.
Ðis is an hæl   earmre sauwle
and þam sorgiendum   selest hihta,
þæt he wunda her   wope gecyðe
uplicum læce,   se ana mæg
aglidene mod   gode gehælan
and ræplingas   recene onbindan . . .

                                        (38–48)

[Don't let any of my abject sins be left in my heart-cave so that a con-
cealed sin does not see the light of day, but let all of the breast, tongue,
and flesh be brought forward in plain words. This is the one cure for the
wretched soul and the best hope for those who grieve, that they may
reveal their wounds with weeping here to the heavenly physician, who
alone may heal with his power the spirit that has stumbled, and instantly
unbind those who are fettered.]

Christ, who ministers to minds diseased, prisoners (*ræplingas*) captured
and bound by the power of the enemy, will not bruise the wounded soul.
Counterbalancing the warlike violence of the experience of temptation
and consent to sin is a Christ who will heal the sinner who makes his
wounds known. The wounds of sin are spiritual analogues to those re-
ceived in actual battle. Just as physical wounds incapacitate the warrior,
spiritual wounds can cause a weakening of valor: consciousness of past
failures can overwhelm the Christian, making further sin more likely.
Untended, such wounds might lead to spiritual death. But since spiritual
wounds can be healed through the sacraments, they need not entail
permanent defeat. This motif dramatizes evanescent processes of psy-
chic health and disease within a context of heroism and valor. Such
rhetoric transforms the commonplace experience of succumbing to
pride, lust, or anger into mythic conflict. Even defeat is provisional, in
that it can help a wounded spiritual warrior become victorious later on.
By enlisting cultural traditions of literal violence, Old English poets
transform the mundane into the mythical.

In the old strife Satan first launched against God and now pursues against man, the *miles Dei* must resist heroically. In *Guthlac*, this notion of the spiritual warrior is connected with the conception of God as a *cyning* who rewards faithful thanes. The whole of heroic society, with all its military actions and obligations, becomes the vehicle for a spiritual trope:

> Sume þa wuniað   on westennum,
> secað ond gesittað   sylfra willum
> hamas on heolstrum.   Hy ðæs heofoncundan
> boldes bidað.   Oft him brogan to
> laðne gelædeð,   se þe him lifes ofonn,
> eaweð him egsan,   hwilum idel wuldor,
> brægdwis bona   hafað bega cræft,
> eahteð anbuendra.   Fore him englas stondað,
> gearwe mid gæsta wæpnum,   beoþ hyra geoca gemyndge,
> healdað haligra feorh,   witon hyra hyht mid dryhten.
> Þæt synd þa gecostan cempan   þa þam cyninge þeowað,
> se næfre þa lean alegeð   þam þe his lufan adreogeð.
>
> (81–92)

[Some dwell in desolate areas and of their own wills seek out and establish homes in remote places. They await a dwelling place in heaven. Often he who strives against their lives brings some hateful danger, sometimes he shows them something terrifying, or an empty splendor, for the skillful slayer has the cunning to do both: he persecutes these anchorites. Angels stand before them, ready with spiritual weapons, mindful of their safety, guarding the life of the holy ones; they know their hope is with the Lord. These are tested warriors who serve a king who never refuses the reward for those who live his love.]

Here, the figure of warfare is used to represent not only the attack of the old enemy, but also resistance to it: the spirits' weapons (*gæsta wæpnum*) in this passage are wielded by angels, not by men. Even though these seasoned warriors are sometimes defenseless, save for angelic assistance, they are represented as heroic. God, as munificent as any Germanic ring-giver from epic tradition, never fails to reward his warriors, however.

Guthlac's own heroic service of God is rendered in detailed battle scenes:

Þær he mongum wearð
bysen on Brytene,   siþþan biorg gestah
eadig oretta,   ondwiges heard.
Gyrede hine georne   mid gæstlicum
wæpnum * * *   wong bletsade,
him to ætstælle   ærest aærde
Cristes rode,   þær se cempa oferwon
frecnessa fela.   Frome wurdun monge
godes þrowera;   we þæs Guðlaces
deorwyrðne dæl   dryhtne cennað.
He him sige sealde   ond snyttrucræft,
mundbyrd meahta,   þonne mengu cwom
feonda færscytum   fæhoe ræran.
Ne meahton hy æfeste   anforlætan,
ac to Guðlaces   gæste gelæddun
farsunga fela.

(174b–89a)

[He became a model for many in Britain when he climbed the hill, holy warrior, fierce in battle. He earnestly geared himself with spiritual weapons . . . he sanctified the place and first reared up the cross of Christ as assistance, where this soldier overcame many dangers. Many of God's martyrs became bold; we give credit to the Lord for Guthlac's precious part in all this. He gave him victory and the power of prudence, the protection of spiritual powers, when a host of devils came with sudden volleys of arrows to begin battle. On account of their hatred they could not leave him alone, but brought many temptations to Guthlac's soul.]

The girding with spiritual weapons and sudden onslaught of diabolical missiles constitute a quite graphic development of the *miles Christi* figure.[11] The mighty protection given to Guthlac is *snyttrucræft*, or *sapi-*

---

11. *Cempa*: Guthlac 153, 324, 402, 438, 513, 558, 576, 580, 688; *Andreas* 230, 324, 538, 991, 1446; *Juliana* 17; *Phoenix* 452, 471; *Solomon and Saturn* 139; *oretta*: *Andreas* 463, 983; *Guthlac* 176, 344, 401, 569. In *Andreas* 982, the saint is called *bearn beaduwe heard*. *Campian*: Guthlac 316, 643; *A Prayer* 12. The following description appears in *The Gifts of Men* 89–90: *Sum bið deormod deofles gewinnes, / bið a wið firenum in gefeoht gearo*. The weapons of the spirit are mentioned in *Guthlac* 89, 177–78, and implied in *Guthlac* 304. One of the more generalized uses of the idea of the weapons of the spirit is found in *Byrhtferth's Manual*, where we are told that we need them in order to understand the complexity of the computus (S. J. Crawford, ed., EETS O.S. 177, 52). The devil too has warriors, e.g., in *Christ* 563 (*deofla cempan*); they fight with weapons in *Christ* 775 and *Andreas* 1291, a variation of the typical motif of the missiles of the devil.

entia, which is represented as an oppositional force. Although Old English poets were quite fond of this notion of the soldier of Christ, critics have not been: summary dismissals of poetry based upon it have been common.[12]

Some of the finer ironic passages in Old English poetry occur when literal and spiritual warfare are juxtaposed. This can occur in two ways: loss in literal battle can be seen as yielding spiritual victory, or victory in literal battle can be seen as producing simultaneous spiritual defeat. Examples of the latter include Hroðgar's stories of Heremod and the hypothetical ruler assaulted by the devil's arrows while at his military and earthly apogee. Although given great power, Heremod grew so bloodthirsty and greedy that he slaughtered his people; Hroðgar's hypothetical ruler also becomes powerful, but his military successes lead to unchecked passions, and thus to his downfall. In *Vainglory*, this theme receives sustained development:

> . . . þonne monige beoð   mæþelhegendra,
> wlonce wigsmiþas   winburgum in,
> sittaþ æt symble,   soðgied wrecað,
> wordum wrixlað,   witan fundiaþ
> hwylc æscstede   inne in ræcede
> mid werum wunige,   þonne win hweteð
> beornes breostsefan.
>
> (13–19a)

[For there are many who plan battle, proud warriors in the festive cities, who sit at feast and tell true stories, conversing, trying to find out what battle place there might be within the hall among the men dwelling there, when wine excites the heart of the warrior.]

Defeat in spiritual combat occurs at the moment these proud war-smiths boast of their heroic military exploits. Their vainglorious behavior constitutes the missiles of the devil which destroy the fortress of the soul. The meek and forgiving man, on the other hand, is represented as one whose

---

12. See the illustrative comments by Rosemary Woolf and Kenneth Sisam which appear in J. P. Hermann, "The Recurrent Motifs of Spiritual Warfare in Old English Poetry," *Annuale Mediaevale* 22 (1982): 21–23. Several more recurrent motifs are also discussed in this article.

battle is internal, whose actions are nonviolent, and whose reward is eternal:

"Ðonne bið þam oþrum   ungelice
se þe her on eorþan   eaðmod leofað,
ond wiþ gesibbra gehwone   simle healdeð
freode on folce   ond his feond lufað,
þeah þe him abylgnesse   oft gefremede
willum in þisse worulde.   Se mot wuldres dream
in haligra hyht   heonan astigan
on engla eard.   Ne biþ þam oþrum swa,
se þe on ofermedum   eargum dædum
leofaþ in leahtrum,   new beoð þa lean gelic
mid wuldorcyning."   Wite þe be þissum,
gif þu eaðmodne   eorl gemete,
þegn on þeode,   þam bið simle
gæst gegæderad   godes agen bearn
wilsum in worlde,   gif me se witega ne leag.
Forþon we sculon a hycgende   hælo rædes
gemunan in mode   mæla gehwylcum
þone selestan   sigora waldend. Amen.

(67–84)

["But it is different with the other sort of person who lives humble-minded here on the earth and always holds peaceful thoughts toward his family and other people, and who loves his friend (who may often have done him injury) with good will in this world. He is able to ascend from here into the joy of glory, the hope of the holy, the dwelling place of angels. This is not the case with the other sort who lives in vainglory with evil deeds and sins; the rewards are not the same with the king of glory." Know by this that if you meet a humble man or thane among the people, there is always a guest with him—God's own son, the desire of the world, if the prophet has not lied to me. Therefore, ever thinking of the plan of salvation, we should always remember the excellent lord of victories.]

The Lord of victories rewards the peaceful and humble man who forgives those who offend him. Those who seek revenge are punished. Such an inversion of epic tradition is a literary transformation of historical significance, a strategic misprision of pagan cultural forms for Christian ends.

The other sort of juxtaposition of literal and spiritual warfare, defeat in literal battle associated with spiritual victory,[13] is found more frequently, as in *Fates of the Apostles*:

> Swylce Thomas eac   þriste geneðde
> on Indea   oðre dælas,
> þær manegum wearð   mod onlihted,
> hige onhyrded,   þurh his halig word.
> Syððan collenferð   cyninges broðor
> awehte for weorodum,   wundorcræfte,
> þurh dryhtnes miht,   þæt he of deaðe aras,
> geong ond guðhwæt,   ond him wæs Gad nama,
> ond ða þæm folce   feorg gesealde,
> sin æt sæcce.   Sweordræs fornam
> þurh hæðene hand,   þær se halga gecrang,
> wund for weorudum,   þonon wuldres leoht
> sawle gesohte   sigores to leane.

(50–62)

[Likewise, Thomas also courageously ventured into other regions in India, where through his holy word the mind was enlightened and thought fortified for many a person. Then by his wondrous power this proud-spirited man brought the king's brother back to life in the presence of multitudes, so that he rose from the dead, the young man brave in battle, and his name was Gad. Then in battle he gave up his life to the people. A sword assault by a heathen hand took his life where the saint fell wounded in the presence of the multitudes. From there his soul sought out the light of glory as a reward for his victory.]

After this proud-spirited warrior preached to the inhabitants of India and raised the king's brother from the dead, he was slain by a heathen swordstroke. His soul, however, sought the light of glory (*wuldres leoht*) as the reward for victory (*sigores to leane*). Defeated in literal combat, he nevertheless achieved a victory of the spirit. This strategic inversion of the Germanic military ethos constitutes a critique of heroic values. Finely calculated to enlist traditional poetic violence for the service of

---

13. This sort of juxtaposition also appears in *The Fates of the Apostles* 44; 70–74; 75ff.; *The Dream of the Rood* 67; *Elene* 623; *Andreas* 59–75; 1404–11; *The Descent into Hell* 39ff.; *Guthlac* 302; *Juliana* 683; *Panther* 64; *Maldon* 173–80. An interesting development of this juxtaposition is the notion of the cross as *sigebeam* in *The Dream of the Rood* 13, 127; *Elene* 420, 444, 665, 847, 860, 965, 1028.

Christianity, it exemplifies the strong misreading of tradition that constitutes poetic achievement for a critic such as Harold Bloom.[14]

A poignant instance of defeat in earthly terms resulting in spiritual victory can be found in the characterization of Christ and the personified Cross in *The Dream of the Rood*:

"Genaman me ðær strange feondas,
geworhton him þær to wæfersyne,   heton me heora wergas
                                                                         hebban.
Bæron me ðær beornas on eaxlum,   oððæt hie me on beorg
                                                                         asetton,
gefæstnodon me þær feondas genoge.   Geseah ic þa frean
                                                                         mancynnes
efstan elne mycle   þæt he me wolde on gestigan.
Þær ic þa ne dorste   ofer dryhtnes word
bugan oððe berstan,   þa ic bifian geseah
eorðan sceatas.   Ealle ic mihte
feondas gefyllan,   hwæðre ic fæste stod."

(30b–38)

["Powerful enemies took me there, made me into a spectacle, commanded me to raise up their criminals. There men bore me on their shoulders, until they set me upon a hill, many enemies set me up there. Then I saw the Lord of mankind hasten with much courage, for he intended to climb onto me. Then I did not dare, against the Lord's word, bend or break when I saw the earth's corners shaking. I could have destroyed all the enemies, yet I stood fast.]

The Cross is the agency of raising (*gestigan*) Christ literally and figuratively, as he suffers the most hideous of torments. Although capable of felling the crucifiers at will, the Cross restrains itself so the *strang ond stiðmod* young hero might mount it. That the lord of mankind had to be raised upon a cross is the supreme instance of the humbling of power. Christ, as well as the Cross, chooses the path of nonviolence instead of destruction of these *feondas*. Such paradoxical reinscriptions of tradition might be viewed as instances of the modern moment in Old English literature, when a powerful irony hollows out the inherited epic language. Such irony is coextensive with allegory itself, a literary mode that acknowledges its artifice and supplementarity as it displaces unmediated origins.

---

14. Further discussion of this recurrent motif appears in chap. 5.

Part 2   Allegoresis

So far *Allegories of War* has dealt with personification allegory, focused first on the psychomachia and *conflictus* traditions, then on the recurrent motifs. But the theme of spiritual warfare was frequently embodied in another variety of allegory, allegorical exegesis. Allegorical exegesis was the dominant hermeneutic method employed by biblical commentators in the early Middle Ages. These medieval exegetes thought of the Scriptures as a source of nourishment enclosed within a tough and sometimes unpalatable exterior. Before they could reach the *medulla*—the life-giving spiritual sense—they first had to strip off the *cortex*—the dead literal sense. Old English poems of spiritual warfare show traces of this tradition of allegoresis: for example, a battle from the Old Testament is sometimes reinscribed as a portrait of *Ecclesia*'s war against the powers of evil.

The remainder of the book treats with examples of the allegoresis of war in *Exodus*, *Elene*, *Andreas*, *Juliana*, and *Judith*. In these works there is a sustained development of a fundamental opposition, as in Prudentius. But the opposition inhabits hagiographic or biblical texts, encoding narrative conflicts as allegories of *Ecclesia*'s struggles against *Diabolus* or *Synagoga*. Exegetical critics have drawn attention to these five poems in ways which allow us to read an allegoresis of warfare, an overarching symbolic structure of the battle between good and evil supervening upon a narrative of historical conflict from the Bible or Church history.

However, there is a double movement to the following chapters, which rely upon the notion of an allegoresis of warfare even as they explore the limitations of Exegetics. Attention is given to allegorical dimensions of the poems, but at a certain stage in the argument a dialectical reversal takes place: the focus then shifts to textual residues resistant to an allegorical perspective. These discussions of the allegory of war in *Exodus*, *Elene*, *Andreas*, *Juliana*, and *Judith* are also archaeological and genealogical projects: each reading of larger rhetorical patterns in Old English poetry is linked to an investigation of formative social and psychological processes.

Before proceeding any further, terminological problems must be addressed. It is often difficult to know what is meant by the elusive and ambiguous term *allegory*. It may mean personification allegory of the sort found in the *Psychomachia*, where characters like *Luxuria* or *Discordia* appear. Or it may mean figural allegory like that in the *Divine Comedy*, where Virgil represents not only the historical poet of Augustan Rome, but a personification like Reason as well. These uses of the term refer primarily to a mode of artistic expression. Yet even when we are referring to allegory as a hermeneutic method the term is ambiguous, since "allegory" also does duty as the second of the four interpretative levels, as in Bede's discussion of *allegoria* in *De Schematibus et Tropis*:

> *Lauda Hierusalem dominum, lauda deum tuum Sion, quoniam confortavit seras portarum tuarum, benedixit filios in te* [Ps. 147.12–13]. De civibus terrenae Hierusalem, de ecclesia Christi, de anima quaque electa, de patria caelesti iuxta historiam, iuxta allegoriam, iuxta tropologiam, iuxta anagogen recte potest accipi.[1]

> [*Praise the Lord, Jerusalem, praise your God Sion, because he has greatly strengthened the bolts of your gates, he has blessed your children within you.* This may rightly be taken to mean the cities of the earthly Jerusalem, the Church of Christ, the chosen soul, and the heavenly fatherland, according to the historical, allegorical, tropological and anagogical levels.]

In other words, the second of the four allegorical levels is the allegorical level. There are schemes for resolving these ambiguities, but they are ungainly or unwieldy, so I have instead chosen to put my readers on notice of the possibility of confusion when this key term occurs. I should also point out that the first allegorical level, which Bede refers to as the historical level, is often referred to as the literal level; I will use both terms.

---

1. In *Rhetores Latini Minores*, ed. Karl Halm (Leipzig, 1863), 617–18. See also the introductory material and commentary in Gussie Hecht Tanenhaus, "Bede's *De Schematibus et Tropis*—A Translation," *Quarterly Journal of Speech* 48 (1962): 237–53.

A further terminological point, dealing with a critical word in the arguments that follow: *sublation* is the English translation I have chosen for Hegel's *Aufhebung*. The word is difficult to render in plain English, variously meaning "lifting up," "negating," and "conserving"—roughly speaking, the incorporation of a prior stage or concept by a subsequent one. One might say that *Ecclesia* sublates *Synagoga* in the Old English *Exodus*, or that the historical level of allegoresis is sublated into the allegorical level(s)—to do so, I would argue, is to broach a fundamental problem in early medieval culture.

Part 2 of *Allegories of War* interrogates sublatory traces in Old English poetry by means of a methodological shift from a predominantly analytic to a predominantly dialectical paradigm. An increasingly strenuous subversion—or sublation—of protocols for reading Old English literature parallels the discussions of textual violence. The shift from analytics to dialectics between Parts 1 and 2 of *Allegories of War* occurs within each of the following chapters as well.

Chapter 3

Exodus

The broad outlines of the Old English *Exodus* were taken from Exodus 13–14 in the Vulgate, which recounts the Israelites' journey from Egypt, pursuit by Pharaoh's army, and miraculous deliverance at the Red Sea. The poem differs from its Old Testament source in two principal ways: by the inclusion of details found elsewhere in the Bible and the adoption of a Christian hermeneutic perspective.[1] *Exodus* foregrounds the allegoresis of its materials,[2] and the fundamental oppositions of the poem are stark, making *Exodus* an ideal place to begin reading the allegoresis of war.

The most striking signal of the way *Exodus* is marked by the tradition of allegorical exegesis is an authorial gloss to the narrative. Notice how the truths revealed to Moses are equated with the truths contemporary men could also find in Scripture:

> Þanon Israhelum   ece rædas
> on merehwearfe   Moyses sægde,
> heahþungen wer,   halige spræce,

---

1. Consult Edward B. Irving, ed., *The Old English Exodus*, Yale Studies in English, 122 (New Haven, 1953) for details added to the Old Testament narrative. Irving's notes and introduction incorporate the results of earlier investigators. See also Irving's "New Notes on the Old English Exodus," *Anglia* 90 (1972): 289–324. For the influence of allegorical exegesis, see J. E. Cross and S. I. Tucker, "Allegorical Tradition and the Old English Exodus," *Neophilologus* 44 (1960): 122–27 and James W. Earl, "Christian Tradition in the Old English Exodus," *Neophilologische Mitteilungen* 71 (1970): 541–70.

2. Much recent scholarship has contradicted Irving's generalization that the poet "is interested primarily in facts, in recreating historical events as accurately as possible. . . . A few phrases in the poem suggest that he was aware of [allegorical tradition] . . . but the whole poem shows decisively that he was not interested in it" (Irving, *The Old English Exodus*, 20). But see Ruth M. Ames, "The Old Testament Christ and the Old English *Exodus*," *Studies in Medieval Culture* 10 (1977): 33–50.

deop ærende.   Dægword nemnað
swa gyt werðeode,   on gewritum findað
doma gehwilcne,   þara ðe him drihten bebead
on þam siðfate   soðum wordum,
gif onlucan wile   lifes wealhstod,
beorht in breostum,   banhuses weard,
ginfæsten god   gastes cægon.

(516–25)

[Thereupon Moses, the man of high rank, declaimed to the Israelites in holy speech eternal counsels and a deep message on the seashore. Nations still invoke the words of that day, as even now they find in the Sacred Scriptures each of those laws which the Lord, with true words, commanded them to observe on that journey, if the interpreter of life, the guardian of the body, bright in the breast, is willing to unlock abundant good with the keys of the spirit.]

The spiritual depth of Moses' words is indicated by the phrases *deop ærende* (deep message) and *ece rædas* (eternal counsels). The conjunction *swa gyt* (even now) bridges the gap between the third and sixth ages of the world: latter day readers can still find *doma gehwilcne* (each of the judgments) revealed to Moses if the soul will unlock lasting good with the keys of the spirit. This metaphor is one of allegoresis—the events of the poem are to be understood *spiritualiter*. Without such a process of decoding, the truth is locked up or, in another trope, left in the dark. The poet's gloss becomes more specific:

Run bið gerecenod,   ræd forð gæð,
hafað wislicu   word on fæðme,
wile meagollice   modum tæcan
þæt we gesne ne syn   godes þeodscipes,
metodes miltsa.   He us ma onlyhð,
nu us boceras   beteran secgað
lengran lifwynna.   Þis is læne dream,
wommum awyrged,   wreccum alyfed,
earmra anbid.   Eðellease
þysne gystsele   gihðum healdað,
murnað on mode,   manhus witon
fæst under foldan,   þær bið fyr and wyrm,
open ece scræf.   Yfela gehwylces
swa nu regnþeofas   rice dælað,

yldo oðð ærdeað. Eftwyrd cymð,
mægenþrymma mæst   ofer middangeard,
dæg dædum fah.   Drihten sylfa
on þam meðelstede   manegum demeð,
þonne he soðfæstra   sawla lædeð,
eadige gastas,   on uprodor,
þær is leoht and lif,   eac þon lissa blæd;
dugoð on dreame   drihten herigað,
weroda wuldorcyning,   to widan feore.

(526–48)

[The mystery will be interpreted and counsel will issue forth; it has wise words within its interior, and wishes earnestly to teach our spirits so we will not lack the mercy of the Lord and divine instruction. He will further enlighten us, but for now scholars will tell us of the better, longer pleasures of life. This life is a transitory joy, corrupted by sins, one allowed to exiles, a biding of time for the miserable. Deprived of our native country, we live in this guest house with sorrow, mourn in spirit, knowing of the dungeon established deep in the earth, where there is fire and serpent, the eternal open pit. They share the kingdom of every evil, just as the consummate thieves old age and early death do now. The judgment day is coming, the greatest of mighty events upon the earth, a day distinguished by significant deeds. The Lord himself will judge multitudes in the assembly place; then he will lead the souls of the righteous, blessed spirits, on high where there is light and life, as well as abundant mercy; that band will praise the Lord in joy, the glorious king of hosts, for ever and ever.]

When the keys of the spirit are used, instruction will follow; we will discover that lasting joys in heaven are preferable to transient pleasures on earth. The work summarizes its *ræd* here, fulfilling the hermeneutic expectations it has aroused. Tropological content is linked to anagogical when the focus shifts to joys *on uprodor* (in heaven, 545b) which will be the believer's *bot lifes* (reward of life). If these lines do not complete the labor of interpretation for the modern reader, they do provide a framework.[3] It is, after all, *lifes wealhstod* (the interpreter of life, 523b) within the breast that must unlock the poem's mysteries—which suggests that no gloss, whether authorial or patristic, can substitute for earnest grap-

3. The notion of a poem containing its own interpretation presents a notorious logical difficulty. The problem is that of invagination, in which the contained becomes the container, as when a glove is turned inside out. See Jacques Derrida, "The Retrait of Metaphor," *Enclitic* 2 (1978): 14–23.

pling with the poem. The intratextual interpretation represents what the devout reader would have already known and must be made to remember: that not only wandering Israelites but Christians as well are *eðellease* (homeless, 534b); that man's true home is in heaven; that Christ leads the souls of the blessed to heaven just as Moses led the Jewish exiles to safety.[4]

A specific instance of the need for an allegorical interpretive framework is Moses' miraculous rescue of the fleeing Israelites from the pursuing Egyptian army, culminating in the miracle at the Red Sea:

> "Hwæt, ge nu eagum to   on lociað,
> folca leofost,   færwundra sum,
> hu ic sylfa sloh   and þeos swiðre hand
> grene tacne   garsecges deop."

(278–81)

["Lo, now you, the most dear of nations, may look upon a great miracle with your own eyes, how I myself and this right hand have struck the ocean deep with this green symbol."]

Virga, the Vulgate's word for the rod Moses uses to part the Red Sea, is rendered by *grene tacne* in the Old English poem. Most editors suspect scribal error, emending *tacne* (symbol) to *tane* (rod), a literal-minded reading first proposed by Franz Dietrich more than a century ago: "nicht mit grünem zeichen, sondern mit grünem stabe schlug Moses das meer; also l[esen] tâne"[5] [Moses struck the sea, not with a green symbol, but with a green staff; therefore, read *tane*]. There is certainly some basis for this conjecture, given the apparent inappropriateness of striking the sea with a "green symbol." But is it really so inappropriate? I have argued elsewhere that the manuscript reading *tacne* is an instance of paronomasia placing the rod of Moses in the very allegorical perspective urged by the authorial gloss. It is both a figure of speech and a figure of thought, both a scheme and a trope, to use Bede's rhetorical terminology, since the rod of Moses is a *tan* which is also a *tacen* in traditional

---

4. See J. R. Hall, "Pauline Influence on *Exodus*, 523–48," *English Language Notes* 15 (1977): 84–88.

5. Franz Dietrich, "Zu Cädmon," *Zeitschrift für deutsches Alterthum* 10 (1856): 346. Of the twelve editors of the poem, all emended in this fashion except Blackburn, Krapp, and Irving.

allegorical commentaries.[6] According to one exegetical tradition it beto-
kens the cross of Christ: "Virga autem qua mare tangitur, sicut supra
dictum est, crux Christi est, quam per baptismum accipimus" [The rod,
however, with which the sea is struck, as has been said earlier, is the
cross of Christ which we accept through baptism].[7] Rabanus Maurus
prefers an alternative interpretation of the rod as symbolic of the knowl-
edge of the law and Scriptures:

> Si Aegyptum fugias, si ignorantiae tenebras relinquas, et sequaris legem
> Dei Moysen, obviet autem tibi mare, et contradicentium fluctus occurrat,
> percute tu obluctantes undas virga Moysi, id est, verbo legis et vigilantia
> Scripturarum.[8]

> [If you want to flee from Egypt, if you want to leave behind the shadows
> of ignorance and follow the Mosaic law of God, yet the sea opposes you
> and the waves of gainsaying counter you, strike the waves rushing against
> you with the rod of Moses—that is, with the word of the law and close
> attention to the Scriptures.]

We cannot determine which of these two interpretations is right for this
virga that is also a *tacen*, nor is it necessary—the play of meanings
between *tacne* and *tane* is significant enough.

Of further interest in this regard is the description of the rod/
symbol as *grene*, since no color is specified in the Vulgate. In a passage
from his *Moralia* explicating Jacob's experimental genetics in Genesis
30, Gregory saw the green sticks peeled to spot Laban's flocks as repre-
sentative of allegorical exegesis.[9] They stand for the words of Scripture
which, according to this well-known exegetical topos, have a cortex
which must be stripped away so the inner whiteness of the medulla—the

---

6. See Bede's discussion of paronomasia and factual allegory in his *De
Schematibus et Tropis*. I first made this argument in "The Green Rod of Moses in the Old
English *Exodus*," *English Language Notes* 12 (1975): 241–43. See also Thomas D. Hill,
"The *virga* of Moses and the Old English *Exodus*," in *Old English Literature in Context:
Ten Essays*, ed. J. D. Niles (Cambridge, 1980), 57–65, 165–67; and Maxwell Luria, "Why
Moses' Rod is Green," *English Language Notes* 17 (1980): 161–63.

7. Pseudo-Bede, *In Pentateuchum Commentarii, Patrologia Latina* 91:310. Here-
after abbreviated *PL*.

8. Rabanus Maurus, *Commentaria in Exodum, PL* 108:67. Cf. Gaudentius, *Ser-
mones de Exodo, PL* 20:848–49.

9. Gregory the Great, *Moralia in Job, PL* 76:187–88.

allegorical significance—may be revealed. In traditional commentaries the rod of Moses is symbolic of either the *verbum legis et vigilantia Scripturarum* (the word of the law and close attention to the Scriptures) or the *crux Christi* (cross of Christ), but it may also refer to the process of allegorical interpretation itself. The color green is put to symbolic work elsewhere in the poem.[10]

I will return to the green rod of Moses later. For now, it is enough to remark that to read *Exodus* along allegorical lines is only to follow the lead of the poem's opening lines, which give notice of a controlling principle of allegoresis:

> Hwæt! We feor and neah   gefrigen habað
> ofer middangeard   Moyses domas,
> wræclico wordriht,   wera cneorissum,—
> in uprodor   eadigra gehwam
> æfter bealusiðe   bote lifes,
> lifigendra gehwam   langsumne ræd,—
> hæleðum secgan.   Gehyre se ðe wille!
>
> (1–7)

[Lo, we have heard heroic men tell of the judgments of Moses far and near over the earth, splendid laws for the generations of mankind—of the reward of life on high for each of the blessed after the dangerous journey, everlasting counsel for each of the living. Let him who is able to, give heed!]

Moyses domas and *wræclico wordriht* are in apposition, and would appear to refer to laws handed down by Moses in Leviticus and Deuteronomy as well as to the Decalogue itself. In parallel construction to *domas* are *langsumne ræd* (long-lasting counsel) and *bote lifes* (reward of life), phrases which serve as a gloss on *domas* and expand its meaning. The *bot lifes* is *in uprodor* (in heaven) for *eadigra gehwam / æfter bealusiðe* (each of the blessed after the deadly journey), indexing the anagogical level. The *langsum ræd* which inheres in *Moyses domas* is not otherworldly, but rather for *lifigendra gehwam* (each of the living) in this life,

---

10. The *haswe herestreata* (284), or path through the Red Sea, is later called *grene grund* (312). Cf. Hugh T. Keenan, "*Exodus* 312: The Green Street of Paradise," *Neuphilologische Mitteilungen* 71 (1970): 455–60 and "*Exodus* 312a: Further Notes on the Eschatological 'Green Ground,' " *Neuphilologische Mitteilungen* 74 (1973): 217–19.

indexing the moral level. The importance of these spiritual levels is underscored by the parabolic topos of line 7b: *Gehyre se ðe wille*, which can itself be heard in various ways.[11]

I

The allegorical levels rarely line up as neatly as in the opening lines. But patterns of diction occasionally do mesh with traditional *Exodus* commentaries and sermons that took the Red Sea crossing as an allegory of baptism.[12] The epithet and antonomasia that characterize Moses and Pharaoh are cases in point. Moses is *leof Gode* (dear to God, 12), *horsc and hreðergleaw* (wise and prudent, 13), and a *freom folctoga* (bold leader of his people, 14). He is *from* (wise, 54) and *frod on ferhðe* (wise in mind, 355)—characterized, in other words, primarily in terms of his *sapientia et fortitudo*. Pharaoh, on the other hand, is twice referred to as *Godes andsaca* (God's enemy, 15, 503), a formulaic expression used elsewhere in the Old English poetic corpus primarily as an epithet for Satan.[13] Traditional allegoresis also identified Pharaoh with Satan. Gaudentius took this position in his *Sermones de Exodo*:

> Exodus ergo beate atque perfecte consummatur in nobis quando verus Moyses de Jordanis aqua sumptus, et . . . Deus, Dominus noster Jesus Christus, virga crucis suae nos per aquam Baptismi de captivitate Pharaonis diaboli educit. . . .[14]

> [The Exodus therefore is blessedly and perfectly brought to fruition in us when the true Moses is taken from the water of the Jordan, and . . . God, our Lord Jesus Christ leads us from the captivity of the devil Pharaoh through the water of Baptism, by means of the rod of his Cross . . . .]

---

11. Such injunctions are found in Matt. 11.15; 13.9, 43; Mark 4.9, 23; 7.16; Luke 8.8; 14.35. Cf. the gloss to Matt. 13.9 in Joseph Bosworth, *The Gothic and Anglo-Saxon Gospels* (London, 1865): *Se ðe hæbbe earan to gehyrenne, gehyre*.

12. But by no means as consistently as allegorical critics would like. See below, chap. 6.

13. Used in the singular, *Godes andsaca* appears ten times in the corpus of Old English poetry. Outside of the citations for Pharaoh in *Exodus*, and two citations for Grendel in *Beowulf* (786, 1682), all other references are to Satan (*Genesis* 442; *Christ and Satan* 190, 268, 279, 339, 717). On Moses' characterization, see R. E. Kaske, "Sapientia et Fortitudo as the Controlling Theme of *Beowulf*," *Studies in Philology* 55 (1958): 423–57.

14. *PL* 20:848–49.

Many other commentaries make this equation as well.[15]
Epithet and antonomasia are used to contrast the Egyptians and
Israelites in a similar way. The Egyptians are *wlance þegnas* (arrogant
thanes, 170), *hare heorowulfas* (old sword-wolves, 181), an *eorp werod*
(dark host, 194). Proleptically termed *deade feðan* (dead troops, 266)
and *wlance þeode* (arrogant people, 487), they are characterized chiefly
by their *gylp* (boasting, 455, 515). Significantly, at one point they are
called *hergas on helle* (armies in hell, 46), in a line which has attracted
more than its share of emendation. Imagery of binding is frequently
associated with the Egyptians. After the early characterization in terms
of his *sapientia et fortitudo* we are told that Moses *"Faraones cyn, / godes
andsacan, gyrdwite band . . ."* (He bound Pharaoh's people, God's ene-
mies, with the rod of punishment, 14b–15). The rod being referred to is
the green rod of Moses, here seen as binding the Egyptians in the Red
Sea. Later they are described as *handa belocene* (with their hands shack-
led, 43). When in the Red Sea, they are *fæste gefeterod* (tightly fettered,
470), *searwum asæled* (cunningly bound, 471), *fæste befarene* (securely
trapped, 498). By contrast, *hæft wæs onsæled* (the bond was unloos-
ened, 584) for the Israelites. In MS. Junius 11, where this poem appears,
several illustrations of bound devils appear.[16] Many other specifically
literary instances of binding imagery in connection with the torments of
hell occur in Old English poems, further proof that the Egyptians are
represented as demonic.[17]

Conventional exegesis read the army of Pharaoh as either past sins
or devils, two closely allied ideas.[18] Rabanus Maurus emphasizes the
latter interpretation, although the view of the army of Pharaoh as past
sins is also found, to a limited degree, in his *Commentaria in Exodum*:

Interfecit quippe exercitum spiritualium Aegyptiorum cum vero
Pharaone, quando diabolum et satellites ejus, cum tota spirituali nequitia

---

15. Cf. Zeno, *Tractatus de Exodo*, *PL* 11:510; Primasius of Hadrumentum, *In Epis-
tolum ad Hebraeos Commentaria*, *PL* 68:769; Isidore, *Questiones in Vetus Testamentum*, *PL*
83:296; Pseudo-Bede, *In Pentateuchum Commentarii*, *PL* 91:310 and *Questiones super
Exodum*, *PL* 93:370; Rabanus Maurus, *Commentaria in Exodum*, *PL* 108:66; *Aelfric's
Catholic Homilies: The Second Series: Text*, ed. Malcolm Godden (Oxford, 1979), 115.

16. They appear on pp. 3, 16, 17, 20, and 36 of MS. Junius 11.

17. E.g., *Solomon and Saturn* 158; *Christ* 365, 562, 732; *Christ and Satan* 38, 58,
103, 323; *Judith* 115; *Descent into Hell* 65.

18. On this relationship, see Franz Dölger, *Der Exorzismus im altchristlichen
Taufritual: Eine religionsgeschichtliche Studie, Studien zur Geschichte und Kultur des Al-
tertums*, 3 (Paderborn, 1909), 25–38.

et multitudine peccatorum in aquis spiritualibus, ubi credentes per similitudinem mortis ejus baptizati a morte peccatorum resurgunt, submersit et aeterno damnavit interitu . . . .[19]

[To be sure, he slew the army of spiritual Egyptians with the true Pharaoh, when he submerged in spiritual waters and damned to eternal ruin the devil and his accomplices—with their whole-hearted spiritual wickedness and multitude of sins—in the very place where believers, through the similitude of his death, rise up baptized from the death of sins.]

More frequently, however, the Egyptians were seen exclusively as past sins destroyed by baptism, as in Isidore's *Quaestiones*:

Hostes sequentes cum rege, qui a tergo moriuntur, peccata sunt prae-terita, quae delentur, et diabolus, qui in spirituali baptismo suffocatur.[20]

[The enemies who follow with their king, they who perish in the rear, are past sins, which are destroyed, and the devil, who is suffocated in spiritual baptism.]

The reference to hell and predilection for binding imagery put the poem squarely in the tradition of Rabanus and Zeno.

The most striking metaphor of the poem, the description of the cloud guiding the Israelites through the desert, also has exegetical signifi-cance:

	hæfde witig god
sunnan siðfæt	segle ofertolden,
swa þa mæstrapas	men ne cuðon,
ne ða seglrode	geseon meahton,
eorðbuende	ealle cræfte,
hu afæstnod wæs	feldhusa mæst. . . .

(80b–85)

---

19. *PL* 108:66. Cf. Zeno, *Tractatus de Exodo*, *PL* 11:510.

20. *PL* 83:296. Cf. Primasius of Hadrumentum, *In Epistolam ad Hebraeos Com-mentaria*, *PL* 68:769; Pseudo-Bede, *In Pentateuchum Commentarii*, *PL* 91:310 and *Ques-tiones Super Exodum*, *PL* 93:370; Aelfric's *Catholic Homilies*, 115. For the influence of patristic onomastics, see Fred C. Robinson, "The Significance of Names in Old English Literature," *Anglia* 86 (1968): 26–29.

[Wise God covered the course of the sun with a sail so that earth-dwellers could not see the rigging or the mast, no matter how skillful they were, how this greatest of tents was fastened there . . . .]

This trope is developed more fully when the Israelites are seen as sailors and the journey to the Red Sea is seen as the progress of a ship, despite the fact that on the literal level they are marching through the scorching desert:

> Forð gesawon
> lifes latþeow   lifweg metan;
> swegl siðe weold,   sæmen æfter
> foron flodwege.

(103b–6a)

[They saw ahead where the guide of life measured out the way of life; the sail marked out the course, while seamen traveled the ocean way behind it.]

The metaphor of *Ecclesia* as a ship is traditional.[21] In contrast, the Egyptians are called landsmen (179), save at the time of their drowning in the Red Sea when, with savage irony, they are called seamen (479). The *Exodus* poet then makes the conventional association of the Israelites with *Ecclesia*. The Israelites, like *Ecclesia*, take life as an exile from their true homeland. *Eðellease* (homeless) in two senses, they are *nydfara* (fugitives, 208), *wræcmon* (exiles, 137), and *wreccan* (wanderers, 533).

The journey of the Israelites is contrasted with that of the Egyptians. Both have allegorical significance. The general metaphor of life as a journey is suggested by *bealusið* (deadly journey, 5), and *lifweg* (road

---

21. On the sea journey as metaphor for the pilgrim Church, see G. Ehrismann, "Religionsgeschichtliche Beiträge zum germanischen Frühchristentum," *Beiträge zur Geschichte der deutschen Sprache und Literatur* 35 (1909): 209–39; Jean Daniélou, *The Bible and the Liturgy* (Notre Dame, Ind., 1961); Wolfgang Harms, *Homo Viator in Bivio: Studien zur Bildlichkeit des Weges* (Munich, 1970); Hugo Rahner, *Griechische Mythen in christlicher Deutung* (Zurich, 1957); G. V. Smithers, "The Meaning of *The Seafarer* and *The Wanderer*," *Medium Aevum* 26 (1957): 145–53; R. E. Kaske, "A Poem of the Cross in the Exeter Book," *Traditio* 23 (1969): 41–71, esp. 54–55; Earl, "Christian Tradition," 562. On the cloud, see Peter J. Lucas, "The Cloud in the Interpretation of the Old English *Exodus*," *English Studies* 51 (1970): 297–311.

of life, 104) echoes the Bible.[22] Many subsequent allusions function on both a literal and allegorical level, such as the description of the Israelites *on langne lust leofes siðes* (in unceasing desire for the dear journey, 53). The journey of the Egyptians, on the other hand, is a *spildsið* (journey to destruction, 153) which ends in drowning, as well as in spiritual death for the *hergas on helle* (46). The Israelites tread the *rihtu stræt* (right way, 126) of the New Testament.[23] And when wandering through the dangerous region of the *Guðmyrce*, they traverse *enge anpaðas, uncuð gelad* (narrow paths and unknown ways, 58).[24] The phrase *uncuð gelad* (313) is later used for the *grene grund* (312) through the Red Sea. The formula *enge anpaðas* evidently refers to the strait way of Matthew 7.14: "Quam angusta porta, et arcta via est, quae ducit ad vitam: et pauci sunt qui inveniunt eam!" [How narrow is the gate, and strait is the way, which leads to life; and few there are who discover it!] Rabanus Maurus draws the same parallel in his *Commentaria in Exodum*. In Exodus 14.1–2, the Lord tells Moses where to set up camp: "Locutus est autem Dominus ad Moysen, dicens: "Loquere filiis Israel: Reversi castra metentur e regione Phihahiroth, quae est inter Magdalum et mare contra Beelsephon . . . ." [The Lord spoke to Moses, saying, "Speak to the children of Israel. Let them turn and camp over by Phiahiroth, which is between Magdal and the sea at Beelsephon . . ."]. After giving standard etymologies for the camps, Rabanus explains them *spiritualiter*:

Ascensio est, et ascensio tortuosa: non enim proclive iter est, quo tenditur ad virtutes, sed ascenditur. Audi etiam Dominum in Evangelio dicentem: *Quam arcta et angusta via est, quae ducit ad vitam.* . . . Multae enim nobis tentationes occurrunt: multa offendicula volentibus agere quaedam sunt. Tum deinde in fide multa invenies tortuosa, plurimas quaestiones, multas objectiones haereticorum, multas contradictiones infidelium.[25]

[There is an ascent, and it is an ascent full of turns and windings. The road toward which the virtues are inclined does not slope downwards, but

---

22. Such imagery is found in Ps. 16.11, Matt. 7.14, and Acts 2.28, for example.

23. E.g., 2 Pet. 2.15 refers to those unjust men who "derelinquentes rectam viam erraverunt, secuti viam Balaam ex Bosor, qui mercedem iniquitatis amavit" [leaving the right way have gone astray, following the way of Balaam from Bosor, who loved the wages of wickedness].

24. The latter line is also found in *Beowulf* 1410, a fact which was central to the old argument over which poem influenced the other.

25. *PL* 108:63.

must be climbed. Listen then to the Lord in the Gospel saying *How narrow is the gate and strait the way that leads to life* . . . . Many temptations work against us; many kinds of stumbling blocks are certain to occur to those who are willing. Then afterwards you will discover many turnings and windings in the faith, many questions, many objections of heretics, many contradictory assertions by infidels.]

That the collocation of the journey of the Israelites with Matthew 7.14 occurs both in the Old English *Exodus* and in the commentary of Rabanus suggests the probable influence of the allegorical tradition Rabanus represents.

In the Old English *Exodus*, the Israelites are represented as an army. Moses even utters a speech which resembles Hnæf's in *The Battle of Finnsburh.*[26] There is faint scriptural basis for this conception, however. In Exodus 12.41, the Israelites are referred to as the *exercitus Domini*, but no description of precisely what sort of army is given. Throughout the Vulgate account of the flight from Egypt they are represented only as the *filii Israel*, a defenseless people who, if not for the Red Sea miracle, could have offered little resistance to Pharaoh's army. Although there were about as many Israelites as Egyptians, their strategic capabilities and ordnance were quite different. The Israelites included large numbers of women and children and traveled by foot, while Pharaoh's army of fighting men was superbly organized and equipped with chariots.[27] The difference is essentially that between an army and a group of refugees.

The Old English poem, however, amplifies the *exercitus Domini* of Exodus 12.41 in the light of battle descriptions in Numbers and Deuteronomy, portraying the Israelites as a *wiglic werod* (warlike host, 233). A *fyrd* (army, 54, 62, 88, 135, 223, 254, 274, 331, etc.), they sing a *fyrdleoð* (war song, 578), make a *fyrdwic* (military encampment, 129), and are even called an *isernhere* (army clad in iron, 348). Their shields are described in lines 113, 125, and 301. They are called *randwigan* (shield-warriors, 126, 134), and make use of the *herebyman* (war trumpet) of Numbers 10.1–10 (99, 132, 159, 216, and 566). Although no battle takes place, the beasts of battle nevertheless make an appearance (162–69). The minute details of the Israelites' organization into a fighting force are

---

26. *Exodus* 218: *habban heora hlencan, hycgan on ellen.*
   Finnsburh 11: *habbað eowre linda, hicgeaþ on ellen.*
27. Cf. *Exodus* 12.37; 14.7.

given (224–233), probably based on the account in Numbers 1. James W. Earl, discussing 565–69, remarks that the diction "is more reminiscent of the series of holy wars conducted later in the exodus . . . . The same is true of the martial imagery throughout the poem, including the division of spoils in the concluding lines."[28] Earl argues that the poem conflates the full account of the exodus that appears in Numbers and Deuteronomy as well as Exodus.

Some of the specific ways the later Pentateuch is utilized have caused a good deal of confusion. Soon after the introduction of Moses, we encounter a battle description based on nothing in the escape narative:

<blockquote>

Heah wæs þæt handlean   and him hold frea,
gesealde wæpna geweald   wið wraðra gryre,
ofercom mid þy campe   cneomaga fela . . .

(19–21)

</blockquote>

[The retribution of his hand was heavenly and his Lord was loyal to him, he granted him victory with weapons against the horror of the fierce enemies, he overcame in battle many nations . . .]

Irving interprets this as "a reference forward in time to the warfare in Canaan" but offers no explanation.[29] Earl observes, "These lines certainly cannot refer directly to the action of the poem, and all the similar diction and imagery throughout the poem must be understood in some other than a literal fashion."[30] He goes on to explain the passage as a conflation of the exodus narrative into the single Red Sea episode. Interpretive problems grow more knotty when the tribe of Judah marches into the Red Sea to do battle with a nonexistent foe:

<blockquote>

    Pracu wæs on ore,
heard handplega,   hægsteald modige
wæpna wælslihtes,   wigend unforhte,
bilswaðu blodige,   beadumægnes ræs,
grimhelma gegrind,   þær Iudas for.

(326b–30)

</blockquote>

28. Earl, "Christian Tradition," 557.
29. Irving, *Old English Exodus*, 67.
30. Earl, "Christian Tradition," 565.

[There was an onrush in the vanguard, hard hand-to-hand combat, brave young warriors unafraid of the slaughter of the weapons, bloody sword wounds, the attack of battle-might, wherever Judah went.]

Several explanations for this bizarre scene were proposed before John F. Vickrey finally solved the puzzle.[31] To follow these attempts at a solution is to learn just how difficult interpreting allegorical poetry can be. Irving observed that "one could easily take the passage as referring to future battles in which the tribe of Judah played a prominent role, the battles mentioned in 20–22, the conquest of Canaan. Or perhaps the courage which Judah displays in entering the sea first can be expressed by the poet only in terms of warfare."[32] On the basis of their influential dictum that "it is reasonable to accept the influence of allegorical tradition particularly to illuminate unrealistic collocations in the poem,"[33] J. E. Cross and S. I. Tucker tendered a third explanation of the crossing: "In the Christian view the catechumen comes to his baptism as a soldier to the colours. . . ."[34] After Cyril of Jerusalem and Gregory Nazianzen are cited to this effect, Augustine and Gregory the Great are enlisted to demonstrate that even though past sins are destroyed in the baptismal font typified by the Red Sea, temptations will continue to occur. Cross and Tucker remark, "It is a short step from enemies *a tergo* and *ante faciem* in the allegorical expositions to the unrealistic situation in the *O.E. Exodus.*"[35] Finally, Earl offered fourth and fifth attempts at a solution, arguing that "This whole line of imagery may be seen as another aspect of the conflation of the exodus story into the one episode,"[36] and that the Red Sea crossing is a figure for the battle between Christ and Satan and thus related to the Harrowing of Hell theme. He admits, however, that "the relationship of this tradition to the 'battle' scene in *Exodus* is perhaps not as direct as the other . . . suggestions I have outlined: Judah's role in the battle, for example, cannot be clearly defined by this tradition."[37]

Taking these attempts in reverse order, it is easy to see that Earl's fifth solution is not really a solution at all, but a way of reinforcing a

---

31. Vickrey, "*Exodus* and the Battle in the Sea," *Traditio* 28 (1972): 119–40.
32. Irving, *Old English Exodus*, 87.
33. Cross and Tucker, "Allegorical Tradition," 123.
34. Ibid., 125.
35. Ibid., 126.
36. Earl, "Christian Tradition," 566.
37. Ibid., 568.

different argument for the influence of the Harrowing of Hell traditions on the poem.[38] His other solution, based on conflation of the exodus, isn't really a solution either, unless one is willing to accept the scene's compositional elements as an answer. To dispose of Cross and Tucker's sacramental explanation of the crux one can simply pose the question, why aren't all the Israelites shown in combat as they cross the Red Sea? Allegories of baptism cannot explain why Judah is singled out. Irving's two explanations yet remain. His first, the same as Earl's theory of conflation of the exodus, is vulnerable to the same objection, namely, that it gives us the elements of the scene's composition, but fails to explain their peculiar combination. Irving's second explanation of the crux in terms of the tribe of Judah is the most interesting of the lot. Although the notion that the poet wishes to stress Judah's courage in leading Israel through the Red Sea is questionable, only Irving's attempted solution looks for a specific poetic purpose in the scene itself, rather than in the allegorical method of some homily or commentary. Just because some details come from an allegorical tradition of the Red Sea crossing as a type of baptism doesn't mean all do.

Cross and Tucker ignore their own precept: "The one general allegory that would cover the events of the poem is the equation of the Israelites' journey from Egypt to the Promised Land with the journey from earthly exile to the heavenly home. . . . The poem is not symbolically about Baptism. . . . There are too many unrelated events to suggest a selection for this purpose."[39] If the poet has chosen to employ details but not the controlling typological theme from the commentaries, and if the journey through a perilous and transitory world to the joy of heaven is the theme of the poem, it remains necessary to ask what relationship the cruces of the poem have, not to the commentaries, but to this very theme.

The martial imagery added to Exodus 13–14 comes from Numbers and Deuteronomy. This material is related to the journey theme in that only the *miles Dei* can succeed in overcoming the obstacles that the seven capital sins (as the seven tribes of Canaan are conventionally allegorized in commentaries on the later Pentateuch) set in the way of the *peregrinus*. Two obstacles confront the soldier of God, either vices or devils. In the first case we have psychomachia or *conflictus*; in the sec-

---

38. Ibid.
39. Cross and Tucker, "Allegorical Tradition," 123–24.

ond, legends of saints entering into combat with devils. The two frequently occur in tandem, as in *Exodus*.

Rabanus Maurus offers the traditional spiritual interpretation of Deuteronomy 7.1, where God names the seven tribes of Canaan and foresees their destruction: "Septem istae gentes septem sunt principalia vitia, quae per gratiam Dei unusquisque spiritualis miles exsuperans, exterminare penitus admonetur. Quod vero majoris numeri esse dicuntur, haec ratio est quia plura sunt vitia quam virtutes."[40] [Those seven peoples are the seven principal vices, which each and every spiritual soldier is admonished to thoroughly expel, overcoming them through the grace of God. They are said to be of a greater number, because there are more vices than virtues]. He goes on to furnish an elaborate list of the major vices and their numerous branches. This is but one example of many which could be furnished to demonstrate that warfare against the seven tribes of Canaan in the latter two books of the Pentateuch was commonly allegorized as the fight of the spiritual warrior against the seven deadly sins.

John F. Vickrey was the first to argue that Judah's battle, inexplicable on the literal level or in terms of baptismal allegory, makes sense in terms of the theme of spiritual warfare against the seven deadly sins.[41] Such warfare requires no physically existent enemy, only fallen human nature. The battle scene in *Exodus* underscores the importance of spiritual struggle to the ongoing baptism and lifelong journey of the believer. Judah enters the Red Sea first because, in the wars against Canaan which were allegorized as spiritual combat, God gives Judah priority: "Post mortem Iosue consuluerunt filii Israel Dominum, dicentes: Quis ascendet ante nos contra Chananaeum, et erit dux belli? Dixitque Dominus: Iudas ascendet: ecce tradidi terram in manus eius" (Judges 1.1–2) [After the death of Joshua, the children of Israel consulted the Lord, saying, "Who will rise up before us against the Canaanites and be the leader of the war?" And the Lord replied, "Judah shall rise up; behold, I have delivered the land into his hands"]. Isidore characterized the tribe of Judah in terms of their fighting ability: "Judas regalis successionis insignis prosapia, cui ducatus bellorum"[42] [Ju-

40. Rabanus Maurus, *Enarratio super Deuteronomium*, PL 108:867.
41. Vickrey, *"Exodus* and the Battle in the Sea."
42. Isidore of Seville, *De Ortu et Obitu Patrum*, PL 83:135.

dah is the family marked out for the kingly succession, and for leader-
ship in wars]. So did the Pseudo-Bede, in a commentary on Numbers
2.3: "Tribus autem Juda ante Isachar ponitur, eo quod Judas fuerit
pugnator"[43] [The tribe of Judah is placed before Isachar, because Ju-
dah was a warrior]. It is not their courage in first entering the water
that provokes the curious battle scene, but their reputation as the
foremost warriors against the seven tribes of Canaan—*spiritualiter*,
the seven deadly sins.[44] Such a collocation of the theme of spiritual

---

43. Pseudo-Bede, *In Pentateuchum Commentarii*, *PL* 91:359.

44. One other aspect of spiritual warfare in *Exodus* shows the influence of allegori-
cal commentaries—the account of the selection of the warriors when battle with the
Egyptians appears imminent:

þæt wæs wiglic werod;	wace ne gretton
in þæt rincgetæl	ræswan herges,
þa þe for geoguðe	gyt ne mihton
under bordhreoðan	breostnet wera
wið flane feond	folmum werigean,
ne him bealubenne	gebiden hæfdon
ofer linde lærig,	licwunde swor,
gylpplegan gares.	

(233–40a)

[That was a warlike army; its military leaders did not allow the weak into that
troop, those who, on account of their youth, were not able to use their hands to
protect men's mail-coats against the hostile enemy, or those who had endured a
mortal wound over the rim of the shield, a burning body wound, the proud play
of the spear.]

Irving's note to this passage explains that "The basis for this idea of careful selection of
fighting men on the part of the Israelites can be found in Num. 1–2 . . . ." Allegorical
commentaries on Numbers by Rabanus Maurus, and the following remark by the Pseudo-
Bede, establish the tropological nature of the selection process:

Ibi ab anno vicesimo annumerantur populi, qui ad proelium eliguntur. Sed cur ab
anno vicesimo, nisi quia ab hac aetate contra unumquemque vitiorum bella
nascuntur. Ideoque ad pugnam eliguntur, ut habeant contra libidines conflictum, ne
luxuria superentur.

[There the people are counted up from the twentieth year, those who are selected for
battle. But why from the twentieth year, unless because from this age on, wars arise
against one of the vices? Therefore they are selected for battle, since they have come
into conflict against the passions, and not been overcome by lechery (*PL* 93:399).]

The *flah feond* (237a) against whom the young could not protect themselves is the *flah
feond gemah* of *Whale* 39, i.e., Satan. The *bealubenn* (238a) which disqualifies a soldier for
acceptance into the *exercitus Domini* is a *hapax legomenon* which can be rendered as
"mortal wound" in modern English, and is probably best understood as "mortal sin." See
J. P. Hermann, "The Selection of Warriors in the Old English *Exodus*, Lines 233–240a,"
English Language Notes 14 (1976): 1–5.

battle with baptismal typology occurs in Rabanus Maurus' *Commentaria in Exodum*.[45]

But the Old English poem devotes more attention to the flight from Egypt, particularly in a well-turned *gradatio* describing the threat of the evil army, than to the crossing itself. And when the crossing is described in Moses' monologue, it is followed by what used to be known as *Exodus B*, recounting the stories of Noah, Abraham, and Isaac. The climax of the poem is not the crossing of the Red Sea, but the destruction of Pharaoh's army.

The problem of spirituality and violence is most evident in the description of this victory. Some sixty-eight lines of epic *amplificatio* describe the incredible horror of the *meredeaða mæst* (greatest of sea-deaths, 465). Earlier the Israelites' fear, caused by lack of trust in God, had been emphasized. When they first caught sight of the Egyptian army, the poet tells us "þa him eorla mod ortrywe wearð" [then men's minds became desperate (154)]. Terror at the power of Pharaoh's army slowly builds, with the beasts of battle thrown in for added effect. The Israelites' camp is filled with weeping at the prospect of impending doom:

---

45. Legitimis tu disputationum lineis rectum fidei iter secabis, et in tantum doctrinae verbo proficies, ut auditores tui, quos in virga legis erudisti, ipsi jam contra Aegyptios velut fluctus maris insurgant, et non solum impugnent eos, sed et superent et exstinguant. Exstinguunt namque Aegyptum, qui non agunt opera tenebrarum. Exstinguunt Aegyptum, qui non carnaliter, sed spiritualiter vivunt. Exstinguunt Aegyptum, qui cogitationes sordidas et impuras vel depellunt ex corde, vel omnino non recipiunt, sicut et Apostolus dicit: *Assumentes scutum fidei, ut possitis omnia maligni jacula ignita exstinguere* . . . . Hoc ergo modo possumus etiam hodie Aegyptios videre mortuos et jacentes ad littus, submergi quadrigas eorum et equos. Possumus etiam ipsum Pharaonem videre submergi, si tanta fide vivamus, ut Deus conterat Satanam sub pedibus nostris velociter, per Jesum Christum Dominum nostrum.

[By lawful lines of disputation, you will decide the right road of faith, and you will advance so much by the word of doctrine that your auditors, whom you instructed in the rod of the law, surely will rise up against the Egyptians like the waves of the sea, and not only assail them, but both overcome and annihilate them. For they annihilate Egypt who do not perform the works of darkness. They annihilate Egypt who do not live according to the flesh, but according to the spirit. They annihilate Egypt, who either drive out filthy and impure thoughts from the heart or do not allow them at all, just as the Apostle says: "Make use of the shield of faith, so you can resist all the fiery darts of the evil one . . . ." Therefore in this way we can see the Egyptians dead and lying on the shore even today, their horses and chariots sunken. We can also see Pharaoh himself drowned, if we live with so much faith that God grinds Satan under our feet quickly, through our Lord Jesus Christ (*PL* 108:67).]

Forþon wæs in wicum   wop up ahafen,
atol æfenleoð,   egesan stodon,
weredon wælnet,   þa se woma cwom.
Flugon frecne spel,   feond wæs anmod,
werud wæs wigblac . . . .

(200–204a)

[Therefore the sound of weeping arose in the camps, the horrifying eve-
ning sound, fears grew, the slaughter net enveloped them. Boastful speech
fled, the enemy was resolute, the troop was splendid in armor . . . .]

Even after an angel intervenes, offering a reprieve, the Israelites con-
tinue to doubt the possibility of deliverance:

Wæron orwenan   eðelrihtes,
sæton æfter beorgum   in blacum reafum,
wean on wenum . . . .

(211–13a)

[They no longer expected the homeland that was their due, they sat on the
hills in dark clothing, expecting misery . . . .]

Moses, recognizing the spread of fear through the ranks, addresses him-
self to alleviating their quite understandable anxiety (259–65). From this
point on, fear is associated solely with the Egyptians. After the drown-
ing scene, the Israelites are left with only the remnants of a purified fear:

Hreðdon hildespelle,   siððan hie þam herge wiðforon;
hofon hereþreatas   hlude stefne,
for þam dædweorce   drihten heredon,
weras wuldres sang;   wif on oðrum,
folcsweota mæst,   fyrdleoð golan
aclum stefnum,   eallwundra fela.

(574–79)

[They rejoiced in battle-song, after they escaped the enemy; the troops
lifted their voices loudly in a glory-song because of the event that had
transpired; the greatest of multitudes, men as well as women, sang a war-
song about the many miracles with reverent voices .]

Their voices are raised in a reverent *hildespell* (battle-song, 574) that
does not celebrate victory in literal war—because, after all, no fighting

ever took place—but in the allegorical warfare of the soldier of God. The *timor Domini* (fear of the Lord) of the Israelites' song is opposed to an *atol æfenleoð* (hideous evening-song, 201a) in their moment of deepest fear. The movement from fear to joyous praise is glossed within the poem: in this short life we (that is, the audience constructed by the work) live in *earmra anbid* (expectation of miseries, 534) and *murnað on mode* (mourn in spirit, 536), because we fear the underground *manhus . . . þær bið fyr and wyrm* (house of evil . . . where the fire and serpent are, 537b). But we too will have our fear turned into songs of joy when the Lord himself leads us to salvation, where *dugoð on dreame drihten herigað, / weroda wuldorcyning, to widan feore* (the band of retainers will praise the Lord in joy / the glorious Lord of hosts forever and ever, 547–48). This transmutation of fear into joy is the fundamental emotional principle of the poem. But it is joy which depends upon violence and destruction.

II

Allegorical commentaries, so alien to modern theological approaches, formed the exegetical milieu for Old English religious poets. The modern critic who suspects an allegorical dimension moves from some puzzling aspect of the poem to the commentaries, then back to the poem, to clarify puzzling elements of plot and characterization. That it took so many years of investigation before Vickrey solved the riddle of Judah's crossing is testimony to the difficulty of the interpretiave problem and the power of the critical method.

But there are limitations to the allegorical approach to *Exodus*. I would begin a counterreading by noting that the sign system of the poem is a classic binary one, based upon conflict between opposed entities. The allegorical approach of the text—and of the modern critic who reflects allegorical textual operations in his own commentary—sublates historical violence into spiritual violence: to read *spiritualiter* is necessarily to transcend the letter.[46] In terms of commentary tradition, the reader's pleasure at the destruction of the Egyptians is a sanctioned triumphing of good over evil. Aggressive instincts are transmuted from the context of literal warfare to that of the spriritual warfare of *Ecclesia*

---

46. "Sublation" refers to the incorporation of a prior stage or concept by a subsequent one. See the introduction to Pt. 2 of this volume.

against Satan, and joy at the destruction of the Egyptians becomes legitimated as joy at the destruction of our own worst instincts. Our reading becomes not critical, but partisan, when we allow the historical imagination free rein in identifying with the readers the text creates for itself.

But should we be complicit in such positioning of ourselves as partisan readers? One reason we might choose not to is that Canaan resists sublation into the promised land of heaven that rewards spiritual struggle:

Swa reordode   ræda gemyndig
manna mildost,   mihtum swiðed,
hludan stefne;   here stille bad
witodes willan,   wundor ongeton,
modiges muðhæl;   he to mænegum spræc:
    "Micel is þeos menigeo,   mægenwisa trum,
fullesta mæst,   se ðas fare lædeð;
hafað us on Cananea   cyn gelyfed
burh and beagas,   brade rice;
wile nu gelæstan   þæt he lange gehet
mid aðsware,   engla drihten,
in fyrndagum   fæderyncynne,
gif ge gehealdað   halige lare,
þæt ge feonda gehwone   forð ofergangað,
gesittað sigerice   be sæm tweonum,
beorselas beorna.   Bið eower blæd micel!"

                                                                    (549–64)

[So he spoke in a loud voice, the mildest of men, confirmed in his powers, mindful of counsels; the army silently awaited the will of their leader, perceived a wonder, the prophecy of the brave one. He spoke to the multitudes: "Great is this company and bold is the Leader, the greatest of helpers, who directs this journey; He has granted us the people of Canaan, their cities and treasures, a broad kingdom; He will now accomplish what he, the Lord of angels, long ago promised with an oath to our forefathers in ancient days: that if you hold fast to his holy teaching you will surpass each of your enemies and dwell victoriously between the oceans in warriors' banqueting halls. Your glory shall be magnificent!"]

Moses speaks after the narrator's allegorical interruption, discussed earlier. Like the narrator's comments, Moses' words also gloss the narrative that contains them. Moses himself is oxymoronic: the meekest of men, yet strengthened in might. But he revels in power, a characteristic previously associated only with the Egyptians. He praises the might of the Jews and their brave heavenly leader, and claims that the people of Canaan have been delivered to them—cities, treasures, the entire kingdom. His proleptic thanksgiving for conquest of the native inhabitants of these lands pleases the internal audience: "*Aefter þam wordum werod wæs on salum*" (After these words the army was joyful, 565). The cycle of oppression begun by the Egyptians will be continued by the Jews. The *beorselas beorna* (banquet halls of men) will be occupied in triumph, Moses says. A historically oppressed people will become historical oppressors themselves.

Such a contradictory logic of meekness and might appears frequently in the Pentateuch. Purely defensive struggle against the Egyptians becomes offensive landgrabbing in Canaan, in a swift reversal of the categories of oppressed and oppressor. The basic structure requiring the oppression of one people by another is left untouched, and is even reinforced, by this rapid change in positions. The divine right which marks the oppressed Jews in their exodus from Egypt will necessarily conflict with the (merely) human rights of peoples who already inhabit the "promised" land.

If he or she does not simply acquiesce in the historical justice of the occupation of Canaan, the complicit (medieval or modern) reader will allegorize this oppression, ignoring a will to power which works through just such textual methods of spiritualizing conflict, whether by oxymoron or allegory. Power grabbing by Pharaoh and the Egyptians is wicked; they are *wlance* (arrogant, 170, 204) and *þurstige þræcwiges* (thirsty for war, 182). Yet domination comes to the meek Moses as the fulfillment of a divine promise, in a mythic (super)naturalization of the violent processes of history. His desire, allegorically desire for the joys of the spirit, is literally a joy in conquest previously associated with worldly Egyptians. But processes of allegorization direct attention away from the historical plane.[47] The absence of any awareness of this contradictory logic of meekness and power in the poem, or in modern

---

47. One might begin the task of historicizing *Exodus* by comparing Bede's attempted justification of the conquest of the Britons: according to the *Ecclesiastical History*, they were insufficiently concerned with the spiritual welfare of the Germanic tribes (I, 22).

criticism of the poem, reflects the success of its fundamental rhetorical processes.

The rhetorical work of the poem depends upon larger textual processes of allegorization through which the historical symbolizes the spiritual. Such an allegorical sublation of Judaism into Christianity is the fundamental textual process of medieval exegesis, within which allegorization in *Exodus* is nested. To read as the narrator prompts us is to understand history as prophetic of a future spiritual holy land—tropologically, the grace-filled soul, anagogically the afterlife. Ultimately, Canaan is heaven for the Christian.

But there is another dimension to this allegory, one in which the literal cannot be completely sublated in the spiritual. It is significant, for example, that heavenly rule and earthly rule are linked early in the poem:

> þær him gesealde   sigora waldend,
> modgum magoræswan,   his maga feorh,
> onwist eðles,   Abrahames sunum.

                                                    (16–18)

[The Lord of victories granted him, their brave leader, the lives of his kinsmen, and to the sons of Abraham He granted landrights.]

The power over the lives of his kinsmen given to Moses is explicitly withheld from Hrothgar in *Beowulf*, a telling contrast in political theories. In addition to this power, victory over enemies and *onwist eðles* (occupation of land or landrights) are given to the Israelites. After following the narrator's advice to grasp the allegorical significance of such empowerment, we should make the effort to rise to the literal level as well. But that step is more difficult than one might expect, since the issue of the origin of landrights in *Exodus* raises the question of the origin of the originary. According to the poem, the Israelites had one father, Abraham, who gave them the landright, an origin marked by violence and patriarchy.[48] The Israelites march into the sea according to the order he had established long before:

---

48. On theological aspects of patriarchy in *Exodus*, see Paul F. Ferguson, "Noah, Abraham, and the Crossing of the Red Sea," *Neophilologus* 65 (1981): 282–87 and Stanley R. Hauer, "The Patriarchal Digression in the Old English *Exodus*, Lines 362–446" in Joseph S. Wittig, ed., *Eight Anglo-Saxon Studies* (Chapel Hill, 1981), 77–90.

An wisode
mægenþrymmum mæst,   þy he mære wearð,
on forðwegas   folc æfter wolcnum,
cynn æfter cynne.   Cuðe æghwilc
mægburga riht,   swa him Moises bead,
eorla æðelo.   Him wæs an fæder,
leof leodfruma,   landriht geþah,
frod on ferhðe,   freomagum leof.

(348b–355)

[One man guided the mighty hosts in their journeys, because he was renowned, the people following the pillar of cloud, tribe after tribe. Each one knew the rank of the tribes as Moses declared it, the noble rank of men. There was one father for all of them, a dear patriarch; wise in spirit, dear to his kinsmen, he had received the landright.]

Abraham is the one father, the *leodfruma* (patriarch), who *landriht geþah* (received the landright) and passed it on to the line of Israelites. A divinely authorized violence is necessitated by *landriht*, which can be realized historically only by the conquest of Canaan. This violence is not only external but internal, marking the *eorla æðelo*, the order of nobility and social status of the tribes.

The miraculous destruction of the Egyptian army through its divine conduit, Moses' green rod, later becomes systematic warfare as Israelite warriors fight to take the land of Canaan away from its inhabitants. Just as landrights cannot be spiritualized without considering the literal remnant, neither can the extreme violence of the Red Sea drowning episode. The Red Sea miracle is recounted as concerted terror, overwhelming in its excess, and upon this terror the joys of Canaan depend. But where an allegorical reading reflects the emotional release of the internal audience, a hermeneutics of suspicion reads against the grain. If one can resist being constructed as an ideal reader by the narrative, the Red Sea crossing disturbs rather than consoles.

The opening lines of the terrifying drowning episode are not a little sadistic:

Folc wæs afæred,   flodegsa becwom
gastas geomre,   geofon deaðe hweop.
Wæron beorhhliðu   blode bestemed,
holm heolfre spaw,   hream wæs on yðum,
wæter wæpna ful,   wælmist astah.

(447–51)

[The people were overwhelmed with fear, the flood horror came to their mournful spirits, the sea threatened them with death. The mountain-waves were steeped in blood, the sea spewed gore, there was screaming in the waves, the water was full of weapons, and the death-mist rose upwards.]

The imposing aural possibilities of the four-beat alliterative line build to to a crescendo of horror. Not only are the Egyptians' mournful souls enveloped in the *flodegsa* (flood horror, 447), but the seas are *blode bestemed* (soaked with blood, 449) and *holm heolfre spaw* (the sea spewed gore, 450). The waves themselves are full of screaming, fear, terror. Repetition of such instances of terror is ritualistic. Particular attention is given to the screams of the drowning Egyptians: *hream wæs on yðum* (there was screaming in the waves, 450); *laðe cyrmdon . . . fægum stæfnum* (the hateful ones cried out . . . in the voices of the doomed, 462–63). These screams blend with the noise of the waters in the *gyllende gryre* (screaming terror, 490). In similar fashion, the vision of bloodstained water is repeated: *flod blod gewod* (blood stained the flood, 463); *wæs seo hæwene lyft heolfre geblanden* (the blue sky was mingled with gore, 477). "Fear," "panic," "terror," "blood," "gore," and "death" are raised to the level of cosmic violence with the description of blood in the sky, as the scene of Egyptian catastrophe winds back upon itself again and again with unmistakable narrative delight.

One reason their slaughter can be presented as delightful is that the Egyptians have been associated throughout the poem with arrogance and cruelty. For example, early in the poem the encamped Israelites await an enemy who had long inflicted violence, oppression, and misery upon them:

> wræcmon gebad
> laðne lastweard,   se ðe him lange ær
> eðelleasum   onnied gescraf,
> wean witum fæst.

(137b–40a)

[. . . the exile awaited the hateful pursuer, he who had long before decreed oppression and misery bound with torments for them.]

Later we learn that the Egyptians who cause so much suffering and pain were ignoring a promise to Joseph made by a pharaoh who had lived long before:

Ealles þæs forgeton   siðöan grame wurdon
Egypta cyn   ymbe antwig;
öa heo his mægwinum   morðor fremedon,
wroht berenedon,   wære fræton.

(144–47)

[The Egyptian people forgot all this when they became enraged at Israel-
ite resistance; then they committed murder against Moses' people,
planned strife, broke their promises.]

The pilgrim Israelites are forced to flee rather than cope with Egyptian
violence and injustice. Yet in terms of poetics, this situation is reversed,
since tone and imagery contradict the fundamental oppositions upon
which the plot is based. Egyptian violence is merely reported, by the
objective voice of historical record, but in the Red Sea drowning episode
there is a sadistic reveling in the violence inflicted upon enemies of
Israel. Although we are informed that the Egyptians are violent, only
the violence characterizing the Israelites—spiritually, *Ecclesia*—is al-
lowed to flower forth rhetorically.

The curious behavior of violence, shifting from side to side of the
slash separating fundamental oppositions, indexes the psychological pro-
cesses at work in the text. The war within the members yields a residue
of violence that can be marshaled against the forces of evil: the threaten-
ing other, whether psychic or social, must be extirpated for the Christian
psyche or society to be constructed. To read early medieval poems is to
witness the violence of the construction of an epoch, as contemporary
pscyhological and sociological realities are grafted onto ancient texts.
Precisely because these texts are rewritten, modern readers have the
opportunity to observe the culturally specific deployment of tradition. In
Exodus, the violent Old English amplification of the gory drowning of
the Egyptians reinscribes the sign system of the original. But to register
the extent to which the Old English text is a palimpsest, critics must
struggle against the idealist temptation to detect again and again only
some transhistorical Judeo-Christian essence passed on across the centu-
ries. To do the latter, to privilege identity rather than difference in the
manner of typological criticism, renders important textual processes in-
visible. We must learn to read what is distinctively Old English in poems
based on ancient sources.[49] But to do so, we must first come to under-

---

49. Kathryn Hume, "The Concept of the Hall in Old English Poetry," *Anglo-Saxon
England* 3 (1974), makes use of the notion of the fallacy of homogeneity (as analyzed by

stand the theoretical chasms that are crossed when typological scholarship becomes typological criticism.

To begin to make sense of the sadistic drowning scene, one must attend to the construction of violence elsewhere in the poem. Violence is reveled in when the poem treats the bloodthristy Egyptian pursuit of the Israelites. The hearts of the enemy are filled with *mihtmod* (violent passion, 149) and *heaðowylmas* (warlike feelings, 148). Descriptions of the battle-lust of the *hare heorowulfas* (grey wolves of war, 181) establish their violence as monstrous. The poem heightens the rapacity of the Egyptians and defenselessness of the Israelites, even though the Bible is already quite clearcut in this matter. In *Exodus*, the good become more good, the evil more evil, highlighting the distinction between the entities on either side of the virgule separating a good peaceful people from an evil violent one, at least until the sudden reversal of categories in the drowning scene.

This shifting of violent imagery from side to side of the slash separating Israelites from Egyptians indexes the poem's construction. Of course there had been earlier preparations for a defensive Israelite counterviolence, as in the scene dealing with the selection of warriors. But beyond the allegory of struggle with sin in the examples of Israelite militancy which are offered, there is a disturbing remnant of historical conflict, for example, when Moses tells his countrymen not to be afraid:

"Ne beoð ge þy forhtran, þeah þe Faraon brohte
sweordwigendra side hergas,
eorla unrim! Him eallum wile
mihtig drihten þurh mine hand
to dæge þissum dædlean gyfan,
þæt hie lifigende leng ne moton
ægnian mid yrmðum Israhela cyn."

           (259–65)

["Do not become more frightened, even if Pharaoh brings vast armies of swordsmen, a countless number of soldiers. Through my hand the mighty

Crane and Greenfield), in alleging that "What we should learn from seeing the many ways in which the idea-complex [of the hall] is used is that simple generalizations about Anglo-Saxon attitudes, whether of author or of audience, are likely to be unsound" (74). In the extended, textual sense which I would give it, the fallacy of homogeneity is the error of transhistoricism, which invokes the panchronic universals of a hypostasized Judeo-Christian tradition in a way that neglects the difficult task of historical contextualization.

Lord will repay all their deeds this very day, so that they may no longer live to oppress the nation of Israel with miseries."]

God is so powerful, Moses tells them, and so willing to use his power, that he will destroy all his enemies. The sublation of aggressivity through the interpretive processes of allegorical exegesis nevertheless allows for divine violence of truly immense proportions. God is represented as being monstrously violent, like Cuchulainn in Irish legend, able to heap seas upon the heads of his enemies. Another example of the insistence of the letter occurs when God rewards the tribe of Judah with the ability to perform triumphant deeds:

> Swa him mihtig god
> þæs dægweorces   deop lean forgeald,
> siððan him gesælde   sigorworca hreð,
> þæt he ealdordom   agan sceolde
> ofer cynericu,   cneowmaga blæd.

(314b–18)

[. . . so mighty God granted {a soldier of Judah} a significant reward for that day's work, when he gave him the glory of victory deeds, so that he would hold the reins of authority over kingdoms and the power of his kinsmen.]

This passage, decribing the march through the *grenne grund*, has been allegorized in Keenan's perceptive reading,[50] but we should also notice that the tribe of Judah is promised *ealdordom* (authority) and *blæd* (power) over kingdoms. Given more power than other tribes, they will rule the rulers of Israel.

The ranking of tribes and marching through the Red Sea makes its appeal to an audience for whom ritualistic order is pleasurable. This measured response to the threat of disorder is patriarchal. The Israelites had one father, Abraham, who held the landright, begat a race of valiant men, and passed his power on until it reached Moses, who presides over the Red Sea crossing. Landownership, in other words, is underwritten by violence and patriarchy. Not to have a homeland is to be oppressed; to have a homeland requires oppression of others. Hebrew power—linked through textual processes of allegory to the power of *Ecclesia*—is

---

50. Keenan, "*Exodus* 312."

transmitted through Moses, the patriarchal channel for divine violence. And writing is the indispensable link between the possession of land and the commemoration of patriarchy:

Cende cneowsibbe   cenra manna
heahfædera sum,   halige þeode,
Israela cyn,   onriht godes,
swa þæt orþancum   ealde reccað
þa þe mægburge   mæst gefrunon,
frumcyn feora,   fæderæðelo gehwæs.

(356–61)

[{Abraham}, one of the patriarchs, gave birth to a race of brave men, a holy people, the people of Israel, the proper people of God, as old men knowledgeably recount, those who have most investigated matters of kinship, the lineage of mankind and each person's paternal ancestry.]

Learned old writers have passed on the tradition of the patriarchal line of landownership from one father. Only one patriarch began the line of descent of *cenra manna* (brave men). Although nobility is represented as a quality of soul in modern democracies, its material origins are in quantities of land. It is writers, says the poet, who have transcribed the origin of the race and of rank, who know *frumcyn* (lineage) and *fæderæðelo* (paternal ancestry or pedigree). And in the work of these writers we can discover the origin of the *landriht* (354) inherited through the patriarchal order. Writing produces aristocratic order by properly recording lines of kinship and affiliation. And this is not only true for the Israelites. For the Old English audience, Church power can be traced back to Christ, and again back to Abraham, in a genealogical line which finds its ultimate origin in the will of Jehovah.

Exodus recounts the supplementary origin for the animals and plants on the ark in the excursus on Noah and his three sons. Their preserving of a canceled world is made possible by their noble lineage, once again traced back to Abraham, originator of Hebrew legal rights:

Swa þæt wise men   wordum secgað
þæt from Noe   nigoða wære
fæder Abrahames   on folctale.
Þæt is se Abraham   se him engla god
naman niwan asceop;   eac þon neah and feor
halige heapas   in gehyld bebead,

werþeoda geweald;   he on wræce lifde.
Siððan he gelædde   leofost feora
haliges hæsum;   heahlond stigon
sibgemagas,   on Seone beorh.

(377–86)

[According to what wise men say in their writings, the father of Abraham was ninth in the genealogical line of descendents from Noah. That Abraham is the very one whose name was fashioned anew by the God of angels; also God entrusted to his care holy groups of men and power over nations far and near. He lived as an exile. Afterwards he led the most beloved of peoples at the command of holy God; kinsmen, they climbed the highlands to Mount Zion.]

The relationship between *werþeoda geweald* (power over nations), the sacrifice of Isaac, and the enumeration of ancestors is plainly spelled out here. The sacrifice of the son is accomplished in the name of God as a Father, a higher father whose will transcends the desire of any earthly father. Yet this canceling of human paternal rights by divine rights serves precisely to reassert the law of the earthly father: it is, as we have learned to recognize, Oedipal. From this law of the father, as seen in the obedience of the first father, Abraham, comes the reward of the land of Canaan. Power over nations is part of the *wære* (covenant, 387), varied as *halige heahtreowe* (high covenant, 388). Property and patriarchy are here grafted onto the theological stem supporting them. Myths of origin, which originate in times of transition, frequently depend upon a metalepsis by which the logically prior is made subsequent: sacred texts themselves organize society through such tropes, erasing the historical origins of the violent expropriation of land by means of a divine inscription of nobility and property rights. In United States history, "manifest destiny" was such a thinly veiled divine inscription, one that, not coincidentally, was supported by Anglo-Saxon racial myths.

The efflorescence of violence in the Old English treatment of the Red Sea drowning releases aggression already inscribed within the fundamental structure of symbolic opposition in the poem. The Israelite/ Egyptian dichotomy involves a tropology for the Old English audience, as it did for Prudentius: the battle against the Satanic, unregenerate parts of the psyche. And the destruction of the enemy within leads to celebration, just as in the *Psychomachia*, when Pax and Concordia sing psalms linked by Prudentius with the Red Sea crossing.[51] Responding properly to the promptings of the devil or the inertia of the Old Man within necessitates the spiritual violence recounted in the many varieties of psychomachia and recurrent motifs of spiritual warfare. This inner drama of the soul has social dimensions as well, as biblical violence is fitted to the template of Germanic poetic tradition, with its ethos of heroism and nationalism. The violence of the war within the members is released in a form peculiar to Anglo-Saxon society, as the valorization of literal violence in Germanic tradition is grafted onto the metaphorical violence of Christian psychomachia tradition. Such cultural violence is thoroughly textual, occurring at the juncture of biblical source, allegorical commentary, and traditional Anglo-Saxon narrative forms. All are implicated in the complex interweaving of fury and turmoil in the Red Sea drownings:

> Flod famgode,   fæge crungon,
> lagu land gefeol,   lyft wæs onhrered,
> wicon weallfæsten,   wægas burston,
> multon meretorras,   þa se mihtiga sloh
> mid halige hand,   heofonrices weard,
> on werbeamas.

(482–87a)

[The flood foamed, those who were doomed fell dead, the water crashed into the land, the air was stirred up; the retaining walls collapsed, the waves burst, the sea-towers crumbled when, with his holy hand, the almighty guardian of the heavenly kingdom, smote the warriors.]

In this brief excerpt from the long and bloody rhapsody, God is the Mighty One who smites doomed, arrogant warriors with His holy hand, destroying them with *gyllende gryre* (screaming terror). Terror comes in the form of a *wæelbenn* (gushing wound) caused by the *ald mece* (ancient sword) of the sea which strikes them. Full requital occurs, and not one survivor is left: *Hie wið God wunnon!* (They fought against God, 515). The message is that the audience had better not, although it might be inclined to do so by yielding to temptation. Resistance in spiritual combat is here bulwarked with fear of giving offense to the Patriarch of patriarchs. To this extent, an Oedipal scene is replayed, with God as the

---

51. Prudentius, *Psychomachia*, 650–57.

Father of fathers who punishes those who do not acknowledge his authority. Only at this point, where the threat of divine paternal interdict is made explicit, does the allegorical level of the text become explicit once again. The necessity for reading with the keys of the spirit is invoked by the narrator at the point of maximum terror for those who strive against the will of God.

This force of heavenly threat makes its presence known on earth in countless ways. The green rod of Moses is allegorical, but it is also emblematic of the phallic authority organizing society and psyche. The road through the Red Sea opened by this multivalent rod produces safety for the Israelites, but death for the Egyptians.[52] The green rod is the staff of authority, with allegorical, sociological, and psychological dimensions. Not only success against the Egyptians, but *landriht* and *onwist eðles* (occupation of land) descend through the patriarchal order represented by the staff. The line of the fathers produces entitlement, but only for those who submit to the will of the father. In psychoanalytic terms, one accedes to authority only through prior acceptance of the limits set by authority. The paternal interdict denies the subject his desire, reforming it as the desire to act according to established rules. Rights descend through the acceptance of this law of the father. Theologically, the origin of patriarchal power is located in heaven: entitlement and empowerment as a subject depend upon the Law of the Father, the eternal source of all earthly authority. The rod representing this Law also inflicts destruction upon those who fail to acknowledge its power.

Hebrew landrights depend upon this rod of authority, no longer to be wielded by Moses, but by Joshua. The originary act of violence producing battle victories against the Canaanites, and hence landownership, is the Red Sea drowning. At this moment of maximum humiliation for the enemies of Israel, Moses prophesies the destruction of Canaan's original inhabitants, recasting them as enemies. But only the aggression of the Israelites, who require a homeland, can position the Canaanites so. These political values, which coexist with psychological themes in the poem, are occulted by the allegorical level emphasized in the text and in contemporary critical readings.

The most important question that Exegetics can raise about the

---

52. For a fuller discussion of phallic authority, castration, and the formation of the subject, see chap. 7.

spiritualizing tendencies of its methodology is: What other values are encoded in the poem along with the allegory? In particular, typological critics should learn to examine the psychological and sociological overcoding of allegory. Pleasure at the destruction of an enemy can be restricted to spiritual joy only by sanitizing an attitude that can always resurface in historical hostilities and encounters. Pleasure at the destruction of the enemy is made safe, even holy, through such textual processes. But encrypted within this religious feeling are implicit political contents. Religious practice embodies psychological and social arrangements, perhaps most certainly in texts where *Ecclesia*'s other is destroyed with a delight both holy and sadistic. To recognize this is to begin to read the repressed history of the allegory of war.

Chapter 4

Elene

Elene follows the outlines of its source, one of the Latin versions of the *Acta Cyriaci*.[1] Besides the addition of an autobiographical, penitential epilogue, Cynewulf's version differs in three significant ways: first, the elaborate battle scenes at the beginning of the poem, including extended descriptions of the approach of the barbarian army (18b–41a), the tentative advance of the Romans (51b–56), and the final battle of Constantine (105–43); second, the rousing description of Elene's sea voyage, evidently worked up out of whole cloth by Cynewulf (212–75); and third, the message to Constantine, followed by his order that a church be built (967–1016). On the more minute level of diction, numerous semantic shifts occurred as the invention legend was transferred from Latin into the Old English heroic poetic. Cynewulf's modifications of the traditional narrative merge the heroic ethos of Anglo-Saxon poetry with the biblical and patristic notion of the spiritual combat.

The first two additions to the source have struck generations of critics as hearkening back to the poetry of Germanic antiquity. The battle descriptions before and after Constantine's vision of the Cross are elaborated upon only the barest hints in the source, the sea voyage description upon none at all. These passages are thematically important as well. It is telling, for example, that Constantine's enemies are called *hæðene* (126) in the description of the slaughter of the barbarian invaders by the Roman forces. At the time of the battle, Constantine himself was a *hæðen* too—so heathen, indeed, that after his victory he had to ask the Roman citizens if they knew what the Cross stood for. *Hæðen* is used elsewhere in *Elene* only once, when the heroine asks Cyriacus to

---

1. For purposes of comparison I have used Alfred Holder, *Inventio Sanctae Crucis* (Leipzig, 1889).

91

find the nails used to crucify Christ (1075). To use this term for both the enemies of Constantine and the crucifiers of Christ is anachronistic: the Romans have prematurely been identified as upholding Christianity, the barbarians as threatening it. This shift in characterization of the barbarians occurs in tandem with redefinition of the Romans, who are already members of *Ecclesia*.[2]

Literal and spiritual battle are closely associated throughout the poem. In the *Inventio*, when Constantine attempts to discover the significance of the Cross, he is told:

> Hoc signum caelestis D[omin]i est. Audientes autem pauci [Christ]iani qui illic erant. eodem tempore uenerunt ad Constantinum regem et euangelizauerunt illi mysterium Trinitatis et aduentum fili[i] D[omin]i quemadmodum natus est et crucifixus est tertia diae resurrexit a mortuis.[3]

> ["This is the sign of the heavenly God." Hearing this, a few Christians who were there at that time came to Constantine the king and taught him the mystery of the Trinity and the coming of the son of God, how he was born, crucified, and on the third day rose from the dead.]

The emphasis shifts in *Elene*, where Constantine is seen as a triumphant warrior-king, to whom the Christians joyfully declare *gastgerynu* (spiritual mysteries). They also tell him that the visionary sign, a token of victory in warfare, set mankind free from diabolical bondage:

> Alysde leoda bearn   of locan deofla,
> geomre gastas,   ond him gife sealde
> þurh þa ilcan gesceaft   þe him geywed wearð
> sylfum on gesyhðe,   sigores tacen,
> wið þeoda þræce.

$$(181-85a)$$

[It set the sons of men and their mournful spirits free from imprisonment by devils, and granted them grace through the same object that was re-

---

2. The existence of an allegorical level on which the Romans and Jews participate in the nature of the abstractions *Ecclesia* and *Synagoga* was convincingly argued by Thomas D. Hill, "Sapiential Structure and Figural Narrative in the Old English *Elene*," *Traditio* 27 (1971): 159–77 and Jackson J. Campbell, "Cynewulf's Multiple Revelations," *Medievalia et Humanistica* 3 (1972): 257–77.

3. Holder, *Inventio Sanctae Crucis*, 2.

vealed to Constantine himself in his vision, the token of victory against the attack of the enemy tribes.]

This latter piece of instruction is absent from the source. Spiritual and physical battle here appear in close juxtaposition, and Constantine moves quickly from ignorance of the meaning of the Cross to deep knowledge of its spiritual significance. Literal and spiritual warfare move on a continuum in the poem: the vision of the Cross, which resulted in literal victory, sets men free from spiritual bondage as well. In Cynewulf's imaginative world things often signify polysemously, and the sudden experience of an expanded vision of history results in conversion, not only for Constantine, but for the Cynewulf of the epilogue as well.

Satan's speech to Judas establishes the relationship between Constantine's literal victory over the barbarians and the spiritual victory symbolized by the Cross:

> "Hwæt is þis, la, manna,   þe minne eft
> þurh fyrngeflit   folgaþ wyrdeð
> iceð ealdne nið,   æhta strudeð?
> Þis is singal sacu.   Sawla ne moton
> manfremmende   in minum leng
> æhtum wunigan.   Nu cwom elþeodig,
> þone ic ær on firenum   fæstne talde,
> hafað mec bereafod   rihta gehwylces,
> feohgestreona.   Nis ðæt fæger sið.
> Feala me se hælend   hearma gefremede,
> niða nearolicra,   se ðe in Nazareð
> afeded wæs.   Syððan furþum weox
> of cildhade,   symle cirde to him
> æhte mine.   Ne mot ænige nu
> rihte spowan.   Is his rice brad
> ofer middangeard.   Min is geswiðrod
> ræd under roderum.   Ic þa rode ne þearf
> hleahtre herigean."

$$(902-19a)$$

["Lo, what man is this who is once again destroying my following by means of the old strife, increasing the old conflict and plundering my possessions? This is an unending battle. Souls which work evil are no longer able to remain in my possession. Now a foreigner has come, whom

I had previously considered steadfast in sins, and he has robbed me of each of my belongings and treasures. This is not a fair thing to have happen. The Savior, the one who was reared in Nazareth, has performed many injuries and cruel acts of hatred against me. After he grew past his childhood, he continually helped himself to my possessions. Now I can not profit from any of my property. His kingdom stretches far and wide over the earth. My authority has diminished under the heavens. I certainly have no need to praise the Cross with jubilation."]

Polysemous battle language abounds in this passage. The *fyrngeflit* to which Satan refers is the "old strife" between the devils and mankind, based upon the recurrent motif of Satan as the *hostis antiquus*.[4] Judas has destroyed the following of Satan, the old enemy, those who are hostile to Christianity. In parallel construction to *fyrngeflit* is *eald nið*, another reference to the old strife. These recurrent motifs of spiritual warfare are given an interesting twist by Cynewulf, who employs them from the standpoint of the devil's view of spiritual struggle: while the members of *Ecclesia* take the old strife to mean the sorties of the *hostis antiquus* against mankind, Satan construes it as of mankind's desire to break free from his power. He views souls bound in sin as his treasures, which Christ, and now Judas, have robbed. Satan's kingdom and authority have been diminished *ofer middangeard* (917), while the kingdom of God has grown in size and power. For this reason, says Satan, he has no cause to praise the Cross (918b-19a), which resulted in the defeat of his minions, the *hæðene*. Satan feels wronged, since his *æhta* (possessions, 904) have been unjustly taken from him, first by the literal victory of Constantine, now by the spiritual victory which radiated from it. Satan does not distinguish literal and spiritual battle in his speech.[5] After an ironic reference to the Cross, he suddenly remembers being shut up in the narrow abode of hell:

> "Hwæt, se hælend me
> in þam engan ham   oft getynde,
> geomrum to sorge!"
>
> (919b–21a)

---

4. The loan translation (*eald feond*) is used in line 207. The devil is referred to as *feond* in *Elene* 899, 953, and as *sceaða* in *Elene* 761.

5. When Satan threatens Judas with the *oðer cyning* who will attempt to torture him into apostasy, his response is so effective that he is referred to as a *hæleð hildedeor* (935).

["Indeed, this Savior has often enclosed me in the narrow abode which brings sorrow to us miserable ones!"]

This dramatic scene recalls the *Acta Pilati*, in which Christ, after chaining Satan, sets up the Cross to remind him of his defeat in the Harrowing of Hell.[6]

Satan, however, makes a final threat, still smarting from his loss in the flyting with Judas, and eager for revenge:

> "Gen ic findan can
> þurh wrohtstafas   wiðercyr siððan
> of ðam wearhtreafum,   ic awecce wið ðe
> oðerne cyning,   se ehteð þin,
> ond he forlæteð   lare þine
> ond manþeawum   minum folgaþ,
> ond þec þonne sendeð   in þa sweartestan
> ond þa wyrrestan   witebrogan,
> þæt ðu, sarum forsoht,   wiðsæcest fæste
> þone ahangnan cyning,   þam ðu hyrdest ær."
>
> (924b–33)

["Yet by calumnies I shall be able to reverse my situation in hell, and I shall raise another king against you who will persecute you, and will abandon your teaching and follow my evil customs, and then send you into the darkest and most hideous sufferings so that, afflicted with sorrows, you will firmly renounce the crucified King whom you once obeyed."]

Most editors take the *oðer cyning* to be Julian the Apostate, who legend held responsible for the martyrdom of Judas. What has not been noted, however, is the figural richness of Satan's description, which leaves the identity of the tormentor of Christians indeterminate. This lack of specificity is significant, and it should not be delimited, for Julian the Apostate was but one manifestation of that other king who is discussed fre-

---

6. "Tunc omnes sancti dei rogaverunt dominum ut victoriae signum sanctae crucis relinqueret apud inferos, ne praevalerent ministri eius nequissimi aliquem retinere culpatum quem absolverit dominus. Et factum est ita, posuitque dominus crucem suam in medio inferni, quae est signum victoriae et usque in aeternum permanebit" [Then all the holy ones of God asked the Lord to leave the sign of victory of the holy Cross among the dead, lest his most evil servants prevail in holding back some condemned soul whom the Lord absolved. And so it was done. In the midst of hell, the Lord placed his Cross, which is the sign of victory and will endure forever (Constantine von Tischendorf, ed., *Evangelia Apocrypha*, 2d ed. [Leipzig, 1876], 430)].

quently in the New Testament—Antichrist. Medieval exegetes were quite familiar with this tradition.[7]

Other references to warfare in the poem show a similar tendency toward polysemy. Jackson J. Campbell has argued convincingly that the episode recounting how the nails of the Cross were made into a bit for Constantine's horse is rich in spiritual significance, however nonsensical it appears when taken literally. Prudentius had associated a fierce unbridled horse with *Superbia*, describing her mount's rage at the presence of the bit in its mouth.[8] Jerome, in his commentary on Zacharias 14.20, a verse which the *Inventio* quotes and Cynewulf elaborates, associates the horse with lasciviousness, lending tropological significance to the bridle. Haymo of Auxerre makes a similar connection, citing Jerome. This evidence leads Campbell to comment:

> Constantine early in the poem was established as the supreme worldly ruler. Once converted, he more than other people needed reminders that secular power is not ultimate. As a Christian ruler, his physical power must be governed by divine principles. Whether the horse is taken as his own pride, or perhaps as the self-centered physical desires of secular humanity, the bodily suffering of Christ on the Cross, recalled by the nails, can conduce to both humility and a healthy, controlled treatment of desire.[9]

It could be noted as well that Cynewulf explicitly glosses this episode from an allegorical standpoint, moving from the bit's power in physical battle to its expanded signficance:

> "He ah æt wigge sped,
> sigor æt sæcce,   ond sybbe gehwær,
> æt gefeohte frið,   se ðe foran lædeð
> bridels on blancan,   þonne beadurofe
> æt garþræce,   guman gecoste,
> berað bord ond ord.   Þis bið beorna gehwam
> wið æglæce   unoferswiðed
> wæpen æt wigge."

(1181b–88a)

---

7. For a convenient collection of exegetes from patristic times to the later Middle Ages who identified Julian the Apostate with Antichrist, see Cornelius à Lapide, *Commentarius in Apocalypsin S. Joannis Apostoli* (Venice, 1717), 171. This passage forms the conclusion to his commentary on Apocalypse 13.

8. Prudentius, *Psychomachia*, 190–94

9. Campbell, "Cynewulf's Multiple Revelations," 274.

["He will have success in battle, victory in warfare, peace everywhere, and protection in battle, he who bears this bridle on his steed, when famous warriors, experienced soldiers, carry shield and spear into battle. This will be for each man an invincible weapon against distress."]

Not only in literal battle, but in any *æglæc* (distress), the bridle will be a sure source of victory for *beorna gehwam* (each man), not only the emperor. Universal applicability is added to the account in the *Inventio*, underscoring the figural dimensions of the image. Taken literally, use of the talismanic *bridels* by all men would be impossible, a fact which discourages a literal-minded reading. This image of the symbolic bridle is an ancient one, occurring in Roman and Christian art. It is conventionally read as a sign of the harnessing of the passions by the spirit, so their energy can be used productively.

A good example of the continuum of literal and spiritual warfare in the poem can be found in the formulaic half-line *sigores tacen* (token of victory). Early in the poem, the angel shows Constantine the *sigores tacen* in the heavens (85). At this point, the expectation of the king is that he will obtain a physical victory over the barbarians invading his kingdom; they have not yet been called *hæðene*. When the Christians inform Constantine that the same object which gave him victory in earthly battle also loosed men from the bondage of devils, they speak of it as a *sigores tacen* (184). Here the literal and spiritual meanings of the Cross coexist. The final use of the formula occurs when the Jews observe the miracle of the glowing nails:

> Leode gefægon,
> weorud willhreðig,   sægdon wuldor gode
> ealle anmode,   þeah his ær wæron
> þurh deofles spild   in gedwolan lange,
> acyrred fram Criste.   Hie cwædon þus:
> "Nu we seolfe geseoð   sigores tacen,
> soðwundor godes,   þeah we wiðsocun ær
> mid leasingum.   Nu is in leoht cymen,
> onwrigen, wyrda bigang.   Wuldor þæs age
> on heannesse   heofonrices god!"

(1115b–24)

[The people rejoiced, the exultant host spoke glory to God with one mind, although previously through the devil's malice they had long dwelled in error, turned away from Christ. They spoke thus: "Now we ourselves see the token of victory, the true wonder from God, although we previously withstood it with lies. Now the course of destiny has come to light, and is revealed. Let there be glory on high to the God of the kingdom of heaven for this!"]

Cynewulf here expands the brief comment in the *Inventio*: "Nunc cognoscimus in quo credimus" [Now we know who it is we believe in]. Through the seductive power of Satan, the Jews withstood Christ with lies, but they finally recognize the true symbol of victory, a victory of the power of grace over that of the Devil. The formula now has no literal referent at all, but signifies only spiritual victory. This movement into continually expanded spiritual meanings epitomizes the way *Elene* sublates physical violence in spiritual warfare.

Although much of the battle diction in *Elene* has spiritual over-tones, one final example will suffice, the description of the sea voyage to Jerusalem which constitutes the second major addition to the *Inventio* narrative. The studies of Claes Schaar and Lee C. Ramsey, which note resemblances between the sea voyage in *Elene* and those in *Beowulf* and *Andreas*, argue that Cynewulf was making use of a type-scene with a long prehistory.[10] Elene and her *eorla mengu* (225) are described as a naval expedition:

> Stundum wræcon
> ofer mearcpaðu,   mægen æfter oðrum,
> ond þa gehlodon   hildesercum,
> bordum ond ordum,   byrnwigendum,
> werum ond wifum,   wæghengestas.
>
> (232b–36)

[From time to time, one troop after another pressed forward over the coastal roads, then loaded the wave-horses with battle-mail, with shields and spears and warriors.]

William O. Stevens captured the flavor of this entire episode when he wrote that "the whole has a distinctly warlike coloring, and suggests an

---

10. Claes Schaar, *Critical Studies in the Cynewulf Group*, Lund Studies in English, 17 (Lund, 1949), 240–44; Lee C. Ramsey, "The Sea Voyages in Beowulf," *Neuphilologische Mitteilungen* 72 (1971): 56.

expedition of viking warriors."[11] But its relationship to the work as a whole has not been grasped, for many critics have viewed it simply as rhapsodic sea poetry in the manner of a John Masefield epigone.[12]

The military tone of the sea voyage description is quite important. After they land, for example, Elene is called a *guðcwen* (war queen, 254), and her *gumena þreat* (band of warriors, 254) is seen as a war band, a *hereþreat* (265):

> Ðær wæs on eorle   eðgesyne
> brogden byrne   ond bill gecost,
> geatolic guðscrud,   grimhelm manig,
> ænlic eoforcumbul.   Wæron æscwigan,
> secggas ymb sigecwen,   siðes gefysde.
>
> (256–60)

[There the linked corselet was easily visible on a man, and the excellent sword, the magnificent battle-dress, many a helmet and the singular boar-symbol.]

Jackson J. Campbell and Thomas D. Hill have seen in Elene's queenliness her figural association with *Ecclesia*.[13] I would add that her *warlike* queenliness is emphasized in the sea voyage episode, figurally, the valor of the Church Militant. Heroic diction here serves a spiritual purpose, for Elene's plans are not represented as literally warlike; military prowess is sublated in the manner typical of allegoresis. The ambiguity of the use of *þeoden* in line 267b is striking:

---

11. William O. Stevens, *The Cross in the Life and Literature of the Anglo-Saxons* (New York, 1904), 14.

12. Consider the view of Kenneth Sisam: "I do not mean that Cynewulf is a slavish paraphraser. He is always ready to develop a hint when he can do it effectively. A well-known example is his description of Elene's voyage, which is barely mentioned in the Latin . . . . In its context this description of a fair-weather voyage is apt and decorative. But, unlike the voyages in *Beowulf*, it is written from the landsman's point of view: there is an elaborate embarkation, a picture of dancing ships with sails set to a fair breeze, as seen by a watcher from the shore; and then suddenly the long voyage is over, the anchors are down, and the pageant of an army marching begins again. The sea-piece is pretty, but slight and obvious" (*Studies in the History of Old English Literature* [Oxford, 1962], 14–15).

13. Campbell, "Cynewulf's Multiple Revelations," 262–64; Hill, "Sapiential Structure and Figural Narrative," 166–67.

Wæs seo eadhreðige   Elene gemyndig,
þriste on geþance,   þeodnes willan
georn on mode   þæt hio Iudeas
ofer herefeldas   heape gecoste
lindwigendra   land gesohte,
secga þreate.

(266–71)

[The blessed Elene, bold in thought and zealous in mind, was mindful of her prince's desire, that she and her excellent troop of warriors, her host of men, should seek out the land of the Jews over the battlefields.]

The *þeodnes willan* may be either Constantine's or God's; the referent is plurivocal, expressing symbolically the need for *Ecclesia* to evangelize the Jews. The *eorlas æscrofe* (illustrious warriors, 275) who accompany Elene are described as a warrior band bent on subjugating some powerful enemy, but their sublated warfare is spiritual, their enemy Satan.

In other words, the elaborate military descriptions added to the source describe an invading force which will never actually be deployed in physical battle. The objective of Elene's powerful army is the conversion of the Jews and the establishment of a model bishopric, which are treated as joyous events. The military imagery of this section of the poem recalls the military imagery of Ephesians 6.11–17: just as Elene is a figural *guðcwen* representing the Church Militant, her warriors are represented as figural *lindwigendas*—that is, the *milites Dei*.

It would be exaggerating to say that the sea voyage parodies the pagan Germanic lay, but the very nature of military force is undermined in the episode. The narrative transmutes military battle, broached only as a fearful necessity against enemy attack, into spiritual warfare. Constantine's message to his invading army, his *secgas ymb sigecwen* (warriors with their victory queen, 260), is significant in light of the heroic vocabulary sprinkled so liberally throughout the poem:

                Heht he Elenan hæl
abeodan beadurofre,   gif hie brim nesen
ond gesundne sið   settan mosten,
hæleð hwætmode,   to þære halgan byrig.
Heht hire þa aras   eac gebeodan
Constantinus   þæt hie cirican þær
on þam beorhhliðe   begra rædum

getimbrede,   tempel dryhtnes
on Caluarie   Criste to willan,
hæleðum to helpe. . . .

(1002b–11a)

[He commanded the battle-renowned soldiers to greet Elene, if the bold
warriors survived the sea and were able to journey safely to the holy city.
Constantine commanded the messengers to ask her to build a church there
on the hillside on the authority of both of them, a temple to the Lord on
Calvary for Christ's sake as a help for mankind . . . .]

In this passage, an episode unique among legends of the Cross and
(besides the epilogue) the final substantial addition that Cynewulf
made to his source, the temporal power of Rome is channeled toward
building a temple on Calvary to aid all men. Through the victory of the
Romans over the heathen Huns proceed further spiritual victories, that
of Judas over the Devil and that which the bridle makes possible for
every man in spiritual battle. Territorial and human possessions which
Satan mentions in his bitter speech to Judas, possessions discussed in
terms more appropriate to a treasure hoard than to human beings, are
from his jaundiced point of view being destroyed. The agent for this
change in the course of history is the power of the Cross, manifesting
itself through Constantine. The *eald nið* to which Satan had referred
has been substantially increased as well, but the rhetorical construction
of the poem is framed so that this can only augur new victories for the
spiritual warriors of *Ecclesia*.

I

The complicity of allegorical readings such as this one with the poem
itself allows the reflection of *Elene* to displace critical interrogation of a
rhetoric of spiritual warfare. As with *Exodus*, the violence of the poem
is accompanied by violent exclusions on the level of the sign. These
exclusions reinscribe the mythic oppositions of the poem by intensifying
contrast, strengthening the slash separating good from evil, *Ecclesia*
from *Diabolus*. Such semiological violence, which makes itself felt in the
treatment of the Jews, presents serious problems for the twentieth-
century reader, although one would not know this from a survey of
Elene criticism. In their eagerness to praise the poem and avoid anachro-

nism, critics have even kept silent about its anti-Semitism. This refusal is the obverse of the failure of *Exodus* criticism to recognize the Jews as oppressors. In both cases, the allegorical approach leads to a critical response that mirrors the rhetorical patterns of the work. The politics of representation are left unread to the extent that one reads *Exodus* or *Elene* allegorically, reflecting textual processes in a critical language complicit with allegorical sublation.

Elene begins to revile the Jews immediately upon landing with her invading army. She tells a group of three thousand Jews that they may have been dear to God in days of old, but *unwislice* (foolishly, 293) they *þære snyttro . . . wraðe wiðweorpan* (fiercely spurned . . . wisdom, 293a-94a). *Modblinde* (spiritually blinded, 306), they *mengan ongunnon* (began to mingle, 306) lies with truth, light with darkness, malice with mercy. Because they crucified Christ, they must suffer *wergðu* (damnation, 309).

As might have been expected, the Jews do not welcome their visitors with open arms after this scolding by the head of an invading army, especially since none of them took part in the crucifixion of Christ. They leave *reonigmode* (downcast, 320), *egesan geþreade* (tormented by terror, 321). Yet not one of the Jews questions the notion that all are to blame for their ancestors' sins. Nor do any of the Christians. Perhaps that is not surprising. But that twentieth-century critics fail to question such a rhetoric of ancestral guilt is surprising.

After this harangue, the Jews split off into a group of a thousand wise men; after another harangue, into a group of five hundred; after yet another harangue, mercifully briefer, they reply that they were not aware they had wronged Elene. Finally, Judas admits to the Jews how wrong it was to murder God's own son, but recommends stonewalling the investigation:

> "Ne bið lang ofer ðæt
> þæt Israhela   æðelu moten
> ofer middangeard   ma ricsian,
> æcræft eorla   gif ðis yppe bið."

(432b–35)

["It will not be for too long after that, that the race of Israelites and their religion would be able to rule over the earth any longer, if this were known."]

The Jews will not be able to rule the earth any more if they don't feign ignorance. Long ago, Judas's grandfather told his father that the Jews would never be able to maintain their power if the murder site were revealed. In this case, desire for political power is ascribed to those who resist Christians, who in turn are represented as merely doing God's will by spreading light and truth. Their political and military power is represented as a benign instrumentality of evangelism. The fundamental sign structure of the poem removes desire for power from Christians at the same time that it blackens the motives of the Jews.

In the midst of Judas's recollection of family tradition, that they had known all along that it was wrong to crucify Christ, Elene sends messengers with a summons. The Jews respond with lies and hate, so *stearce* (obstinate, 565) are they. Elene warns them that if they continue their deceit, they will all be burned to death. This threat of mass execution, which can be justified by the complicit critic as anagogical, produces results. But perhaps letter is not so completely sublated in spirit as the complicit critic might imagine.

II

I will try to make sense of the politics of allegory in *Elene*, and in *Elene* criticism, by working from within allegorical readings by Earl Anderson, Stanley Greenfield, Catherine Regan, and Daniel Calder. In his book on Cynewulf, Earl Anderson mirrors a textual construct in which the humiliation of the powerless Jews is accepted as proper. He explains how *amor* and *terror* function as aspects of royal *potestas*, and how "the king's *terror*, properly maintained, leads to peace."[14] Such reflection of the text never leads to examination of the role that rhetorical constructs play in valorizing the use of raw power to enforce ideology. At the end of *Elene*, for Anderson, "*imperium* and *sacerdotium* [are] brought into harmony in their relationship to the *populus Dei*" (133): here social harmony (like the artistic unity of the Cynewulfian corpus throughout the book) is privileged. That such rhetorical patterns erase political (and poetic) differences is never a subject for sustained questioning. In large part, this is due to the conventions of Anglo-Saxon criticism. The critical persona of curator of historical antiquities is frequently bothersome in

---

14. Earl Anderson, *Cynewulf: Structure, Style, and Theme in His Poetry* (Rutherford, N.J., 1983), 129. Further references to this book, as to other books and articles mentioned in this chapter, are given parenthetically.

Old English studies, usually for its fustiness. However, the lack of critical attention to textual politics representing torture as productive of social and poetic harmony is far more disconcerting. Anderson's reading practice is by no means unusual. My own identification, earlier in this chapter, of an allegory of war in *Elene* ignores, or evades, the cruelty that Anderson reflects.

Stanley Greenfield writes, "One may see, in fact, the struggle between good and evil that preoccupied Cynewulf here presented thematically as a contrast between darkness and light, both on a physical and a spiritual level."[15] The passages in which Elene flexes her muscles against the Jews, says Greenfield, "are usually slighted in criticism as a 'rather tedious dialectic' . . . but they have a distinct literary if not necessarily poetic power. Elene's first speech to an assembled 3,000 Jews calls attention to the darkness-light dichotomy" (116). In this half-hearted defense of *Elene* against a "slight," the "power" Greenfield mentions turns out to be light imagery. But the accusation of tedium is curious. Surely terror ought to elicit an emotional reaction more specific than boredom.

The "power" Greenfield discovers in light imagery is "literary, if not necessarily poetic." This quibbling over the denomination of power is odd, not only because the distinction between the two is obscure, but because literary power in the passage depends on sociopolitical power. Greenfield's New Critical reflection of textual oppositions never questions this other kind of power. For example, he can call Saul's stoning of Stephen "a foreshadowing of Judas's own hardheartedness toward Elene" (116). Hardheartedness is, of course, one way of looking at Judas's reaction to his persecutor. But such a comment itself might be considered hardhearted, and establishing the structural parallel leads Greenfield to adopt the terrorist position.

Catharine Regan displays the perils of the *lexicon rhetoricae* of sublation in her analysis of the torture of Judas, his confession, and the identification of the Cross. The lynchpin of Regan's argument is a figural reading of the poem in terms of the baptismal liturgy. But, as I have argued, the interpretative power of figural readings stems from serious limitations on our role as readers. Critics of Old English poetry would do well to examine the politics of textual sublation that figural readings

---

15. Stanley B. Greenfield, *A Critical History of Old English Literature* (London, 1966), 114.

reflect. Since the poem's source makes use of symbolic incidents, Regan asserts, "When one realizes that Cynewulf is primarily concerned with the spiritual meaning of the Invention of the Cross legend, *Elene* becomes a poem about the Church and its mission to lead men to salvation through acceptance of the Cross, the symbol of the redemptive act."[16] In other words, one "realizes" that Cynewulf is "primarily" concerned with events seen *spiritualiter*, and thus the poem "becomes" pure theology. Her implicit assumption is that the critic's job is to discover authorial intentions on this abstract theological level, not to question textual structures. Indeed, if the poem is about the redemptive act, questioning its politics is low-minded. Yet from Regan's perspective, torture itself becomes a symbolic aspect for contemplation: since the poem is not really about the Jews persecuted throughout the Middle Ages, but about the Old Man in Everyman, violence is not all that upsetting. For Regan, "Elene's relationship with Judas is emblematic of the relationship of the Church with its members. There is mutual need. Elene needs Judas' assistance to locate the Cross, and Judas needs Elene's prodding to acknowledge the truth" (31). But is "prodding" the right word for seven days in a pit without food or drink? If the literal treatment of Judas and the Jews is seen as primarily symbolic, perhaps such diction is acceptable. But it proves dangerous to move so quickly to a symbolic level that justifies torture as service to the victim. According to Augustine's *De libero arbitrio*, which Regan finds applicable to Judas, "the sinner's intellect is darkened and he suffers pain, tribulation, and sorrow, the signs that right order has been violated" (31). But how relevant is this quotation to a poem in which Elene tortures Judas? Augustine's sinner suffers for his mistakes without the intervention of physical torment. Augustine's commentary might be applicable to the pangs of conscience, but surely not torture.

The sublation of the Old Testament into the New provides Regan with her understanding of references to wisdom in the poem, which "can be fully understood only in terms of Cynewulf's vision of the unity of the two testaments" (32). As with Anderson's privileging of artistic and social harmony, this "vision of unity" is obtained at a price. Indeed, allegorical exegesis is itself a work of ideological appropriation of the Judaic text for the purposes of a Christianity increasingly severed from

16. Catharine A. Regan, "Evangelicalism as the Informing Principle of Cynewulf's *Elene*," *Traditio* 29 (1973): 29.

its cultural base in Judaism. Since Regan does not question an emplotment which construes violence as productive of unity, she becomes a partisan reader who can claim that Judas "like the other Jews, blatantly lies by categorically denying knowledge of the Cross" (34). But the absence of qualification in this assertion betrays the presence of Elene's tonal register in Regan's own critical discourse.

The power to ask questions, and to force answers, is central to the way societies define themselves, as Michel Foucault has argued.[17] Power works through language in *Elene*, in sometimes horrifying ways. As we have seen, the nails of the Cross will eventually be used as a bit for the Emperor's horse. Everyman can use this bridle, as we have also seen. But Constantine can use it as well, in the literal battles he fights. The Church Militant is an important symbolic dimension, here as elsewhere in the poem; however, there is also a history to this politics of figuration. After we grasp the symbolic dimension of battle, we must rise to the literal level. The nails of the Cross, tools for inflicting violence upon Christ, will be used by Christians to inflict violence upon those who fail to recognize the truth of the Gospel. Spiritual warfare also prepares the troops for literal warfare.

In the torture scene, an inverted passion,[18] Elene does not suffer torture, she inflicts it. This formal difference indicates cultural changes so great that traditional hagiographic structure can be reversed. Regan comments on this shift in generic expectations: "Judas is a potential saint and Elene's punishment is the means by which he comes to acknowledge the Cross and thereby achieve sanctity" (35). For Regan, torture "may be more appropriately considered a dramatization of the relationship between the teaching Church and the individual soul" (35). But for whom would such a reading be more appropriate? An economy of violence is implicit in the Christian appropriation of Jewish history in allegoresis: "That Judas should be set apart from the others for his instruction by Elene and later completely isolated in the pit is in keeping with the Augustinian principle of the personal nature of man's relationship with God in the formative stage of man's spiritual development"

---

17. Especially in *Madness and Civilization: A History of Insanity in the Age of Reason*, trans. Richard Howard (New York, 1973); *Discipline and Punish: The Birth of the Prison*, trans. Alan Sheridan (New York, 1979); and *A History of Sexuality*, vol. 1: *An Introduction*, trans. Robert Hurley (New York, 1980).

18. This term was first applied to *Elene* by Rosemary Woolf, "Saints' Lives," in *Continuations and Beginnings: Studies in Old English Literature*, ed. E. G. Stanley (London, 1966), 46–47.

(37). Such an optimistic reading of torture and confinement, which scarcely illustrates Augustine's point, is made possible by symbolic recuperation. Once this hermeneutic machinery has been put to work, even death threats can be read as charity: "On the literal level, Elene is trying to force Judas to confess his knowledge of the Cross, but as a figure of the Church Elene is concerned with the fate of Judas' soul" (37). Such acquiescence in a symbolic practice, without attending to the human costs of terror, is an impoverishment of reading. Even horror becomes benign, giving off sweetness and light: "The nature of the queen's power is the lawful authority of the Chuch to be heard and obeyed. Judas seems cognizant of Elene's authority, but his lack of the higher wisdom prevents him from comprehending it fully" (38). The notion that the Church has lawful authority to imprison and torture, and that Judas lacks the higher wisdom to grasp this, illustrates the sedimentation of imperial violence within Christian hagiography, and within Exegetics as well.

Regan claims that Judas interprets Elene's words symbolically: "Judas' reply . . . shows that he has understood the meaning of Elene's alternatives of life or death. He has interpreted her words symbolically and replies in similarly symbolic terms" (39). In other words, death threats can cause those benighted by the Old Law to undergo miraculous spiritual development, which can only mean the ability to interpret and speak symbolically. Actual violence is erased in this precipitous ascent to symbolism, most notably by the torture victim himself. The language of power, it turns out, was never meant to cause physical harm. Even to have thought so was typical Jewish literal-mindedness.

When Judas firmly refuses to reveal the location of the Cross, Regan says "For the Jews and Judas alike, explanation of the meaning of the Cross and Crucifixion triggers vitriolic response because they are not yet ready to succumb to both the demands and the freedom which recognition of the Cross will bring" (42). One might reply that Elene appears rather more vitriolic, even though she represents the Church, and that the reponse she elicits is eminently sane: the Jews resist having their culture discredited by an invading army. Who would not be suspicious of a truth people must be terrorized into accepting? Yet Regan reflects the text in condemning the Jews' attempt to preserve their culture. Such a rhetoric of religion serves historical oppression.

The poetics of terror in *Elene* depends upon a symbolic positioning of opposed elements which are then subjected to a rhetoric of sublation. Although Elene is represented in contention with the forces of darkness, the issue might just as well be conceptualized as the ideological re-inscription of an historic people. Representation in the poem must be questioned rather than succumbed to. Regan goes on to say, "The temporal Church is the Church Militant, and Elene's earlier struggle with the rebellious Jews and now with Judas illustrates the conflict inherent in the pilgrim Church. Before she can emerge as the Church Triumphant, the Church as *Miles* must, like her model Christ, undergo the strife and pain of temporal life" (43). "Rebellious" seems an odd choice of words for the behavior of the Jews. And in the inverted passion, violence is not suffered, but inflicted, by the Church. However, in order to pursue a figural reading, Regan reads suffering inflicted by the Church as an *imitatio Christi*. When Elene has Judas bound with fetters and cast into a dry pit, Regan writes that Judas's punishment "has important thematic implications" (43). These implications involve the hermeneutics and poetics of sublation: "Judas' pain is specific preparation for his Baptism. It must be remembered that one did not simply 'join' the early Church. The candidate underwent a traumatic change in his life. . . . Fasting was one of the principal means used by the Church to free the Catechumen from the bonds of Satan" (44). But torture in the name of a Higher Truth is not the same as fasting voluntarily chosen. Only the attempt to establish a symbolic baptismal parallel requires such a questionable argument.

According to Regan, "When the poet records Judas' confession, he is in fact describing the conversion of a soul to the Christian faith" (45). He is "in fact" doing a good deal more (or less, depending upon one's perspective): he is describing forced conversion, seen by Regan as "just punishment assigned to him by Elene for his refusal to submit to the rightful authority of the Church" (44). Regan assumes Judas's guilt, echoing his transformation into the New Man without questioning its rhetorical production. His "long and moving prayer" at Calvary, which "illustrates his spiritual growth" (46), demonstrates "how far he has risen above self" (46). That is doubtless one way of putting it. But this illustration is staged to demonstrate the beneficial effects of terror upon the psyche of the victim, whose "subconscious yearning for truth" (44) can be rendered conscious through torture.

Why is the Cross, as Regan observes, "reburied in jewels by Elene" (48)? Judas himself alludes to the bones of Joseph which, according to the Talmud, were revealed to Moses, who reburied them in the Promised Land. But the encrustation of the Cross in valuable gems is also its symbolic reburial in the Promised Land of the Christian *imperium*. The wealth gained by a Church no longer under persecution, but persecuting others, covers the Cross. It transforms the Cross into a representation of power, a *sigores tacen* (symbol of victory). Such signifying practice gives evidence of a bidirectionality in allegoresis. The critique of sublation de-sediments historical and political dimensions of the spiritualized text. In so doing it resists the exegetical mechanism enabling power to etherealize itself. *Elene* celebrates spiritual warfare at the same time that it justifies literal conversion by force. And such symbolic encoding is necessary for the literal violence to take place. But this curious tension of literal and spiritual warfare can become a subject for investigation only if a descent into history accompanies the upward thrust of allegorical criticism. Regan objects to Arthur G. Brodeur's claim that *goldhord* is used with "striking inappropriateness" to denote the Cross. She claims that the compound is perhaps "a striking metaphor which not only signifies Cynewulf's attitude toward the Cross . . . but [also] connotes the redemptive merits gained by Christ's death on the Cross" (48). Her reading thus spiritualizes the cross's association with gold. But the *goldhord* of tradition also associates the Cross with the worldly power this symbol of the crucifixion produced for Constantine, and for the English Church as well. The Anglo-Saxon *goldhord* was not desired as capital in the modern sense, but as a representation of past victories, as well as of the future victories its distribution to warriors would make possible. A conventional sublatatory reading like Regan's necessarily spiritualizes this *goldhord*, removing gold to a symbolic plane where only religious associations are presumed relevant.

Regan concludes that, for Elene, "the actual discovery of the Cross is subordinated to its symbolic significance. Finding the true Cross is important only insofar as it is a symbol of the spiritual discovery of the Cross which each man must make for himself" (52). But there are aspects of this discovery—for instance, the nails which form the bit of Constantine's bridle, to be used in actual battles—which are not simply spiritual. The subordination of real history and politics to theological symbolism should not go unchallenged. The historical effects of typology have been insufficiently thought through.

I would attempt to historicize typology in *Elene* by returning to Earl Anderson's article,[19] which focuses on the poem's thematic organi-

---

19. Earl Anderson, "Cynewulf's *Elene*: Manuscript Divisions and Structural Symmetry," *Modern Philology* 72 (1974): 111–22.

zation. And I would begin with his discussion of the organic metaphor of the Cross as:

> mærost beama
> þara þe of eorðan   up aweoxe,
> geloden under leafum . . .
>
> (1224b–26a)

[the most famous of trees which have sprung up from the earth, growing beneath their leaves . . .]

Anderson reads the leaves of the Cross in terms of the "typological association of the Cross with the Tree of Life and the Tree of Knowledge of Good and Evil, seen in visual art as well as in literary texts" (115). He sees its metaphorical reblooming as suggesting renewal of life in an instrument of death. But, as mentioned earlier, Anderson detects political dimensions in the poem as well. The Old English poet represents Constantine as an ideal king, who serves as "a terror to his enemies and a comfort to his people, thereby inspiring, through the exercise of kingly virtues, *amor* and *terror*—a concept of continuing importance in English and Continental thought about kingship from the time of Isidore of Seville to Sedulius Scottus" (117). The political elements that Regan's typological reading transcends furnish the ground for Anderson's reading, which reveals a typology intermixed with less sublime elements.

Anderson points out in a telling phrase that Elene is "the emperor's surrogate" (118). As *Ecclesia*, she is not only representative of the body of Christ, but of the body politic as well. Most allegorical commentaries keep these levels separate, following an Augustinian theoretical caution ignored by a popular hermeneutics complicit with secular power. When critics enlist traditional allegory maintaining Augustinian protocols in order to understand syncretist hagiography like *Elene*, they deflect interpretation toward highly spiritualized readings. In *Elene*, Church means not only those motivated by *caritas*, as in Augustine, but something more worldly as well. Hence the importance of descriptions of battle, of torture descriptions, of the sea-journey of Anglo-Saxon traditional epic, of the bit for the emperor's horse. Like Regan's, my reading earlier in this chapter of an allegory of war in *Elene* spiritualized conflict. Given the genealogy of Anglo-Saxon studies, such misreading seems almost inevitable, a stage that must be incorporated into our understanding of the poetry before it can be transcended.

Ecclesia has manifold ties to violence and power in *Elene* which are defused by the typological orientation. Traditional allegoresis attempted to spiritualize Old Testament violence by relating it to the soul's struggles against Satan, while later poetic allegoresis refashions the politics of typology: less reluctant to conflate the spiritual and the political, it is less scrupulous about the relationship between theology and state power as well. The Cross does indeed bloom in *Elene*. But among its new leaves are oppression and torture.

Anderson discusses the relationship between *imperium* (empire), *studium* (learning), and *sacerdotium* (priesthood), the three powers that "through their harmonious cooperation, sustain the life and health of Christendom" (120), emphasizing how Cynewulf's alterations highlight Constantine's significance. Although his reading supplies the social and political context missing in Regan's, Anderson does not read rhetorical processes critically. There are important dissonances in the poem's harmony as well, and hearing them means questioning the harmonious principles of closure privileged by New Critical perspectives. In *Elene*, the harmonious cooperation of the three powers is produced by negating the Jews who, after the defeat of the barbarians, must be tortured into submission. In so doing, the Cross must be turned into a weapon for advancing the reign of Christianity. Reburied in the gold of empire, it becomes an emblem of imperial will.

Constantine was seen as the first Christian king, the patriarchal origin of political authority in the postpagan era. His victory over the barbarians establishes the Roman *imperium*, "but the failure of his 'witangemot' to inform him fully about the Cross . . . indicates that the *studium* is not yet one of the supporting powers of Christendom" (121). Since the Jews possess the *studium*, but have perverted it, God must bring about a *translatio studii*, "the Pauline doctrine of the supersession of the Old Law by the New" (121). In such textual processes one witnesses an historical tendency that will continue for centuries. Indeed, Regan reduplicates this *translatio studii* in her own hermeneutic of sublation. And for Anderson, "the incident of the discovery and disposition of the nails of the Cross, furthermore, neatly illustrates the harmonious cooperation of *imperium*, *studium*, and *sacerdotium*" (122). But he does not notice that this neat harmony is produced through violence, as Christianity triumphs by allying itself with imperialism. The rhetoric of *Elene* continues the *translatio*, even to the extent of explicitly justifying a violence implicit in typology and allegory. Typology already opens onto violence, since it is the mechanism for one culture's reappropriation of another: Christianity, no longer simply a variety of Judaism, cancels its origins through typology. This typological supersession is so successful that the Jew suffers a *translatio* into the hated symbol of the Old Man. Violence in *Elene* has psychological as well as sociological dimensions, with a justification of oppression written into its operations at the level of the sign.

For Daniel Calder, Constantine's battle is "a germinal episode that sets the thematic pattern for the whole: radiating from this initial episode is a series of circles that duplicates the original pattern."[20] The Rood is both revelation and "proof of God's wish to aid man in his struggle against sin, and its presence presages the triumph of good over evil" (202). A sympathetic reader, Calder mirrors Cynewulfian sublation in his own discourse. His rhetoric of praise of the poem, "a strangely neglected treasure," is based on the claim that it is "highly wrought" (201). These are the enabling rhetorical topoi of New Criticism in Anglo-Saxon studies. In the New Critical paradigm, texts are evaluated on the basis of complexity, subtlety, and intricate design; Old English studies based upon this model seldom move beyond a subordinate relationship to the text, and the tonal register of critical discourse is usually confined to discreet encomium.

This approach to Old English texts produces remarkably sanguine readings. For Calder, *Elene* is "about the perceiving of a pure and visionary truth . . . . It is Elene who, on Constantine's request, shoulders the burden of strife as she journeys to Jerusalem" (202). But this passage from secular to religious struggle is not as complete as Calder thinks, since a residue of violence in the service of state power is never transcended. Rather than harmony between secular and spiritual levels, there is tension between them, resulting in an incomplete transformation into pure truth. Like Anderson, Calder privileges harmonious cooperation without considering its costs. For Constantine and Elene, the rhetoric of the Satanic serves as an ideological weapon for textualizing all who resist. For if anyone can be said to "shoulder the burden of

---

20. Daniel Calder, "Strife, Revelation, and Conversion: The Thematic Structure of *Elene*," *English Studies* 53 (1972): 201.

strife," it is the Jews. This burden will continue to oppress all peoples who resist the encroachments of imperial Christian culture. After mentioning Elene's desire to meet with Jewish wise men, Calder comments: "The irony is pungent; the men who supposedly know most deeply the secrets of God in reality know nothing, since they have not received the light of faith to see into the real mystery of divinity. The wisdom of men is limited, and its deliberate contrast in the poem to the wisdom achieved from God's bright revelation points up the monolithic stature of the one Christian truth" (203). Who is speaking here? Does Calder believe in the descriptive adequacy of a rhetoric in which the wisest Jews "in reality know nothing?" What is the status of "reality" in this passage? Who claims that Christian truth is monolithic? Calder's rhetoric uncritically replicates the poem's: "The series of imagistic correspondences is intricate, and arises from the light of revelation which enabled Constantine to know, to penetrate the mystery and arrive at truth. Thus light, truth, and wisdom become attached to the Christian revelation; darkness, error, and blind ignorance remain the portion of those who in the battle between Christ and Satan still adhere to the night of the Fallen Angel" (203). Instead of interrogating the textual production of value along the cleavage of a binary opposition, Calder sees such a *fundamentum divisionis* as sanctioned. This failure to read critically provokes the eloquent conclusion to his sentence, a triumph of partisan rhetoric. The implicit notion that other religious and cultural traditions "adhere" to darkness and evil must not be echoed by the twentieth-century critic. Cynewulf constructs a representation of the Jew as ignorant, dark, in error, but modern critics need not become spokesmen for his values.

For Calder, the strife of light and darkness continues when Elene "meets only recalcitrance and refusal in her attempt to learn the hiding place of the Cross . . . . [The Jews] have abandoned wisdom in spurning Christ. Thus it is deeply ironic that she calls them into council at all; in their utter error they can know nothing, can perceive nothing of the revelation of Christ's Godhood" (204). For whom is the behavior of the Jews recalcitrance? For whom is it deeply ironic that she even calls them into council? Irony can occur only from the viewpoint of those terrorizing the Jews with a convincing show of military force and a heavy dose of propaganda. Calder goes on to assert that "The values of the Jews are those of darkness and their belief in wisdom is only the acceptance of ignorance. Again Elene points directly to the spiritual errors in the souls of the Jews."[21] But must contemporary criticism join in this pointing? Just who claims that the values of the Jews are those of darkness? Such questions are a way of focusing attention on the typical paraphrastic methodology of Anglo-Saxon studies, which leads to imaginary identification rather than critical distance, and to justification of violence in response to Jewish resistance: "For Elene, already imbued with the wisdom of the spiritual mysteries, there is only one path open—direct encounter in mortal strife with the forces of darkness and unwisdom" (204). The notion of inevitable mortal strife seems curious rhetoric for an invasion by a superior army with the force of Empire behind it.

Calder adds, "With almost pitiful impotence the Jews reassemble" (204) after listening to Elene berate them. But if they are impotent, in what sense is the strife mortal? And why is their impotence *almost* pitiful? Calder's language has little room for sympathy with the victims of power, because imaginary identification with Cynewulfian rhetoric never permits the Jews to be seen as anything other than creatures of error, ignorance, recalcitrance, and lies: "Their impotence is real in the presence of Elene who, without allowing them a chance to demonstrate their wisdom, harangues them with proof of their ignorance . . ." (205). Indeed. Elene terrorizes the Jews, denying them the opportunity to speak in their own defense, because their benightedness remains a foregone conclusion. Calder says that the Jews consider it "their duty to strive aginst Elene and Christ" (205). But since their strife, which is nonmilitary, is in response to invasion, their duty would appear to be understandable, although not in terms of the rhetoric of the text.

Calder is representative of the curious critical concordat Old English scholars forged in the course of negotiating the passage from philology to New Criticism. He argues, "Judas's entombment is, first, the final and most effective device which Elene has at her disposal to force him into submission, and, second, a symbolic parallel to Christ's burial" (206). What he fails to notice about this "parallel," however, is that the positions of torturer and tortured are reversed. Consequently, it is better understood as a profound historical chiasmus.

---

21. Calder sees light/dark imagery as "of course, archetypal, but it also has important and specific sources in the broad literary tradition of Christianity" (203). Calder cites the Platonic context, but to notice specific sources in philosophical tradition is not necessarily to grasp the consequences of such rhetorical structures. Calder echoes the figures and dualities of the poem, but does not question them. Derrida's "White Mythology: Metaphor in the Text of Philosophy" has examined the mythic use of light, clarity, and whiteness in Western discourse (*Margins of Philosophy*, trans. Alan Bass [Chicago, 1982], 207–71).

Elene is a poetic celebration of forced cultural change. Like Re-
gan, Calder tries to demonstrate the theological depth of force, citing
Augustine's *Descende ut ascendas, humiliare ut exalteris* (Descend if you
would ascend, be lowly if you would be exalted.) But surely the involun-
tary descent of a torture victim is not "a poetic enactment of Augustine's
dictum" (206). This would be to make the quite different argument that
typological supersession of the Jews is already potential historical sup-
pression. Calder sees resemblances between Judas's pit, Christ's tomb,
and the grave where the Cross is buried, but ignores differences. For
him, "the wisdom once so obviously lacking in Judas is now his in full
measure . . . and the poem has returned full circle to the beginning of
the thematic pattern where a new warrior has picked up the standard of
the Christian fight" (207). But this new warrior has been produced by
military intimidation: victimization is transformed into spiritual insight,
oppression into inspiration. Such rhetorical validation of force posits an
ideal reader who is complicit with the power of Church and State to
construct him as subject.

There is a textual politics here, a pattern for Church-State rela-
tions and for the construction of the subject deferring to institutional
power. The political dangers of its representation of the Jew are latent,
and will germinate later in English history.[22] Still, there are immediate
social and psychological uses for this representation as well. For the Jew
functions as the other, within and without, which must be assimilated
through the use of force. The subject of Elene/*Ecclesia* must become
transformed by a Church with juridical power, especially the capacity to
inflict suffering. In the broader historical context, social control pro-
ceeds from control over the subject of *Elene*—that is, the ideal reader
constructed by the poem:

> The will of God has been revealed and fulfilled, the people converted, and
> the faithful gathered into His army. Then the poem returns to the ever-
> present need of facing the enemy within the domain of time. Though
> Judas and his people see deeply with the light of faith, there are many . . .

---

22. There are no large-scale Jewish settlements in England until after the Norman
Conquest. On Christian attitudes toward the Jew, see Bernhard Blumenkranz, *Les auteurs
chrétiens latins du Moyen Age sur les Juifs et le Judaisme* (Paris, 1963); James Parkes, *The
Conflict of the Church and the Synagogue: A Study in the Origins of Antisemitism* (London,
1934); Jacob R. Marcus, *The Jew in the Medieval World* (New York, 1938; reprint, West-
port, Conn., 1975); Norman Cohn, *The Pursuit of the Millennium: Revolutionary Millenar-
ians and Mystical Anarchists of the Middle Ages* (New York, 1970).

who would keep the truth of the Christian faith hidden, like the Cross and the Nails, in the occlusion of ignorance so that they may persist in the night of their own error. Against such as these there is no respite from the battle for the Christian armed with the true faith. The ending of the narrative, with its stress on the battle between good and evil . . . is the spiritual reflection of the opening martial encounter between Constantine and the Goths. What was only a heroic skirmish . . . has been carefully transformed by revelation and the acceptance of truth into a war against the very portals of hell (208).

That this careful transformation is one the twentieth-century critic should not simply identify with does not appear to have occurred to Calder, unless we find traces of uncertainty in his pulpit rhetoric. He trumpets the poem's values without considering his own position as an ideal reading subject constructed by the text. As an ideal writing subject constituted by the field of Old English studies, I can identify with Calder's predicament, because it has been my own as well. Although he is one of the most theoretically astute Anglo-Saxon critics, it would have been surprising if Calder had avoided such complicity with the poem's values.[23] The careful construction his writing praises is the craftsmanlike design of an instrument of ideological violence. The imperialistic will gains strength through the rhetorical construction of a battle against the forces of darkness: the resistance of the other necessitates violent erasure of difference in the name of the selfsame. In the role of cultural curator, the critic of Old English poetry can too easily dwell only upon the uplifting aspects of literary artifacts. But museums preserve a past open to reinterpretation, and curatorship of the *Elene* section involves understanding a verbal torture instrument. Connoisseurship, at the very least, demands accurate labelling, so that sympathy for the past will not diminish *Elene*'s importance for the present.

For Calder, the epilogue continues a regular progression toward psychomachia: "Though Cynewulf shares an existence of strife with the other characters, his wrestling is of an interior sort. The poem is transformed steadily in this direction, from the purely military struggle of Constantine, through Judas's duel with Elene, to the inner world of psychological disruption and the chaos of sin in Cynewulf's heart" (209).

---

23. On Calder's eloquent plea for theoretical questioning in Anglo-Saxon studies, see the Afterword.

But the Cynewulfian battle in the epilogue "is cast in the past tense" (209). Cynewulf is delivered from sin "through the revelatory power of poetry . . . the very power of art to transform the soul of the poet and make known to him the wisdom of faith" (209). Reverence for early medieval rhetoric shifts to reverence for the revelatory power of art, a textual move conflating the theological and the literary within Calder's argument. It is true that peace has replaced warfare in the course of the poem. But by allowing his own discourse to succumb to the arc of emotion the poem charts, Calder has failed to question the peace achieved by the revelatory poetic process. For violence against the Jews, and by implication against all non-Christian cultures, makes possible the peace produced through the poem's symbolic action.

III

The language of *Elene* is forceful and moving, but the twentieth-century critic able to resist its charms ought to question the way its Christian harmony, peace, and unanimity are achieved. Such qualities depend, in an essential way, on the repression of difference. In *Attitudes Towards History*, Kenneth Burke makes a distinction between factional and universal tragedy that is particularly applicable to *Elene*:

> In universal tragedy, the stylistically dignified scapegoat represents everyman. In his offence, he takes upon himself the guilt of all—and his punishment is mankind's chastening. We identify ourselves with his weakness (we feel "pity"), but we dissociate ourselves from his punishment (we feel "terror").[24]

Dissociation coexists with association. Repelled and attracted by the universal scapegoat, we observe and participate in his suffering. But the factional scapegoat is different, "closer to the strategy of satire":

> The crucifixion of Christ might, by our distinction, be considered as a universal tragedy made factional by the processes of bureaucratization. That is, Christ died for all—but insofar as all were not believers, the tragedy called for "action" with respect to the non-believers. Thus, the Jews that crucified him ceased to represent all mankind, becoming instead a faction of mankind. (189–90)

24. Kenneth Burke, *Attitudes Towards History*, 3d ed. (Berkeley, 1984), 188.

Elene represents the Old English stage of these "processes of bureau-cratization." The only good Jews, according to *Elene*, are the ones who become Christians. Their conversion must be brought about by force if necessary. Although Gregory I condemned them, forced conversions were commonplace in the early Middle Ages. To mention only one example, the Council of Toledo (694) "reduced to slavery all those in the Visigothic kingdom still found to be practicing Judaism. Their children were to be taken away to be brought up by Christians and to be married off to Christians. Property owned by declared or suspected Jews was confiscated."[25] The violence of forced conversions marks the difference between the early Christian period and the early Middle Ages. A verbal action with social and psychological consequences, *Elene* underwrites the use of force, which extends to the non-Christian other within and without. It sanctions terror, which we associate today with totalitarians of the right and left. As Pope Nicholas I wrote in A.D. 866:

> A confession must be voluntary and not forced. By means of torture an innocent man may suffer to the uttermost without making any avowal—in such a case what a crime for the judge! Or a person may be subdued by pain, and acknowledge himself guilty, though he be innocent—which throws an equally great sin upon the tribunal.[26]

A twentieth-century audience ought to wince at descriptions of the interrogation and torture of Jews; evidently, some highly placed members of the ninth-century audience might have as well. *Elene* embodies the philosophy of torture in all its unsubtle grandeur: your opponents will come around if you punish them enough. That so little attention has been paid to these unsavory aspects of the work is a result of philological, formalist, and allegorical critical models. My readings of allegorical readings have been a departure from the critical norm, largely because they breach protocol. But I think such critique of the critics necessary if we are ever to make sense of the institutional positioning of the reader of Old English poetry, or to bring about a historicization of *Elene*'s hagiographic practice.

---

25. *Encyclopaedia Judaica*, 5:547.
26. This translation from the *Responsa ad consulta Bulgarorum* appears in William Stearns Davis, *Life on a Mediaeval Barony* (New York, 1923), 166. For further information on forced conversions in the early Middle Ages, see the works of Blumenkranz, Parkes, and Marcus previously referred to.

Chapter 5

Andreas

The fundamental textual oppositions of *Andreas* are more difficult to unravel than those of *Elene*. In both of these works, the sometimes bizarre forms of a popular hagiographic practice complicate the basic symbolic register found in a poem like *Exodus*. After Thomas Hill first drew attention to typological aspects of *Andreas* by reading the flood as baptismal, critics followed with typological studies of the other two parts of the poem, Matthew's rescue from prison and Andreas's conversations with Christ. The cannibalism of the Mermedonians, like Andreas's Christlike passion, have also been read from the vantage point of Exegetics.[1] But the typological framework which makes it possible to read the allegory of war in *Andreas* also tends to privilege the theological and suppress the sociopolitical level, as was the case with *Exodus* and *Elene*.

At the end of the work, Andreas wreaks miraculous destruction upon *þæs weorodes eac ða wyrrestan,* / *faa folcsceaðan feowertyne* (the worst of that troop, fourteen bitter enemies of the people, 1592–93). He then prays to God, commanding these *geonge* (young) Mermedonians to rise from the dead. According to the poet, *ðær wæs eall eador* / *leoðolic ond gastlic* (they were completely put back together, bodily and spiritually, 1627b–28a), a reuniting of dead matter and living spirit that leads to the baptism of these newly arisen youths, the conversion of the Mermedonians, the construction of a church, and the organization of a

---

1. Thomas D. Hill, "Figural Narrative in *Andreas*: The Conversion of the Mermedonians," *Neuphilologische Mitteilungen* 70 (1969): 261–73. Important typological studies by Walsh, Hieatt, Earl, Casteen, and Boenig are discussed in the course of the chapter. A translation of the *Recensio Casanatensis* of the Greek *Acts of Andrew and Matthew Among the Cannibals* can be found in Michael J. B. Allen and Daniel G. Calder, trans., *Sources and Analogues of Old English Poetry* (Totowa, N.J., 1976).

diocese. This reunification of soul and body is echoed in the mass conversion requested by *eorlas anmode, ond hira idesa mid* (earls with one mind and their women as well, 1638). A series of ritual baptisms marks the transformation of violence, disunity, and difference into peace, unity, and identity. The constitutive violence of this harmonious transformation disappears in recent criticism, which reinscribes the rhetorical arc by which Andreas's miracle first causes, then cancels Mermedonian deaths. Sorrow has turned into joy, darkness into light, paganism into Christianity—all the fundamental oppositions have been reversed.

But many Mermedonian deaths aren't canceled. Only some of the young Mermedonians are brought back to life.[2] Underscoring the typological dimensions of a death by water which brings new life to a savage race, critics have ignored or sublated the literal violence implicated in the final coherence. As with *Elene*, force remains crucial for the conversion of an alien people who eventually come to appreciate the opportunity of being terrorized for Christ. The Mermedonians' attempt to preserve their traditional culture appears reprehensible, largely due to the bizarre extremity of their characterization as magicians, sadists, and anthropophagi. The violence of the poem, which can be traced to Matthew's attempt to wean the Mermedonians from old religious patterns, differs from the violence of *Elene* in one significant respect: divine punishment takes the place of military force in the ideological reprogramming of a non-Christian people.

The intersection of spirituality with politics emerges in the way the Old English *Andreas* constructs the differential category of the foreigner.[3] The meeting with the other must be conflictual in traditional Western narrative. Indeed, literature which does not observe this convention seems pointless to Westerners. At the beginning of *Andreas*, the twelve apostles are presented as *twelfe . . . tireadige hæleð* (twelve glorious heroes, 2), *frome folctogan ond fyrdhwate, / rofe rincas* (brave chieftains and valiant, bold warriors, 8–9a). This recurrent motif of the *miles Dei* involves acts of literal and symbolic violence against the heathen. The assaults of the other can be represented as stemming from two

---

2. Marie Michelle Walsh, "The Baptismal Flood in the Old English *Andreas*: Liturgical and Typological Depths," *Traditio* 33 (1977): 157.

3. Constance B. Hieatt was the first critic to grasp the importance of the category of the *elpeodig*, which is variously applied to Mermedonians, Christians, and Jews ("The Harrowing of Mermedonia: Typological Patterns in the Old English *Andreas*," *Neuphilologische Mitteilungen* 77 [1976]: 54–55).

liminal regions, the margins of the psyche or the borders of the known world. Originating in a realm of propagandistic fantasy generated by the twin fears of the *eald feond* and the monstrous races, the Mermedonians—who feast on the bodies of strangers—are not quite otherworldly devils, but they come close. Their polyvalency is difficult to read: is symbolism in the service of the historical level in *Andreas*, or is it the other way around? Typological studies decode unidirectionally, inevitably displacing the literal level to reveal the typological. Moving in the opposite direction, however, reopens the historicity of the poem's rhetoric of the foreign.

The foreigners of *Andreas* are presented not merely as symbols, but as a historical race of cannibals. They have a worldly as well as a theological function. A complex metalepsis informs their characterization, since what the poet takes to be actual historical existents is only the ideological production of an appropriate blocking agent from the symbolic resources of tradition. For the typological critic, these races are symbolic. But in the poem they are regarded as frighteningly real. As we know from the *Marvels of the East*, Anglo-Saxons believed such monstrous, demonic races really existed somewhere out there, at the margins of the world. You could sail there to meet them, if you were foolhardy enough.

Mermedonians are violent because it is the *þæs folces freoðoleas tacen* (savage mark of that people, 29) to be violent. They blind Christians, and brew magic potions that pervert the reason, making men bloodthirsty or vegetarian. The Mermedonian dietary options of hay or human flesh occupy marginal sites at the lower and upper limits of the alimentary code. Such degeneration connotes spiritual wickedness, of course, and resembles what happened to Nabuchodonosor. But this symbolism also reinforces the literal monstrousness of alien cultures. The Christian saint journeys overseas to encounter a people portrayed as so overwhelmingly other and monstrous that contact with them can result in human transformations as weird as any in *The Odyssey*. Or even more so. As Constance Hieatt puts it, "Mermedonia is hell."[4] Further work with allegorical commentary tradition will continue to refine our understanding of the diabolical resonance of the hideous Mermedonians. But a historical residue lingers in the presentation of the

---

4. Hieatt, "Harrowing of Mermedonia," 53. As Hieatt points out, the identification of the Mermedonians with devils is also made by Alvin A. Lee, *The Guest-Hall of Eden* (New Haven, 1972), 91.

foreigner as monstrous, one which typological scholarship must not be allowed to negate.

Jewish otherness represents another important aspect of the rhetoric of the foreign in *Andreas*.[5] After his sparkling irony in praising Andreas for calming the sea, Christ himself calls the Jews *arleasan* (impious, 559), *inwidþancas* (evil-minded, 559), *unsælige* (wretched, 561), *grome gealgmode* (hostile, gloomy-minded, 562), and *fræte* (perverse, 571). Christ's torrent of vituperation is provoked by "their" failure to recognize his divinity. Jewish rejection of Christ is not presented universally, as criticism levied against unregenerate humanity, but factionally, just as it was in *Elene*. That Christ himself indulges in scapegoating constitutes a rewriting of Christianity with serious political and theological consequences. The typological critic can always justify Christ's language as a reference to the old man within. Unfortunately, this procedure wagers a totalizing interpretation on the basis of just one textual dimension. *Andreas* utilizes typology to occupy a literal site with exemplary historical and political consequences. In a poem with this kind of pretence to historical specificity, putting anti-Semitism into God's mouth provides divine sanction for hostility to non-Christian cultures. A partisan typological reading is, at the very least, impoverished criticism.

Christ's racist criticisms of the Jewish people occur in a humorous narrative context, since Andreas himself shares the trait of nonrecognition of Christ: the saint too is implicitly impious, wretched, hostile, perverse. Christ manipulates Andreas's nonrecognition, in an urbane ironizing of the gap between divine essence and literal embodiment.[6] Hence, Andreas's ability to respond to the presence of divinity suffers only a glancing blow, and the list of negative traits which Christ considers an essential characterization of the Jews will turn out to apply only tangentially to him. That Andreas does not object to this harangue is not surprising, since he is about to meddle with a wicked race of people too, and there is no hagiographic precedent for such a critique of divinity.

Christ's racist anger is no one-time divine lapse. He continues to

---

5. On the Jews in *Andreas*, see James W. Earl, "The Typological Structure of *Andreas*," in *Old English Literature in Context: Ten Essays*, ed. J. D. Niles (Cambridge, 1979), 72, 76; Thomas Hill, "Hebrews, Israelites, and Wicked Jews: An Onomastic Crux in *Andreas* 161–67," *Traditio* 32 (1976): 360; and Constance Hieatt, "Harrowing of Mermedonia," 60.

6. The typological, or post-figural, parallel here is the apostles' failure to recognize Christ on the road to Emmaus (Luke 24.13–35).

speak of the Jews with vehemence while discussing their council of elders:

> "Me þæt þinceð,
> ðæt hie for æfstum   inwit syredon
> þurh deopne gedwolan.   Deofles larum
> hæleð hynfuse   hyrdon to georne,
> wraðum wærlogan.   Hie seo wyrd beswac,
> forleolc ond forlærde.   Nu hie lungre sceolon,
> werige mid werigum,   wræce þrowian,
> biterne bryne   on banan fæðme."

(609–16)

["It seems to me that they devised malice because of their envy, their deep error. Those doomed men listened too eagerly to the wrathful troth-breaker. This is what deceived, seduced, and misled them. Now, criminals among criminals, they must soon endure vengeance, bitter fire in the embrace of the Slayer."]

Prompted by the devil, the guileful Jewish *bisceopas*, *boceras*, and *ealdormenn* who maliciously plotted against the Christian truth—evidence of their deep error—now suffer bitter burning among the damned. This divinely paranoid reconstruction of the biblical account sees a wicked plot where the Christ of the gospels saw only the ignorance of those who crucified him. The failure to grasp divinity, which in the New Testament had characterized mankind, is now radically delimited to a Jewish conspiracy theory, one advanced by Christ himself in the midst of a conversion narrative.[7]

Damning information about the Jews is elicited through a question-and-answer session with the marked catechetical redundancy of ideology. When Christ interrogates Andreas in the manner of the

---

7. Modern critics often adopt the questionable rhetoric of their sources. For Earl, "Andrew, fulfilling Christ's *bysen*, liberates the captives as Christ harrowed Hell, and he accomplishes the conversion of his tormentors as Christ too will bring about the conversion of His tormentors, the Jews, before the establishment of the Kingdom of God at the Final Judgment" ("Typological Structure," 72–73). It is difficult, from the vantage point of typological criticism, to recognize the institutionalized rhetoric of vilification of the Jews as ideology. It is not a mere quibble to point out that the torture of Christ was carried out by Romans, or that *some* Jews collaborated with them; for Gregory the Great's position on this matter in his *Moralia in Job*, see Bernhard Blumenkranz, *Les auteurs chrétiens latins du Moyen Age sur les Juifs et le Judaïsme* (Paris, 1963), 86.

classroom teacher, Andreas replies with the formulaic answers of the well-programmed pupil. According to Andreas, the high priest accused Jews who favored Christianity of obeying the teachings of an *elþeodig* (stranger, 678). This emphasis on group identity and exclusion recurs in the accusation of disloyalty that the high priest levels at those who would depart from the customary practice of their people. Although his identification of difference with decadence and treason is treated as benighted, *Andreas* manifests no compensatory awareness of the way it rhetorically maligns strangers. Both the high priest and the Old English poet employ the same rhetoric of hostility to the foreign to accomplish their ends. Although the vilified high priest, presented *as* a deceitful stranger, accuses Andreas and the other apostles of following the teachings *of* a deceitful stranger, the poem dissociates its own rhetorical processes from those of Jewish resistance to Christ. The chief priest's deployment of a rhetoric of accusation appears as the conscious duplicity of the *domgeorn* (ambitious, 693). The text consistently embodies a failure to think through the implications of its categories, which dismantle early Christian conceptions of Jew and gentile. The high priest and Jews are represented as ambitious, but the extent to which the ambition of Christianity in its expansionist missionary phase relies on identical textual strategies goes unexamined. Unacceptable aspects of Christianity's will to destroy other belief systems are attributed to the other. The poem thereby maintains Christian purity of motive by sullying the other, whether Jew or Mermedonian.

Christian identity, not an essence but the result of an ongoing historical process, is constructed upon a rhetorical blind spot in *Andreas*: if strangers are Christian apostles, they are lightbringers; otherwise, they are darkness incarnate, inhuman and monstrous. This logic disposes of the dark side of Christianity's will-to-power through the power of semiology. But, to paraphrase Barbara Johnson's reworking of Montaigne's maxim, differences *between* Christians and non-Christians are differences *within* each of the opposed categories. Strategies for representing Mermedonians in the poem are homologous with the prior institutional model of the Jew. Typological processes that sublate Jewish tradition are reenlisted for the suppression of an alien gentile culture. The Jew, much more than the heathen, loomed as an alien presence threatening the early Christian order. The threat they posed was internal as well as external: that part of the fledgling Jewish convert which refused to put on the New Man. Although the threat of Judaism became predominantly internal after the triumph of Christianity, the Jew continued to serve a structural purpose, one testifying more to the way Christianity conceptualized itself than to any challenge Jews presented to the new Christian *imperium*. Early on, Christian tradition made the Jew into a factional scapegoat, despite the teachings of theologians who recognized the error of locating evil within Judaism proper. The enemies of *Ecclesia* can be so localized only within an impoverished and anti-Augustinian theology; yet even the Augustinian tradition maintained the existence of a deformed spiritual Jewishness while disclaiming direct revenge against actual Jews.[8] Jewish evil mirrors the self-imputed purity of Christianity. Scapegoating allows the other within to be located without, differences within to be rewritten as differences between opposed categories. The ambition of Christianity works through just such textualization of the other, whether Jew or Mermedonian. That this rhetoric has led, and continues to lead, to actual persecution of Jews illustrates its potential for quite concrete effects.

Historically, the key element shared by Mermedonians and Jews was thought to be cannibalism. Medieval Christian evidence for the existence of Jewish cannibalism, often elicited in the aftermath of pogroms, rested upon confessions and eyewitness accounts. Not surprisingly, these beliefs are based on no supporting evidence that modern researchers would accept. William Arens sees "racism" inherent in *all* accounts of supposed cannibalistic practices, although "a nicer term might be cultural eccentricity or prejudice."[9] Evidence for the tendency

---

8. See Hill, "Figural Narrative," 268–69 on "the Pauline theme of the death of the Old Man and birth of the New Man" in *Andreas*. On representations of Judaism in early medieval Christianity, see Blumenkranz, *Les auteurs chrétiens latins du Moyen Age* and Parkes, *The Conflict of the Church and the Synagogue*. The policy of Gregory the Great, which would become the official position, is discussed by Jacob R. Marcus, *The Jew in the Medieval World* (New York, 1938; reprint, Westport, Conn., 1975), 111–14.

9. Elisabeth Rosenthal, "Myth of the Man-Eaters," *Science Digest* 91 (April, 1983): 12. See also William Arens, *The Man-Eating Myth: Anthropology and Anthropophagy* (Oxford, 1979). John Casteen, "*Andreas*: Mermedonian Cannibalism and Figural Narration," *Neuphilologische Mitteilungen* 75 (1974): 74–78 discusses the theology of cannibalism as punishment for a nation's sins. On medieval Christian accusations of Jewish cannibalism, see the *Encyclopaedia Judaica*, s.v. "blood libel." These allegations survive even in more recent times, as evidenced by the fact that "in this century a non-Jewish German scholar who wrote on this phenomenon actually entitled one chapter of his book 'Is the Use of Christian Blood Required or Allowed for Any Rite Whatever of the Jewish Religion?' " (Arens, 19) Greek allegations of Jewish cannibalism predate the Christian era: "Pagan incomprehension of the Jewish monotheist cult, lacking the customary images and statues, led to charges of ritual killing. At a time of tension between Hellenism and

to rewrite other cultures as cannibalistic can be seen in Pliny's letter to Trajan, in which he must defend Christians against the accusation.[10] Although the potential for physical violence in such rhetorical strategies is not always actualized, cultural violence always accompanies the accusation of cannibalism, whether directed against Mermedonian, Jew, or Christian.

The elemental signifying processes of *Andreas* announce themselves in an extended semiotic fugue occupying the central portion of the poem. It begins with a bizarre scene recounted by Andreas: a sculpted angel leaps down from a wall to address the ambitious and wicked Jews. Christ himself arranged things so that an *onlicnes* (likeness, 731) uttered *soðcwide* (true speech, 733), Andreas tells the miracle's author, whom he does not yet recognize. Through divine power, the exigencies of representation and interpretation can be eliminated at will. Meaning(s) need no longer be decoded, given such a miraculous short-circuiting of the path from signifier to signified—a miracle made necessary by the hermeneutic depravity of (Jewish) sinners, who would not receive *soðra swa feala / tacna* (so many true tokens, 710b–11a) of divinity. Jews are represented as more culpable than heathens, who had access only to the belated language of missionaries, discourse about Christ substituting for his presence. These representations remained invalidated by heathen sinners because they could not interpret them properly as revelations of pure Logos; hence, this sculpted angel which speaks for itself, a figure for the hermeneutic dream of a pure logos underlying representation. The sculpture's ability to detach itself from its background signifies a fantasy of representation immune to the failings of ordinary processes of interpretation—immune, that is, to the opacity of its material cause. This overdetermined scene obviates the need to question the mediated

---

Judaism, it was alleged that the Jews would kidnap a Greek foreigner, fatten him up for a year, and then convey him to a wood, where they slew him, sacrificed his body with the customary ritual, partook of his flesh, and while immolating the Greek swore an oath of hostility to the Greeks. This was told, according to Apion, to King Antiochus Epiphanes by an intended Greek victim . . ." (*Encyclopaedia Judaica*, 4.1120). The metonymic link of Mermedonians and Jews in the Greek *Acts of Andrew and Matthew Among the Cannibals* resembles that in the *Pseudo-Methodius*, a work translated from Greek into Latin in Paris during the eighth century. In it, the lost tribes of Israel were identified with the peoples of Gog and Magog who lived off "human flesh, corpses, babes ripped from their mothers' wombs" (Norman Cohn, *The Pursuit of the Millennium: Revolutionary Millenarians and Mystical Anarchists of the Middle Ages* [New York, 1970], 79).

10. Pliny, *Letters*, X, 96–97, cited by Robert Boenig, "*Andreas*, the Eucharist, and Vercelli," *Journal of English and Germanic Philology* 79 (1980): 314.

presence of Christ in the language of missionaries. Christians' "true tokens" are underwritten by the Logos, and if the opacity of the signifier makes interpretation of the kerygma dangerous, such interpretation can be dispensed with in a transparent presentation of signifieds.[11]

The secondariness of the sculpted angel, an artistic product that contains life within it, is miraculously erased. If such transparency of logos is possible for a man-made artifact, *a fortiori* it must be true of the word of God. Christian representation thus differs fundamentally from other representational systems. These differences make interpretation almost unnecessary, since Christianity uses true tokens underwritten by the authority of the Logos. There is no need for critical resistance, or pluralist reception of these tokens, whether artistic or inartistic. In *Andreas*, those who resist the kerygma do so out of depravity. From a less partisan perspective, however, Christian representation betrays its weakness in mandating such circumscribed reception, and in using such questionable narrative devices. This rhetorical patterning produces social patterns as well: since there is no need to resist those who speak in the name of Christ, audience resistance merits condemnation. The miracle renders the villainous Jews who would not accept incarnate truth quite monstrous, just like the Mermedonians. At the same time it unifies the contemporary Christian audience, who have not seen yet have believed.

Alteration of representational conventions in the sculpted-angel scene is homologous with violence to ordinary modes of representation in the theology of the Incarnation, which treats Christ as both true Logos and true man. While Apollinarianism saw his humanity as mere representation, and Arianism took his divinity as unauthorized representation, the orthodox mystery of the Incarnation sees divinity and humanity fused in Christ. Not only a theology, but a theory of the sign as well is involved here. The problem centers on the relation between the material signifier and the transcendental signified: if the vagaries of interpretation are to be kept from the origins of Christianity, Logos must permeate its signifier thoroughly, nullifying the interpretative gap between matter and spirit in Christ's nature. Although sinners would not receive Christ's

---

11. The dream of a transparent signification is associated with the recurrent light imagery of the poem, as in the *hador sigel* "bright sun" (89) which precedes the unmediated voice of God. Its opposite is the evil Mermedonian writing of *run* and *rimcræft* (134). On the metaphorics of light, see Jacques Derrida, "White Mythology: Metaphor in the Text of Philosophy," in *Margins of Philosophy*, trans. Alan Bass (Chicago, 1982), 207–71.

soðe tacen (true tokens), the voice of the likeness nevertheless uses *sweotule tacen* (clear tokens, 742) to teach the Jews. When true tokens spoken by Christ himself are not heeded, a statue must utter them, lending magic to the mystery of the Incarnation by opening a potentially infinite regress of signification. Although the Incarnation conflates transcendental signified and signifier, interpretative resistance necessitates a continuing series of representations, such as *Andreas* itself, to reassert an originary dispensation from the defilement of mediation.

This circumvention of the material signifier for the transparent conceptual signified prompts quite worldly consequences, however. The voice of the likeness that Christ summons up is remarkably shrill, condemning the Jews, who are *unlæde* (wretched), *earmra geþohta / searowum beswicene* (tricked by the snares of miserable thoughts), and *mode gemyrde* (disturbed in mind, 744–46). The miraculous transcending of representation meshes with a factionalizing political rhetoric. The angel of Christian—and Jewish—tradition has been reduced to a hectoring accuser.

In a paradox of narrative self-referentiality, the Jews reject the miracle of the sculpted angel, misreading it as magical enchantment. The accusation of magic had been leveled against the Mermedonians earlier, with the full authority of the poem behind it; here the Jews employ it against Christ's miracles. To call those magical is evidence only of hate, doubt, and blasphemy. Only the wicked doubt the ability of Christianity to re-present the Logos. After all, such re-presentation occurs not merely in ad hoc miracles, but in the Eucharist, where the true essence of Christ appears in the form of bread. Calling the miracle of the statue magical casts doubt upon that other transformation as well. For the Christian poet, such doubt is culpable. Those who do not acknowledge what is clearly divine, whether *in propria persona*, sacrament, or sign, can only be blind or, in the case of the Mermedonians, blinding.

Resurrection is the second theme in the semiotic fugue, reendowing the dead signifier of the body with spirit. When Abraham, Isaac, and Jacob are raised, the Jews acknowledge them only with terror. Such narrative resurrection is a biological elaboration of textual processes of typology and sublation, the emplotment of a hermeneutic strategy. The narrative invents the miracles which sustain and authenticate it. Abraham, Isaac, and Jacob honor Christ in an apocryphal episode adduced to silence the Jews' objections. That the truth of Christianity requires fictional support at such crucial moments is by no means limited to *Andreas*, as the *Ecclesiastical History* or *Dialogues* show. The word of God, for the Anglo-Saxon, depends upon just such fictional props.

When Andreas finally realizes that he has been in Christ's presence, he tells the others that he knew his speech, even though his countenance was concealed. Since the countenance of Christ is ordinarily concealed, requiring a process of decipherment, we must suppose Andreas to mean that Christ's divinity had no striking manifestations. Christ appeared as an ordinary human, a revelation in the everyday that itself constitutes concealment. Andreas's decipherment of divinity occurs by decoding language, not countenance. *Andreas* finds several ways for evading the strictures of representation, because surfaces are suspect: they reveal depths only at the risk of concealing them in the opacity of signifiers. An augmentation of this problem of Christ's concealment in an ordinary body follows:

> "Us sæwerige   slæp ofereode.
> Þa comon earnas   ofer yða wylm
> faran on flyhte,   feðerum hremige,
> us ofslæpendum   sawle abrugdon,
> mid gefean feredon   flyhte on lyfte,
> brehtmum bliðe,   beorhte ond liðe.
> Lissum lufodon   ond in lofe wunedon,
> þær wæs singal sang   ond swegles gong,
> wlitig weoroda heap   ond wuldres þreat."
>
> (862–70)

["We were so weary of the sea that sleep overcame us. Then eagles came flying over the surging of the waves, their feathers making a clamor. They drew our souls out of us while we were sleeping, and carried them away in the air with joy, noisily happy, gleaming and kind. They adored lovingly and praised unceasingly, where there was perpetual song and the circuit of the heavens, a splendid throng of heavenly hosts and glorious multitudes."]

His companions tell Andreas that eagles carried their souls away while they slept, enabling them to witness thousands of angelic thanes honoring their lord. At this stage of the semiotic fugue, heavenly joy may be the carrot, but the stick is not far behind:

"Þam bið wræcsið witod,   wite geopenad,
þe þara gefeana sceal   fremde weorðan,
hean hwearfian,   þonne heonon gangaþ."

(889–91)

["Exile will be ordained and torment will be opened up for those who become estranged from those joys and depart in misery when they go away from here."]

Those who become estranged from such joys can expect exile and torment. Even the joys of heaven presuppose the social violence of exclusion. The heavenly vision of Andreas's companions depends upon the structural privilege allowing essences to be separable from accidents in the Christian dispensation, and Christians to be exempt from the normal interdependence of body and soul. But its social practice is based on mechanisms of a more common kind.

After Andreas's confession of faith, Christ returns as a boy, a corporeal transformation which constitutes the final theme in the semiotic fugue.[12] The bodily surface can be altered to reveal the logos within; the signifier can be displaced to demonstrate the living spirit of the transcendental signified informing it. Christians have access to the signified without passing through the defiles of the signifier, where the letter can become opaque and access to spirit can be blocked. The danger of signifiers lies in the possibility of multiple signifieds. But here, plural signifiers have only one signified, an intensification of Christian power over ordinary operations of the sign. *Andreas* bypasses the problem of letter and surface. Its rhetorical strategies require a programmatic dismissal of both the exigencies of representation and the perils of interpretation. What the world adds up to is Christophany, and textual operations must reflect this revelatory hermeneutic.

The doctrine of the Eucharist, where the signifiers of bread and wine lose their essence and take on that of divinity, is the privileged ritual exemplar of Christian violence to ordinary notions of representation. In *Andreas*, the saint's explicit mention of bread and wine is situated between two anti-Semitic outbursts uttered by Christ himself. The symbolism of spiritual food is associated here with hatred for those who would

---

12. However, Andreas's invisibility (985–89) can be read as a subsequent narrative development of the transformations in the semiotic fugue. The only actual quadruple fugue I am familiar with is the last, unfinished piece in J. S. Bach's *The Art of Fugue*.

not—and will not—allow themselves to be properly fed. The absence of bread and water on the island of the Mermedonians makes typological sense. It is, of course, nonsensical that a people could live without food, just the sort of interpretative lemma that ought to lead readers to ponder Eucharistic symbolism. What doesn't make sense in medieval literature often doesn't fit into the patterns that moderns bring to texts, which is not to say that the criticism of medieval literature cannot accommodate the patterns moderns bring to texts. Life without food qualifies as the sort of symbolic notion that demands the attention of the contemporary typological critic. But after recognizing the role of the symbolic, the historical level must be recuperated once again. For there is a politics to this Eucharistic material which associates monstrous resistance to Christianity with Jews as well as Mermedonians. The intelligent, urbane irony of the Eucharistic symbolism in this passage is overemphasized by those who have focused upon typological dimensions.[13] The Old English *Andreas* reifies this symbolic practice, giving it existence in the world of time and space, not merely in that of contemplative thought.

When the sabre-rattling of the Mermedonians is presented in the style of traditional Germanic verse, their Grendel-like cannibalism spurs the poet to draw the parallel to Christ's sufferings at the hands of the Jews. The Mermedonians enact a Eucharistic parody, the effect of which depends upon the reader's awareness of sacramental language and symbolism. Controversy over the Eucharist in early Middle Ages dovetails with problems of typology, as Robert Boenig taught us to recognize. At the core of the First Eucharistic Controversy is a miraculous vision of the unmediated truth of the Eucharist. Paschasius Radbertus describes the experiences of the Abbot Arsenius, who believed that the bread was the body of Christ only in figure, and two monks who disagreed with him:

> The eyes of their understanding were opened, however, when the bread was placed on the altar, and there appeared to them a vision just like a small boy lying on the altar, and when the priest had extended his hand in order that he might break the bread the angel of the Lord descended from heaven having a knife in his hand, and he sacrificed that small boy, and truly his blood was being caught up in the cup. Moreover, when the priest had broken the bread into small pieces, the angel also cut up the boy's

---

13. As, for example, the typological studies of Robert Boenig, "*Andreas*, the Eucharist, and Vercelli" and David Hamilton, "The Diet and Digestion of Allegory in *Andreas*," *Anglo-Saxon England* 1 (1972): 147–58.

members into moderate pieces. Therefore when the old man had approached in order that he might accept the Holy Communion only the bloody flesh was given to him. Because he had seen, he became very afraid and exclaimed, saying, "I believe, Lord, that the bread which is placed on the altar is your body and the cup is your blood," and immediately that flesh was made into bread in his hand according to the mystery, and he took it into his mouth giving thanks to God. And the old man said to them, "God knows human nature, that it is not able to eat bleeding flesh, and on account of this he transformed his body into bread and his blood into wine"—these things which that one looked up to in faith, and they gave thanks to God for that old man, how God did not allow his labor to be destroyed, and all went back with joy to their cells.[14]

As Boenig comments, "The underlying cannibalism is strong here, and notable is Radbert's rather surprising statement that the sole reason for the bread and wine on the altar is the inability of our human stomachs to accept real human flesh and real human blood."[15] The Radbertian problematic can be rephrased as a question: Is the literal level still present when the symbolic makes its entry, or have transformation rules reduced it to purely conceptual form?

Ratramnan, another monk of Corbie, opposed Paschasius Radbertus, arguing that the Eucharistic bread and wine are Christ's spiritual body and blood, a "figure" of what once existed physically. His opposition to Radbertian thinking attempts to dispose of the literal by preserving it only in figure, sublating the bleeding body of Christ into spiritual corporality. Such a figural reading sustains itself by recourse to the rhetorical figure of oxymoron. Responses of this sort gave rise to the First Eucharistic Controversy, in part a language controversy concerned with the hermeneutic sublation of letter into allegory. The reified symbolic of *Andreas* exemplifies crucial problems of representation in early medieval culture.

Identity and difference between Christian and Mermedonian are rather more difficult to determine than one might imagine. The Mermedonians eat the dead, a bizarre practice meant to be seen as gruesomely non-Christian. But this difference cannot elide its identity with the commemorative Eucharist. The symbolic Eucharistic dimen-

---

14. Because of the length of this passage, I have supplied Boenig's English translation (*"Andreas*, the Eucharist, and Vercelli," 316). The original can be found in *PL* 120:1318–19.

15. Boenig, 316.

sion is invoked in the course of a rhetorical expression of the otherness of Christianity itself, in what can be read as an attempt to defend itself against the cannibalism implicit in the Eucharist. Each the other's obverse, Christian and Mermedonian cannibalism become as hard to differentiate as Christian and Mermedonian magic. The Mermedonians and Jews are paralleled in their use of magic, attributed to non-Christian others in order to contrast their corruption with the purity of Christians. But Radbertus himself conjures up magic to bolster the doctrine of Real Presence. So important is magic as a textual prop that much Anglo-Saxon and early medieval Christian narrative would founder without it. Accusations of magic would become a standard Protestant line of attack against Catholics who held on to the ritual practice of the Middle Ages. For those who disclaimed the doctrine of the Real Presence, the notion of transubstantiation seemed so much hocus pocus from a superstitious medieval church. Just as the accusation of magic was an important strategy of resistance to the authority of Rome, early medieval theological accusations of magic have complex political affiliations.[16]

Andreas employs magic politically in several ways. At the beginning of the poem, as we have seen, Mermedonian magicians supposedly use sorcery after they blind the elpeodige, creating magic potions which pervert the mind, causing animality to supplant rationality. Similarly, Jewish galdorcræftas (magic arts, 166) are said to have been withstood by Christ, in a textual move similar to the earlier linking of Mermedonian with Jewish foreignness. Since Judaism plays an important role in the self-construction of Christianity, as the foundation which it erects itself upon and against, the expulsion of Jewish magic serves to purge Christianity of the difference it bears within itself. Such self-definition continues in the narrative rejection of Mermedonian magic. Since the Church represents itself as practicing authentic Judaism, its magic is reconceptualized as miracle or mystery. The semiotic fantasy, claiming of unmediated access to truth and presence, invalidates censure; it is criticized only by an unreliable internal audience, when the Jews raise the accusation of magic against the sculpted angel likeness speaking soðcwidas (true sayings, 733) and sweotule tacen (true tokens, 742). The critique and accusation are made by those lacking faith, effectively disposing of any doubts contemporary readers might have had about magical textual effects.

---

16. See Arens, *The Man-Eating Myth*, 94–95.

Magic is associated with Christianity once again when Andreas becomes invisible, a hoary plot device that looks backward to Homer and forward to H. G. Wells. Andreas even speaks while invisible, a comic touch causing no end of consternation for the devil and Mermedonians. It provides yet another example of the alteration of ordinary relations obtaining between accident and essence. Earlier the voice of God had told Andreas how easy it would be to avoid a long sea journey, since divine intervention could bring Mermedonia to Achaia instantaneously. And magic is hardly forsworn when Andreas is later teleported to Mermedonia, although it had been explicitly stated that this sort of miracle would be eschewed. Such textual ambivalence toward the miraculous bespeaks a conflict within the sublatory processes of theology. Christianity itself relies on "white" magic, miracle or mystery invoking an essence without accident, whether for the body of Andreas as he journeys through the city or the body of Christ in the Eucharist. Later, when Matthew and his fellow prisoners are led out of prison by Andreas in an antitype to Christ's harrowing of hell, the clouds which cover them resemble those in *Exodus*. Such protection prevents wicked enemies from assailing them with arrow volleys, either literal or symbolic.

The devil will accuse Andreas of being a magician. Since Christian magic is reinscribed as miracle, the accusation is meant to be taken as unfounded. Yet the climax of the work consists in a Christian magic spectacle, the pillar which floods the city. Although the destruction it causes is later canceled, it serves its purpose in terrorizing the Mermedonians. Originally the pillar of the Law of the Jews, but now in Christian control, the Exodus-like punishment it inflicts on the Mermedonians associates them once again with the Jews. Typology is indeed important, as later when the fiery angel torments the Mermedonians into having a change of heart. But typology does not exhaust the significance of a kerygma represented as less persuasive than redoubled violence from heaven.

The attribution of magic to the enemy provides a way of eliding Christianity's own "magical" operations: the cancelation of the letter— and its preservation on a higher level—which allows Christianity to found itself. Eucharistic theology also works by such magical transcendence of literality in the name of essentiality. One response to the questions such a signifying practice might raise would be to vilify such operations in the foreign other. The ideological violence of representation in Radbertus's image of the Eucharist extends to the sublatory processes of typology which erase the literal in the name of divine essence. The reinscription of Judaism for Christian ends expresses cultural violence, Christian self-authorization by textual processes which sublate the historical people of God. Such violence at the level of the sign appears in *Andreas* as narrative violence that attributes magic and cannibalism to the alien culture, thus legitimating the violent imposition of Christianity upon heathens. The message of love, nonviolence, and compassion identified with Christ is transformed by an imperialistic Christianity extending its influence to the furthest corners of the earth. This early medieval appropriation of Christianity occurs in ways which the reader of Old English allegories of war is uniquely positioned to witness.

Andreas foregrounds textual operations at the level of the sign, as semiological violence plays itself out in an extraordinary narrative violence. The description of bizarre bloodthirsty foreigners invites Christian counterviolence, which occurs only after it has been well prepared for. When Andreas, *Cristes cempa* (Christ's warrior, 991), finally arrives at the prison gate, with the help of magical invisibility, he does not need to act violently himself:

> Ealle swylt fornam,
> druron domlease.   Deaðræs forfeng
> hæleð heorodreorige.
>
> (994b–96a)

[Death took them all away, and they died ignominiously. Sudden death seized the blood-stained warriors.]

The death of his enemies is magical; instead of hand-to-hand combat, we encounter divine retribution in the form of "sudden death." Slaughter of the heathens, who are sleeping and *dreore druncne* (drunk with blood, 1003), moves Andreas to prayer. He and Matthew are transfigured by violence:

> Syb wæs gemæne
> bam þam gebroðrum,   blis edniwe.
> Æghwæðer oðerne   earme beþehte,

cyston hie ond clypton.   Criste wæron begen
leofe on mode.   Hie leoht ymbscan
halig ond heofontorht.   Hreðor innan wæs
wynnum awelled.

(1013b–19a)

[Peace was mutual between the two brothers, happiness was renewed. Each threw his arm about the other, and they kissed and hugged. Both were dear to Christ's spirit. Light shone about them, holy and heaven-bright. Their breasts welled joyfully within.]

As they kiss and hug, they glow. Without a human intermediary, God has wrought death and destruction, a rhetoric of literal violence which brings about the peace and joy that will flood the poem. Love, peace, and happiness are dependent upon the (justified) violence of *Andreas*.

Further slaughter of the Mermedonians is explicitly framed as justi- fied counterviolence. After binding the hands of *sigerofne* (victory- brave) Andreas, the heathen drag him about in a hideous torture session lasting an entire day:

Heton þa lædan   ofer landsceare,
ðragmælum teon,   torngeniðlan,
swa hie hit frecnost   findan meahton.

(1229–31)

[Then the bitter enemies ordered him to be taken and dragged again and again over the landscape, in the most cruel manner they could devise.]

He is dragged repeatedly through mountain caves, over rocky slopes, and along cobblestone streets in the cruelest manner they, and textual *inventio*, can devise. All this punishment has its desired effect:

Wæs þæs halgan lic
sarbennum soden,   swate bestemed,
banhus abrocen.   Blod yðum weoll,
haton heolfre.

(1238b–41a)

[The body of the holy man was soaked from horrible wounds, steeped in blood, his bone-house broken; blood gushed out in waves of hot gore.]

Torture is embellished with the linguistic repetition compulsion that colored the drowning of the Egyptians in *Exodus*, a scene which will also be replayed in *Andreas*. And this is only the beginning of the torture session, which continues when he is scourged once again:

> Swat ýðum weoll
> þurh bancofan,   blodlifrum swealg,
> hatan heolfre   Hra weorces ne sann,
> wundum werig.

> (1275b–78a)

[Blood gushed out in pulse-waves from his bodily frame, flowed out in clots of hot gore. Although weary from wounds, his body ignored the pain.]

To notice only the typological association with Christ's passion is to limit the possibility of reading textual processes at work as Andreas's blood gushes out in waves. The text deploys torture factionally in this propaganda scene, which serves the pragmatic purpose of mobilizing audiences into unity.[17] Alluding to Christ's passion in the manner of *Andreas* reinscribes typology as ideology, transforming the critique of violence against God into the legitimization of violence by God.

Clearly, the intertwining of spiritual warfare with literal narrative violence makes it difficult to separate *machia* from psychomachia. After a dose of martial imagery, Andreas is told by the *meotud mihtum swið* (the Lord strong in might, 1207) to make his mind steadfast against difficulties: *þinne modsefan / staðola wið strangum!* (1209b-1210a). This advice is repeated:

> "herd hige þinne,   heortan staðola,
> þæt hie min on ðe   mægen oncnawan."

> (1213–14)

["Make your intention harder, make your heart firm so they can recognize my power in you."]

---

17. The parallel to Christ's passion has been noted by Earl, "Typological Structure," 72 and Hieatt, "Harrowing of Mermedonia," 52.

Andreas is told to strengthen his mind and heart so his enemies can perceive God's power. If the spiritual heroism of the *æðele mod* (noble-spirited man, 1241) fails to console readers troubled by the sufferings of a Christian saint, there is the added pleasure of revenge. The Mermedonians can expect massive reprisal for their exceptionally brutal treatment of the saint. Evil will be punished with even more evil.

Winter is used in symbolic association with the sufferings of Andreas,[18] which as we have seen includes scourging in a parallel to Christ's passion. The hero reacts to this Christ-like punishment with Christ-like steadfastness in battle. In Andreas's prayer to God in his misery (1281–95), several of the motifs of spiritual warfare cluster: God as protector, the weapons of the foe, Satan as the murderer of mankind. After urging emblematic mouth punishment to discourage such prayerful reliance upon God, the Devil returns with six others; the battle imagery that follows supports the diabolical version of sacred history.[19]

The Devil accuses Andreas of being a magician who misleads men, in yet another attempt to dispose of the threat of the other by the accusation of magic. That such accusations of magic take place on both sides of the virgule separating Christian from non-Christian never leads to the interrogation of such a rhetoric of vilification. The Devil is called by epithet the author of bitter strife (1386–87), in reference to the recurrent motif of the *ealdgewinn*, but acts as a coward when he flees Andreas's speech of deliverance. There follows a third attempt to weaken Andreas's steadfastness, but he remains a patient thane. He is bound, like Christ and Satan, who were referred to earlier. He cries out to God, describing his sufferings: his limbs have been wrenched apart, his body broken, his sinews destroyed, his blood shed, his hair strewn across the earth (the earliest reference to scalping in English poetry) in typological elaboration of Christ's passion. That the desire for revenge which this lurid violence provokes ends in the establishment of a Christian mission to the Mermedonians does not erase the fact that a good deal of Christian violence, including numerous Mermedonian deaths, is also necessary to save the alien race of Mermedonians. Like Christ, Andreas questions God in his time of suffering; unlike Christ, he is

---

18. See Thomas D. Hill, "The Tropological Context of Heat and Cold Imagery in Anglo-Saxon Poetry," *Neuphilologische Mitteilungen* 69 (1968): 522–32.

19. This is part of the *bysen* of Christ's passion, first noted by Earl, "Typological Structure," 71–72. On emblematic mouth punishment, see chap. 1.

suicidal. Yet he is referred to as "the resolute man" when God speaks to him, an ironized motif of spiritual victory in literal defeat, since Andreas is anything but resolute at times.

Flowers spring up where the saint's blood falls, emblems of the terrible beauty born of violence: the poem describes this magical narrative device as an actual miracle the saint witnesses.[20] When, for the fourth time, the heathens attempt to batter down his steadfastness, Andreas again refuses to budge. God finally shows up personally to rescue Andreas: his wounds are healed, his wholeness restored.[21]

In the cannibalistic parody that follows, violence is linked with scapegoating and the Eucharist. Lots are cast to see who will be first to offer himself as food for the others, but the lucky nobleman who wins offers his son in his place. The Mermedonians consider this a fine idea, since they are hungry and uncivilized, a combination of traits that seldom results in good table manners. God's intervention halting this sacrificial parody gives way to a liturgical formula of thanksgiving which breaks the narrative surface:

> Gode ealles þanc,
> dryhtna dryhtne,   þæs ðe he dom gifeð
> gumena gehwylcum,   þara þe geoce to him
> seceð mid snytrum.   Þær bið symle gearu
> freod unhwilen,   þam þe hie findan cann.
>
> (1150b–54)

[Let thanks be given completely to God, the Lord of lords, because he gives justice to each man who in wisdom seeks his assistance. Unlimited peace will always be at hand for him who knows how to find it.]

The reassurance of sacred formula, familiar from the Roman liturgy, interrupts the fictional plane with the apotropaic power of ritual. Scapegoating elicits the divine intervention prompting this prayer. The mecha-

---

20. According to Earl, "God strengthens [Andreas] by showing him the fruits of his suffering—literally!—blossoming groves springing up where he had left his bloody tracks" ("Typological Structure," 86).

21. But see Kenneth R. Brooks, ed., *Andreas and the Fates of the Apostles* (Oxford, 1961), 111–12 on faulty counting in the poem. On Germanic heroic tradition, see Leonard J. Peters, "The Relationship of the Old English *Andreas* to *Beowulf*," *Publications of the Modern Language Association* 66 (1951): 844–63.

nism of scapegoating operates by means of two separate techniques: it can be either ideological or random. The randomness of the Mermedonian casting of lots vanishes in ideologically motivated scapegoating, which shores up the identity of the social group by choice, not chance. Unlike random scapegoating, an interpretation of tradition provides supernatural justification for ideologically motivated sacrificial murder; ideological scapegoating rests upon the semiological attribution of one group's unacceptable qualities to the other. The casting of lots emphasizes societal rather than personal need, but by selecting a victim from within the social group rather than from without.[22] In *Andreas*, the societal need for a factional scapegoat occurs by means of the abyssal structure which scapegoats Mermedonians and Jews by presenting them *as* random scapegoaters. Christian scapegoating takes place *via* condemnation of the supposedly historical sortilege indulged in by Mermedonians, or the crucifixion of Christ by Jews. Accusations of this sort illustrate the Christian need for a scapegoat, which is shifted to alien cultures since it is not in keeping with Christianity's self-definition. If the evil within *Ecclesia* were to be faced, rather than deflected by such textual strategies, factional scapegoating would become universalized: humanity itself would then be characterized as deniers of Christ, not just Mermedonians or Jews.

The Eucharist erases the corporality of the crucifixion, but in *Andreas* the ritualistic slaughter it represses returns on the side of the other. The violence of the Crucifixion has often elicited contradictory interpretations: emphasis can be placed upon Christ's choice of suffering, or upon society's need for a victim. In *Andreas*, a non-Christian nation endures violence and terror because they practice violence and terror themselves. Although state violence was directed against Christians in the early Christian era, *Andreas* celebrates the violence of Christians. Worse yet, they are supported in their violence by God himself, an anti-Semite. To construct the Mermedonians as scapegoating cannibals is itself scapegoating, legitimizing violence against monstrous heathen who exemplify the depravity of non-Christian cultures.

The spectacular violence of the poem's conclusion follows a self-reflecting narrative interruption:

---

22. Christ's slayers cast lots for his clothes; in *Andreas*, lots are cast for the victim. On the tradition of the *sortes apostolorum*, see Brooks, ed. *Andreas*, xxvii.

Mycel is to secganne,
langsum leornung,   þæt he in life adreag,
eall æfter orde.   Þæt scell æglæwra
mann on moldan   þonne ic me tælige
findan on ferðe,   þæt fram fruman cunne
eall þa earfeðo   þe he mid elne adreah,
grimra guða.

(1481–87a)

[To tell all that {Andreas} suffered in this life from the beginning is a
great task and an exhausting study. Some earthly man more learned in
the law than I consider myself will find in his heart that he knows from
the very beginning all the hardships, the grim battles, that he endured
with courage.]

Someone more learned in the law than Cynewulf himself will discover
"in his heart" all the fierce battles Andreas endured. James Earl reads
this passage in terms of hagiographic nonrealism:

> The poet here expresses a notion which should startle the modern reader:
> that a man wise in the Law will *already know* this tale in his heart. Strange
> as it is, the idea that the tale itself can be known through wisdom or piety,
> even without historical knowledge, is actually a *topos* in medieval hagiog-
> raphy. . . . The saint's life is ultimately devotional rather than historical
> in our sense of the word; it is more concerned with the truths which
> underlie Christian history . . . than with the particulars of actual historical
> events.[23]

The *grime guðe* (grim battles) Cynewulf mentions would include spiri-
tual warfare, which the learned heart knows any saint would have to
fight, even without sufficient historical evidence. But hagiography con-
tains political elements as well, which deserve attention precisely be-
cause they are dependent upon typological practice. Can we revise our
expectations of the genre by learning to read the history embedded
within a spiritualizing hagiographic practice?

The agency of destruction at the conclusion of the poem is water
which pours out from a pillar, an antitype of the water which sprang
from a rock in Exodus. The pillars are addressed in a symbolic manner:

---

23. Earl, "Typological Structure," 69.

"Læt nu of þinum staþole   streamas weallan,
ea inflede,   nu ðe ælmihtig
hateð, heofona cyning,   þæt ðu hrædlice
on þis fræte folc   forð onsende
wæter widrynig   to wera cwealme,
geofon geotende.   Hwæt, ðu golde eart,
sincgife, sylla!   On ðe sylf cyning
wrat, wuldres god,   wordum cyðde
recene geryno,   ond ryhte æ
getacnode   on tyn wordum,
meotud mihtum swið."

                                        (1503–13a)

["Now let streams well out from your foundation, a raging river, now that
the almighty king of heaven commands you that you quickly send forth
widespreading water upon this perverse nation, a gushing sea which will
destroy these men. Indeed, you are more precious than gold or treasure-
gift. On you the King himself, the God of glory, wrote and revealed in
words his mysteries and betokened his righteous law in ten command-
ments, the Lord mighty in his powers."]

Destruction of a "perverse nation" will come from the Old Law, utilized
by the New in the course of making its point. A lengthy passage cele-
brates the Mermedonians' destruction in the ensuing deluge:

                    Stream ut aweoll,
fleow ofer foldan.   Famige walcan
mid ærdæge   eorðan þehton,
myclade mereflod.   Meoduscerwen wearð
æfter symbeldæge,   slæpe tobrugdon
searuhæbbende.   Sund grunde onfeng,
deope gedrefed.   Duguð wearð afyrhted
þurh þæs flodes fær.   Fæge swulton,
geonge on geofone   guðræs fornam
þurh sealtne weg.   Þæt wæs sorgbyrþen,
biter beorþegu.

                                        (1523b–33a)

[A stream welled out and flowed over the ground. Foamy waves covered
the earth at dawn, and the flood grew ever greater. After the feast day
came the the day of deprivation of mead-joy; the warriors started up out
of their sleep. The sea, deeply stirred, encroached upon the land. The

people were terribly frightened at this sudden danger of the flood. The doomed died, the battle-onrush of waves swept away the young men in the salt wave. That was a burden of sorrow, a bitter beer-drinking.]

Andreas underscores the terror and sorrow of the warriors, as did *Exodus*. The phrase applied to the flood from the pillar, *biter beorþegu* (bitter beer-drinking, 1533), ironizes the destruction of the Mermedonians in a clever deployment of epic tradition. When old warriors try to flee the flood, an angel spreads fire over the city to prevent their escape:

Wægas weoxon,   wadu hlynsodon,
flugon fyrngastas,   flod yðum weoll.
Ðær wæs yðfynde   innan burgum
geomorgidd wrecen.   Gehðo mændan
forhtferð manig,   fusleoð golon.
Egeslic æled   eagsyne wearð,
heardlic hereteam,   hleoðor gryrelic.
Þurh lyftgelac   leges blæstas
weallas ymbwurpon,   wæter mycladon.
Þær wæs wop wera   wide gehyred,
earmlic ylda gedræg.

(1545–55a)

[The waves towered, the breakers resounded, sparks of fire flew, the flood welled up in surging waves. Within the city it was easy to find a sorrowful lamentation being sung. Many a frightened person lamented his sorrow, singing the song of death. The fearful flame was quite clearly visible, dire devastation, and terrifying noise. Through the air blasts of flame enveloped the walls, and the waters surged higher. The weeping of men was widely heard, the miserable lamentation of men.]

Fiery flames, towering waves, deafening uproar, cries of fear, and songs of death are followed by more fiery blasts, surging water, terrifying weeping, and miserable lamentation. As in *Exodus*, the linguistic relish in this repetitive destruction of the enemy is sadistic. All this horror has its desired effect upon the heathens, who realize that peace will come only if they free Andreas. When they do so, the roaring of the flood ceases, the Mermedonians rejoice, and an abyss opens up, swallowing the waves along with *þæs weorodes eac ða wyrrestan, / faa folcsceaðan, feowertyne* (the worst of that troop, fourteen bitter enemies of the people, 1592–93). Terrified at this display of saintly vengeance, the Mermedonians turn to the religion of their oppressors:

>   Hie ða anmode   ealle cwædon:
>   "Nu is gesyne   ðæt þe soð meotud,
>   cyning eallwihta,   cræftum wealdeð,
>   se ðisne ar   hider onsende
>   þeodum to helpe.   Is nu þearf mycel
>   þæt we gumcystum   georne hyran."

(1601–6)

[Then they all spoke out with one mind: "Now it is clear that the true Lord, the King of all creatures, rules in his might, he who sent this messenger here in order to help his people. Now there is great need for us to eagerly obey this most excellent man."]

All this fire and flood, interpreted by the Mermedonians as clear proof of God's power, demonstrates how effective slaughter can be in changing cultural values.[24] They witness "with one mind" (*anmode ealle*, 1601) to the necessity of obeying the "most excellent" representative of a God of such immense power.

Although the suffering inflicted upon the Mermedonians is later canceled, it contributes crucially to the harmonious ending of the poem. Freud's work on dream narrative has taught us that after negation, the unnegated original—introduced into discourse only to be removed—still remains to be accounted for. The act of negation signals the importance of the original. *Andreas* recasts violence by miraculously negating it, a rhetorical magic that allows sadistic pleasure at the destruction of the heathen to become righteous satisfaction at their enlightenment. Yet such violence plays an important role before the text erases it, and its negation—or sublation, the typological reflex of this narrative device—must not cancel a reading of its textual effects.

Literal and symbolic warfare encode the politics of enforced cultural change throughout *Andreas*, not only in the flood scene. The metaphorics of spiritual warfare are the agency for its representation of con-

---

24. On the angel with fire that keeps them from the places of refuge, see Hill, "Figural Narrative," 264–66.

version.[25] Andreas parallels Christ as *wigendra hleo* (protector of warriors). This consoling Germanic militarism assumes that misery is appointed for backsliders, as for heathens. The vilifying of the other culture in *Andreas* vilifies the other within Christian psyche and society too. Christian identity is produced by such rhetorical acts of fending off difference, and the textual politics of conversion require an organization of the other within and without. The recurrent spiritual warrior motif in *Andreas* is plurivocal, as when Andreas's *eorlas, geonge guðrincas, þegnas þrohthearde* are told to wait on land for their lord:

> "Hwider hweorfað we hlafordlease,
> geomormode, gode orfeorme,
> synnum wunde, gif we swicað þe?
> We bioð laðe on landa gehwam,
> folcum fracoðe, þonne fira bearn,
> ellenrofe, æht besittaþ,
> hwylc hira selost symle gelæste
> hlaforde æt hilde, þonne hand ond rond
> on beaduwange billum forgrunden
> æt niðplegan nearu þrowedon."
>
>   (405–14)

["Where shall we turn—lordless, sad in mind, lacking in good, wounded by sin—if we abandon you? We shall be hated and despised by people in each country, when the sons of men, famous for their courage, debate which has best served his lord in battle when hand and shield battered by swords endured hardship in deadly play on the battlefield."]

These are the exiled warriors of Germanic tradition, incapable of conceiving life apart from their lord. Many of the poem's Germanic heroic aspects have been catalogued by earlier scholars researching its affinities with *Beowulf*. That such material is now often recognized as having a symbolic function reveals the increasing critical sophistication of

---

25. Hieatt says, "it is, unfortunately, notable that modern readers often look no further than the 'literal' meaning of the verbal surface. . . . The heroic vocabulary . . . is no ill-adapted hand-me-down garment: like the eucharistic imagery, the typological echoes of the passion, and the structural parallels between sections, it is carefully chosen to illuminate what is central to the poem—Andrew's reenactment of the role of Christ" ("Harrowing of Mermedonia," 61). It is also unfortunate that the literal meaning of the poem is ignored in modern criticism.

Anglo-Saxonists. But it is not easy to decide whether this imagery is literal or metaphorical. Ignoring its symbolic dimension entails reading as merely awkward a passage which relies upon a metaphoric code; yet reading the complaint of Andreas's warriors solely in relation to spiritual combat forecloses aspects of language which extend beyond theology into history.

Symbolic elements of the poem are more densely interrelated with the historical level than has been recognized. The rhetoric of the foreigner as enemy in *Andreas* applies to Jews as well as Mermedonians, and even Christ uses battle imagery to describe Andreas's trials. This is not surprising in and of itself. When the Christ of *Andreas* links Jews as factional scapegoats to battle imagery, however, something significant has occurred within the field of the allegory of war:

> "Nu ðu, Andreas, scealt   edre geneðan
> in gramra gripe.   Is þe guð weotod,
> heardum heoruswengum   scel þin hra dæled
> wundum weorðan,   wættre geliccost
> faran flode blod.   Hie þin feorh ne magon
> deaðe gedælan,   þeh ðu drype ðolie,
> synnigra slege.   Ðu þæt sar aber;
> ne læt þe ahweorfan   hæðenra þrym,
> grim gargewinn,   þæt ðu gode swice,
> dryhtne þinum.   Wes a domes georn;
> læt þe on gemyndum   hu þæt manegum wearð
> fira gefrege   geond feala landa,
> þæt me bysmredon   bennum fæstne
> weras wansælige.   Wordum tyrgdon,
> slogon ond swungon,   synnige ne mihton
> þurh sarcwide   soð gecyðan.
> Þa ic mid Iudeum   gealgan þehte,
> (rod wæs aræred),   þær rinca sum
> of minre sidan   swat ut forlet. . . ."

(950–68)

["Now, Andrew, you must quickly venture forth into the grasp of your enemies. Battle is destined for you, hard sword strokes; your body will be dealt wounds, and your blood will flow out in a stream just like water. They will not be able to give you over to death, even though you will suffer blows and beating from those sinners. Endure that suffering; do not allow the might of the heathens and the terrible spear-battle to change you

so you abandon the Lord God. Be eager for glory; be mindful of how it
has become known to many people in many lands that unblessed men
mocked me, bound me tightly. They taunted me with words, struck and
buffeted me; sinners could not declare the truth with hostile speech. Then
I was hung among the Jews on the gallows, (the cross was raised up),
where one of the men let the blood flow out of my side . . ."]

Christ, a Jew, nevertheless talks of hanging *among* the Jews on the
gallows: *"ic mid Iudeum gealgan þehte"* (966). This language recurs so
often in Christian tradition that it may not seem as strange to readers as
it ought to. Christ does not say that he was hung among "men," but
among "Jews." The crucifixion, the process by which he becomes a
universal scapegoat, taking upon himself the sins of the world, is re-
ferred to by Christ himself in a way that turns Jews into factional scape-
goats. Although Jews are repeatedly presented as factional scapegoats in
Andreas, nowhere is this process more striking: Christ's *guð* (battle)
with the doubting, poisonous, blasphemous Jews (767–72) is intended as
a pattern for Andreas in his conflict with the heathen enemy. The differ-
ence between Mermedonian and Jew is that Mermedonians allow them-
selves to be forced into conversion, but Jews in the early Middle Ages
usually did not. That Jewish sublation into *Ecclesia* occurs in typology,
but not in historical fact, means that Mermedonian violence against the
apostles can be negated in a way that Jewish violence cannot. The divine
language of warfare Christ uses to send Andreas into the breach con-
nects with the rhetoric of warfare throughout the poem, a verbal assault
which reflects the violence of the fundamental signifying practice that
both inscribes and erases Jewish and Mermedonian resistance.

Violence against the Mermedonians is finally canceled when the
young men are raised from the dead, then baptized. Or almost canceled,
since seven deaths that happen during the rescue of Matthew from
prison, as well as those of the fourteen bitter enemies who die in the
flood, are not canceled. According to Andreas, the Mermedonians
"chose destruction" (*fell curen*, 1609). Yet miraculous violence circum-
scribes the survivors' decision to become Christian, overwhelming any
objections they might have had. All Mermedonians are represented as
united in the harmonious social fabric produced by acts of violence from
on high. The harmony made possible by canceled (and uncanceled)
Christian violence is institutionalized when Platan is named bishop of
the new diocese so Andreas can continue his missionary travels:

Sægde his fusne hige,
þæt he þa goldburg   ofgifan wolde,
secga seledream   ond sincgestreon,
beorht beagselu,   ond him brimþisan
æt sæs faroðe   secan wolde.

(1654b–58)

[He said his mind was eager to go—that he wanted to leave the wealthy city, the hall-joys of warriors, treasure, and the glorious hall where rings are distributed—and that he would seek out a ship for himself at the seashore.]

Everything Andreas is said to want to leave is part of the formulaic treasury of warfare handed down in Germanic poetic tradition. In this case, such formulas index the sublation of the glorious Germanic heroic past in the name of the Christian mission. Andreas's role as a leader is heroic: a protector of warriors, a thane of Christ, he must return, God tells him, to establish firmness in his flock. Like Elene, Andreas also casts down heathen temples: his spiritual warfare against heathen divinities is so effective that *næfre feondes ne bið, / gastes gramhydiges, gang on lande* (a fiend, hostile spirit will never pass through the land, 1693b–94). When Andreas dies "in battle" (*beaducwealm*, 1702) while seeking Achaia, his treacherous slayer is destined for an eternity in hell, a final rhetorical flourish to convince those with any doubts still left that the violence of God surpasses that of the wicked. The poem ends with a heroic ship burial, in which the memorializing ritual of pagan Germanic tradition bows to Christian values. Accompanying this rewriting of pagan tradition is a Christian liturgical tag that finally buries the narrative invention of *Andreas* in the stasis of an eternal language of sacred repetition.[26] Such ritual phrasing furnishes a pole of order and comfort, its very monotony emblematic of the secure resolution of narrative conflict.

Typological studies have taught us much about the symbolic patterns of *Andreas*, but the language of Christian imperialism stubbornly inheres in its language of spirit. Warfare is symbolic in the poem, but is deployed in order to legitimate literal conflict. The conversion of Jew and heathen by military force was attempted regularly in the early Mid-

---

26. Several of the liturgical formulae (those which appear in ll.118–21; 225–29; 595–600; 977–80; 1053–57; 1150–54) would seem to be the additions of the Old English poet.

dle Ages, despite Gregory the Great's recommendation that Jews ought to be persuaded (although heathens might be forced if language proved insufficient).[27] The slippage inherent in metaphoric processes allows for a bidirectionality in the language of spiritual warfare. In the semiotic fugue, for example, the violent Christian disruption of ordinary signifying processes is interwoven with the poetics of historical violence. Eagles carry off the souls of Andreas's followers to a Germanic heroic heaven:

Utan ymbe æðelne   englas stodon,
þegnas ymb þeoden,   þusendmælum,
heredon on hehðo   halgan stefne
dryhtna dryhten.   Dream wæs on hyhte.

(871–74)

[Around their Prince angels were standing, thanes around their Lord by the thousands, and they praised him with holy voices on high, the Lord of lords. The joy was blissful.]

This Christian valhalla has a *þeoden* (lord) who is *sigedryhten* (lord of victories, 877), and surrounded by his *dugoð domgeorne* (warriors eager for fame, 878), his *þegnas, orettan, hæleð*. No *gewinn* (strife) disrupts this troop of warriors. It will be recalled that this description of a harmonious valhalla is followed by a warning of torment for those who would shatter its unity. The semiotic fantasy allows the magic of body/soul separation and otherworldly travel, but the ultimate destination of these miracles remains a metaphorized scene of violence. In *Andreas*, we can trace the extent to which semiological violence, necessary to the foundation of Anglo-Saxon Christianity, is also memorialized in its destiny, as Germanic poetic and cultural tradition are enlisted to reenact a conflict within *Ecclesia's* language of self-definition. This conflict is both symbolic and literal, staged on a historical site opened by a multivalent typology.

---

27. Gregory the Great, Epistolae, *Patrologia Latina* 77:509–11. On Gregory's proposal to tempt Jews to Christianity "even by offering fiscal alleviations," see *Encyclopaedia Judaica*, 8.657 and Parkes, *The Conflict of the Church and the Synagogue*, 212. A weakening of Pope Gregory I's relatively humane policy "was exemplified when Pope Leo VII (937) advised the archbishop of Mainz to expel the Jews from his diocese if they continued to refuse baptism" (*Encyclopaedia Judaica*, 5.537). Early medieval legislation affecting the Jews is discussed by Parkes, 379–91.

Chapter 6

Juliana

How are we to understand the now alien mode of medieval hagiography that informs Cynewulf's *Juliana*? Or, to phrase the question differently, how can we make sense of it? The first question sometimes leads critics into thinking that their task is to "understand" texts somehow already possessed of meanings which they then "discover;" the second question emphasizes the active role of the critic in making meaning. Although, as I have been arguing, criticism of Old English poetry is largely of the former variety, recent discussions of *Juliana* within those theoretical limits have contributed to our understanding of the work and appreciation of Cynewulf's artistry (in recent Old English criticism these two activities are often taken to be interchangeable).[1] But if our readings of this poem are ever to move beyond the reflection and reenactment of its form and values, both types of questions ought to be asked. The play of language and religion in *Juliana* suggests two interrelated projects: the discussion, in traditional terms, of alterations Cynewulf made to the original legend, as well as the investigation, using the untraditional critical approaches applied to *Elene* and *Andreas*, of the hagiographic strategies implied by those changes.[2]

1. Daniel Calder, "The Art of Cynewulf's *Juliana*," *Modern Language Quarterly* 34 (1973): 355–71; Joseph Wittig, "Figural Narrative in Cynewulf's *Juliana*," *Anglo-Saxon England* 4 (1975): 37–55; Claude Schneider, "Cynewulf's Devaluation of Heroic Tradition in *Juliana*," *Anglo-Saxon England* 7 (1978): 107–18; R. Barton Palmer, "Characterization in the Old English *Juliana*," *South Atlantic Bulletin* 41 (1976): 10–21; Raymond C. Saint-Jacques, "The Cosmic Dimensions of Cynewulf's *Juliana*," *Neophilologus* 64 (1980): 134–39.

2. According to my colleague Joe Hornsby, Angus Cameron once suggested that Cynewulf may not be a single person, but the name for a school of writers. I adopted a less radical position in criticizing Earl Anderson's argument that "the stylistic and thematic unity of the Cynewulf corpus is the result of the poet's own conception of his career as a didactic ministry." I argued that such emphasis upon the career of the individual poet was

One of Cynewulf's more significant omissions of source material occurs just after his heroine's imprisonment. She had previously been stripped, beaten, scourged, suspended by the hair, and scalded in a huge metal pot. Cynewulf includes this series of punishments, which seem excessive to contemporary taste—although, mercifully, he does leave out the metal pot. In the *Vita*, however, she then utters a lengthy prayer asking for divine protection, during which she alludes to the passage of the Israelites through the Red Sea: "Deduc me in portum voluntatis tuae, sicut deduxisti filios Israel fugientes ex Aegypto per mare sicut per terram, inimicos autem illorum operuit mare; ita me Domine exaudire dignare, et extingue minas tyranni, qui contra me exsurrexit, et destrue potestatem ejus ac mentem . . ."[3] ["Lead me into the harbor of your will, just as you led the children of Israel through the sea as if it were land when they were fleeing Egypt, but overwhelmed their enemies in the sea. In just this way deign to listen favorably to my prayer: destroy the threats of the tyrant, who rises up against me—destroy his power and even his mind . . ."] Those familiar with typological criticism of Old English poetry will have no difficulty in grasping the significance of Cynewulf's failure to mention such an instance of divine protection, an alteration all the more striking in light of his subsequent description of the destruction of Eleusius and his warrior band:

Þa se synscaþa
to scipe sceohmod   sceaþena þreate
Heliseus   ehstream sohte,
leolc ofer laguflod   longe hwile
on swonrade.   Swylt ealle fornom
secga hloþe   ond hine sylfne mid,
ærþon hy to lande   geliden hæfdon,
þurh þearlic þrea.   Þær XXX wæs

inappropriate, and that "the sociology of the monastic group" should have been invoked instead (J. P. Hermann, Review of *Cynewulf: Structure, Style, and Theme in His Poetry*, by Earl R. Anderson, *Journal of English and Germanic Philology* 84 [1985], 252).

3. Chap. 1, sec. 5. References to the *Vita* are to the chapter and section of Jean Bolland's *Acta Sanctorum* as reprinted in William Strunk, ed., *The Juliana of Cynewulf* (Boston, 1904), 33–49. It is possible that the *Vita* is not the exact version of the legend Cynewulf used, although most scholars believe that Cynewulf used it, or a closely related version, as his source. The *Vita* probably took final form in the sixth century, although it might well have been written in the fourth or fifth. On the style and function of saints' lives, see James W. Earl, "Typology and Iconographic Style in Early Medieval Hagiography," *Studies in the Literary Imagination* 8 (1975): 15–46.

ond feowere eac   feores onsohte
þurh wæges wylm   wigena cynnes,
heane mid hlaford,   hroþra bidæled,
hyhta lease   helle sohton.
Ne þorftan þa þegnas   in þam
                                    þystran ham,
seo geneatscolu   in þam neolan scræfe,
to þam frumgare   feohgestealda
witedra wenan,   þæt hy in winsele
ofer beorsetle   beagas þegon,
æpplede gold.

(671b–88a)

[Then the sin-stained wretch Eliseus, the coward, sought out the ocean stream by ship with a band of warriors, and for a long while tossed upon the ocean, on the swan-road. Death took them all with severe punishment, the crew of warriors and himself with them, before they had arrived at land. There the lives of thirty-four warriors were taken through the billowing of the wave, and the despised men along with their lord, deprived of joys and hopes, sought out hell. There was no need for the thanes in that dark abode, the troop of retainers in that deep hole, to expect their lord to dole out treasures, or that they would receive rings and embossed gold on the beer-bench in the wine-hall.]

In this elaborate set piece, which must have had an archaic flavor even for Cynewulf's contemporaries, Eliseus and his evil troop toss about on the swan-road before arriving at their infernal destination, where the hapless retainers will have no need to petition their diabolical chieftain for gold rings. Here we find a specifically Cynewulfian addition to the account supplied by the *Vita*. Yet Cynewulf has omitted the parallel earlier in his source which would have given the passage typological significance. A recent reading of *Juliana* which argues for the presence and significance of figural elements asserts:

The very manner of Heliseus's death recalls a passage from the book of Wisdom, parts of which were read on feasts of martyrs:
. . . transtulit illos per mare Rubrum et transvexit illos per aquam nimiam. Inimicos autem illorum demersit in mare. Et ab altitudine inferorum eduxit illos . . . [. . . she led them through the Red Sea and conveyed them across that great body of water. Their enemies, how-

ever, she drowned in the sea. And she led them out of the depths of the
infernal regions . . . (Wisdom 10.17–20).]
This notion might well underlie the poem's presentation of Heliseus's end.
Juliana embodies the wisdom of God's people. On the one hand, she leads
the good to baptism and salvation, even to the possession of Heliseus's
city; on the other, she brings a watery death to those too perverse to
survive the figurative crossing of the Red Sea.[4]

However, Cynewulf's omission of Juliana's earlier allusion to the Red
Sea crossing seems curiously difficult to account for if such a typological
reading is accepted. Indeed, one might prefer to abandon such a reading
rather than go to the lengths required to justify such an omission. While
figural elements can be found in the poem, they do not loom as large as
they do in *Exodus*, *Elene*, or *Andreas*. These elements tend to be magni-
fied by modern typological commentary, however, unless the critic is
particularly vigilant in resisting the force of his own interpretative
method. *Juliana* is an allegory of war which does not elaborate the
implicit conflict of *Ecclesia* vs. *diabolus* in the same manner, or to the
same extent, as the other poems discussed in Part 2 of *Allegories of War*.[5]

If Cynewulf's text ignores the key figural element in his source that
would allow us to make a connection with typological interpretations of
Exodus, what, then, does he choose to emphasize? To begin with a
rather modest example, Cynewulf seems interested in a quality which
might be termed "firmness." Only three instances of this attribute are
found in the *Vita*. The first occurs when the devil describes how he and
his brothers enter men's souls: "Et ubi invenerimus prudentem ad opus
Dei consistere, facimus eum desideria multa appetere . . ." [And wher-
ever we find a prudent man who stands firm in the work of God, we
make him long for many desires . . . (2.9)]. The second occurs when
Juliana is being tortured: "Beata autem Juliana stabat immobilis in fide
Christi, contrita corpore sed rigida fide" [However blessed Juliana stood
firm, unmoveable in the faith of Christ, with contrite body but unbend-
ing faith (3.14)]. The final instance takes place during Juliana's speech
before she is decapitated: "aedificate domos vestras super firmam pe-
tram, ne venientibus ventis validis disrumpamini" [build your houses

---

4. Wittig, "Figural Narrative," 54. My translation.
5. As I will argue in chap. 7, the interpretative category of the subtext can be
helpful in making sense of typological critics' reinscriptions of implicit allegory left undevel-
oped on the textual surface.

upon firm rock, so they will not be smashed to bits when the strong winds come (3.20)]. Here is the way Cynewulf translates the devil's speech:

"Þær ic hine finde   ferð staþelian
to godes willan,   ic beo gearo sona
þæt ic him monigfealde   modes gælsan
ongean bere   grimra geþonca . . ."

(364–67)

["Where I find him making his spirit steadfast according to the will of God, I am immediately ready to incite manifold lusts of the heart and hostile thoughts . . ."]

He also includes a plethora of other references to firmness. *Ferð staþelian* (to make the spirit steadfast), or a similar phrase, probably would have been used to translate the second instance as well, which would have appeared in the second missing leaf of *Juliana*; this formulaic half-line is repeated several times.[6] Cynewulf translates the final example thus:

"Forþon ic, leof weorud,   læran wille,
æfremmende,   þæt ge eower hus
gefæstnige,   þy læs hit ferblædum
windas toweorpan.   Weal sceal þy trumra
strong wiþstondan   storma scurum,
leahtra gehygdum.   Ge mid lufan sibbe,
leohte geleafan,   to þam lifgendan
stane stiðhydge   staþol fæstniað . . ."

(647–54)

["Therefore I want to teach you, dear people, in fulfilling the law, to make your houses firm, lest the winds destroy it with their fierce gusts. A strong wall can more firmly withstand the blasts of storms and vicious thoughts. In the peace of charity and in the light of faith, resolute in mind, make your foundation firm upon the living rock . . ."]

---

6. E.g., *ferð staþelian* (270, 364); *mod staþelian* (222); *hyht staþelian* (437); *fæste gestaþelian* (107). Especially significant is the devil's use of such language to describe his devotion to Satan (*hyht staþelie*, 437b). Cynewulf's interest in firmness is discussed by Daniel Calder, *Cynewulf* (Boston, 1981), 94–95.

The two ways of referring to firmness here, *gefæstnige* (to make firm) and *stapol fæstniað* (to make the foundation firm) will be repeated frequently.[7] Also noteworthy is the saint's use of *stiðhydge* (resolute, 654), as well as analogous epithets occurring elsewhere in the poem.[8] Often, the notion of Juliana's exemplary firmness is developed by reference to the devil's attempt to break down such Christian fortitude by changing the spirit (*mod oncyrran*).[9] All told, Cynewulf makes some fifty references to this notion of firmness, as opposed to the three in his source. I am no great believer in criticism-by-numbers, but these figures invite critical attention. Evidently, one of Cynewulf's chief concerns is his heroine's steadfastness, her refusal to allow her faith to be changed by any external or internal force. She builds spiritual bulwarks against the intrusion of the pagan forms of worship characteristic of the late Roman Empire, and Cynewulf honors her success in resisting alteration by the world and the devil. Her imperviousness to temptations of the flesh, of course, goes without saying. Here, then, is an example of what sparked Cynewulf's imagination in the *Vita*, leading to amplification, while a key figural parallel was omitted.

Concern with the heroine's steadfastness occurs alongside a contrasting focus upon the haste and rashness of the evil characters. Opposing Juliana's fixedness, the devil tells her to be in haste (*on ofeste*, 253) to sacrifice to the pagan gods. Later, he will describe his method of changing the mind of hitherto steadfast Christians in order to make them yield quickly (*hrape*, 370) to the promptings of sin.[10] For Cynewulf, firmness is associated with Juliana and Christianity, haste with the powers of evil opposing her. One motive for this emphasis is supplied by Cynewulf's vocation (most scholars have concluded that he was a monk) and his poem reflects many of the concerns of monastic spirituality, chief among which in the *Benedictine Rule* is the vow of *stabilitas*.[11]

The spiritual firmness his text recommends is not achieved easily,

---

7. E.g., *gefæstnian* (400, 499, 649); *stapol fæstnian* (654); *fæst* (535, 625); *fæste* (42, 107, 234, 284, 389, 433, 522); *fæstlice* (270); *stapolfæst* (374); *wærfæst* (238); *soðfæst* (325, 337, 348, 362, 426, 438).

8. E.g., *unwaclice* (50); *anræd* (90); *unbrice* (235).

9. E.g., *mod oncyrran* (226, 326, 363, 439); *mod gemyrran* (412); *onwendan* (57, 144); *acyrran* (139, 411); *oncyrran* (144); *ahyldan* (171); *hweorfan* (275, 381, 390); *mod ahwyrfan* (326, 360); *mod oðcyrran* (338).

10. E.g., *hrape* (254); *ofestlice* (582); *fromlice* (40, 89); *snell* (60); *recene* (62); *næs to læt* (573); *scyndan* (489).

11. The monastic vows of stability, conversion of life, and obedience are discussed in chap. 58 of the *Benedictine Rule*.

of course. It can be maintained only by the peculiar sort of spiritual violence that, as we have seen, characterizes a good deal of Old English Christian poetry. Indeed, one might plausibly argue that the most significant of the Cynewulfian additions to the *Vita* is the theme of spiritual warfare.[12] The role it plays runs deeply, to the very heart of the learned rhetoric of spirituality in the poem. In the passage which describes the spiritual combat in greatest detail (345–417a), the devil explains how he tempts the warrior of Christ, after being asked by the heroine to reveal his tactics. He replies that his spiritual assaults are aimed at those who attempt to remain firmly committed to Christ (*ferð staþelian*, 364); he attacks those who cannot remain steadfast (*staþolfæst ne mæg*, 374) in their commitment, but is unable to defeat those who make a stand (*bidsteal gifeð*, 388) by taking their positions firmly in the army of the *milites Dei* (*fæste on feðan*, 389). He must seek others to defeat who, although they might try to put up some resistance, are vulnerable because their spiritual fortresses have not been well maintained. Like several other alterations Cynewulf made, the full importance of firmness and *stabilitas* becomes evident only when we attend to the play of meanings associated with spiritual warfare in the poem. For example, when Juliana questions the demon, she addresses him as the enemy of souls (*sawla feond*, 348); previously, the narrator had referred to him as the enemy of heroes (*hæleþa gewinnan*,345), epithets from one of the most important classes of the recurrent motifs of spiritual warfare that were examined in chapter 2.[13]

The narrator next uses these motifs in referring to the devil as the author of ancient sins (*fyrnsynna fruman*, 347). They are "ancient," or "former," because they stem from the conflict between God and Satan, the *hostis antiquus*, that took place before the creation, and resulted in

---

12. Critics have often drawn attention to the more obvious examples of this theme in the poem. In addition to the works by Calder, Wittig, Schneider, Saint-Jacques, and Palmer mentioned previously, see Martin Irvine, "Cynewulf's Use of Psychomachia Allegory: The Latin Sources of Some 'Interpolated' Passages," in *Allegory, Myth, and Symbol*, ed. Morton W. Bloomfield (Cambridge, Mass., 1981), 39–62. On possible Germanic aspects of Juliana's characterization, see Helen Damico, "The Valkyrie Reflex in Old English Literature," *Allegorica* 5 (1980): 149–67.

13. *Juliana* makes use of such terms as *se feond* (350, 573); *feond moncynnes* (317, 523, 630); *sawla feond* (348); *sawla gewinna* (555); *hæleða gewinna* (243, 345); *hettend* (663); *wiðerbreca* (269); *wiþerfeohtend* (664); *gæsta geniðla* (151); and *gæstgeniðla* (245). Elsewhere in his poetry, Cynewulf employs *feond* (*Elene*, 207, 899, 953; *Christ II*, 569, 623, 733, 770) and *sceaða* (*Christ II*, 775; *Elene* 761).

the war in heaven and the fall of man.[14] The devil's purpose in this ongoing *bellum intestinum* is, as we have seen, to inflict wounds of sin (*synna wundum*, 355).[15] These enable him to cause the *soðfæst* man (362) to change his spirit (*mod oncyrre*, 363). Cynewulf's recurring interest in spiritual firmness, as well as the paradoxical nature of the concept, motivates the devil's remarks about the man whose spirit remains firmly attached to God's will (*ferð staþelian / to Godes willan*, 364b–65a): the devil launches delusions against him (*dyrnra gedwilda . . . gedwolena rim*, 368).[16] He sweetens the pleasures of sins for such a man so that he quickly obeys teachings which urge him to wicked mind-love (*mæne modlufan*, 370), a term which recalls the Augustinian distinction of *cupiditas* and *caritas*. A lover of paradox himself, the devil too emphasises firmness when he describes how his victim, who was once firmly attached to God's will, can no longer remain steadfast (*staþolfæst ne mæg . . . lenge gewunian*, 374b–75b) in the place of prayer, due to his love of vices. On the other hand, the devil tells Juliana, when he finds a courageous soldier of the Lord (*ellenrofne . . . modigne metodes cempan*, 382–83b), his evil designs lose their potency. He then goes on to discuss the shield and spiritual armor (*bord, haligne scyld, gæstlic guðreaf*) of the *miles Dei*.

The devil's description of the soldier of Christ and his spiritual armor is specifically limited, however, to those capable of withstanding the storm of arrows (*flanþræce*, 384).[17] When he encounters a warrior who puts up resistance (*bidsteal gifeð . . . fæste on feðan*, 388b-89a), he must lament his inability to overcome his opponent in battle (*guðe widgongan*, 393), and must seek a less courageous and alert warrior

---

14. In *Juliana*, Cynewulf employs *eald nið* (623); *lað leodgewin* (201); *wræce ræran* (333); *sceþþan* (349); *beadu* (385); *guð* (393, 397); *gewin* (421); *gemot* (426); *hildewoma* (663). Although it has overtones of spiritual combat, *gewindæg* (611) refers primarily to literal violence. Elsewhere, Cynewulf makes use of this motif in *Elene*, 903 (*fyrngeflit*); *Elene*, 904 (*eald nið*); *Elene*, 905 (*singal sacu*); *fæhð* is used in this sense in *Christ II*, 617. On *fyrnsynn* (347), see Rosemary Woolf, ed., *Juliana* (London, 1955), 88.

15. The notion of the wounds of sin occurs when Affricanus and Eliseus are referred to as *synnum seoce* (65); in the epilogue, Cynewulf will refer to his own "working" of the wounds of sin (*synna wunde*, 710). Elsewhere, he employs the figure in *Elene*, 514 and in *Christ II*, 763, 770.

16. E.g., *gedwola* (13, 138, 202, 301, 368); *dolwillen* (202, 451); *misgedwield* (326); *gedwild* (368, 460); *scinlac* (214). An exceptional example of the notion of diabolical delusion is found in ll.297b–301, where Satan is seen as a *drys* (sorcerer) who attacks through *gedwolan*.

17. See Stephen Morrison, "OE *Cempa* in Cynewulf's *Juliana* and the Figure of the *Miles Christi*," *English Language Notes* 17 (1979): 81–84.

(*ellenleasran . . . cempan sænran*, 394, 395) to incite with his leaven (*beorman mine*, 396) and hinder in battle (*agælan æt guðe*, 397). Such a warrior is seen as less courageous in the war-hedge (*cumbolhagan*, 395), a graphic illustration of the corporate nature of resistance: the *milites Dei* form part of Christ's body, and only the fearful, who cannot remain firm in the place of prayer, that literal or figurative place where the Church Militant takes its stand, can be defeated. Although this less courageous warrior might have some good qualities, the devil can examine the way his inner defenses are secured (*hu gefæstnad sy ferð innanweard, / wiþsteall geworht*, 400–401a). These defenses no longer involve the armor of the *miles Dei*, but the alternate figure of the soul as a fortress.[18] After the gate of the wall is opened, the tower is pierced and a flight of arrows (*eargfare*, 404), varied as bitter thoughts, is sent into his breast. As a result, he is turned away (*acyrred*, 411) from Christ's law, his mind led astray (*mod gemyrred*, 412).

Using such a close reading of the various images of the spiritual warfare appearing in this passage as a paradigm, one might trace the significance of these themes and motifs elsewhere in *Juliana*. And such an exercise would be of no small value in approaching *Juliana*, since it seems fair to say that the notion of spiritual warfare constitutes the most significant addition which Cynewulf made to the original legend. The *hostis antiquus*, the *bellum intestinum*, the wounds of sin, the arrows of the devil, the *miles Dei*, the spiritual armor, and the soul as a besieged fortress are central to Cynewulf's reworking of the *Vita* for an Old English audience. Even when he discusses Juliana's earthly antagonists, he employs terms like *feond* (enemy), *cempa* (warrior), *hererinc* (warrior), *þegn* (thane), and *duguþ* (army) which associate her earthly opponents with the powers of spiritual wickedness on high. One might also show how Cynewulf's concern with this theme can be traced in the many references to peace and victory in the poem, which signify in terms of the polar opposites to which Cynewulf's attention is usually drawn.[19] Similarly, the notion of God as *cyning* has specifically Anglo-Saxon connotations, and cannot be seen simply as a version of God as the *rex gloriae* or *rex victoriae*, since the context of the alliterative Anglo-Saxon

---

18. James F. Doubleday, "The Allegory of the Soul as Fortress in Old English Poetry," *Anglia* 88 (1970): 503–8.

19. E.g., *sib* (200, 219, 540, 652, 655, 668, 698); *frið* (320); *sigor* (224, 361, 561, 668, 705); *sigortifr* (255).

poetic determines much of the force of the epithet.[20] And, finally, one might argue that only when we understand the way Cynewulf uses motifs of spiritual warfare to transform the legend can we focus on the many ironic versions of this theme in *Juliana*. Raymond Saint-Jacques has shown how literal references to warfare work in terms of the cosmic dimensions of the poem. But the poem also sets into play further ironies based on the notion of warfare. For example, when Eliseus orders Juliana to be beaten and scourged, he is called a *hererinc* and refers to torture as a battle: "þis is ealdordom uncres gewynnes / on fruman gefongen!" (190–91) ["In this way the leadership in our strife is seized from the very beginning!"] In this instance, Trautmann was undoubtedly correct in arguing that Cynewulf probably read *principatus* (leadership) for the *Vita*'s *ecce principium quaestionis* ("behold, this was only the beginning of our questioning"); but we should see the misprision of *quaestio* (questioning) as *gewin* (strife) in terms of the theme of spiritual combat, and consider the resonance of *ealdordom* within the Anglo-Saxon word-hoard as well. This *hererinc* has seized the *ealdordom* of the struggle in the most ironic of ways: not only is his stripping and scourging of the defenseless girl exceptionally unheroic and cowardly, but Cynewulf has emphasized the fact that the struggle exceeds Eliseus's power of comprehension. And this is merely one of the many ironies of the poem which Cynewulf limns through his alteration and revision of the original legend.[21] Cynewulf's additions exemplify a pervading intertextuality in which patristic psychology and Anglo-Saxon poetic resources are grafted onto the *Vita*. The specific modes of rhetorical operation associated with this graft in Cynewulf's text invite the kind of critical attentiveness that ramifies beyond further elaboration of motif, theme, and parallel. Such traditional research accomplishes most, I think, when it opens onto a different sort of critical questioning.

---

20. God is referred to as a ruler in such phrases as *cyninga wuldor* (279); *beorna hleo* (272); *gæsta hleo* (49); *meotud moncynnes* (436, 666); *dryhtna dryhten* (594); *cyninga cyning* (289); *heofoncyning* (360); *rodorcyning* (447); *wuldorcyning* (238, 248, 428); *brego engla* (666); *heofena helm* (722); and *meahta waldend* (723). The devil is called *hellwarena cyning* (322, 544). See James Walter Rankin, "A Study of the Kennings in Anglo-Saxon Poetry," *Journal of English and Germanic Philology* 8 (1909): 413 and Fred Robinson, *Beowulf and the Appositive Style* (Knoxville, 1985), 29–59.

21. E.g., the cowardly *hæleð* (609) who deliberate her death and the thanes who spring from the race of warriors (*wigena cynnes*, 680) who are distinguished largely for their torture of a helpless girl. The militaristic atmosphere of the consultation of Eliseus and Affricanus is discussed by Calder, *Cynewulf*, 86.

II

Heroic vocabulary throughout *Juliana* is related to the fundamental operations of the work's rhetoric of spirituality. I would begin to read *Juliana* by questioning the play of figuration in the poem. What is the theoretical status of *Juliana*'s rhetoricity? What societal and psychical sanctions are invoked through its emplotment? Whose interests are served? *Juliana*, for instance, makes continual use of the classic dualities of Church/State, saint/devil, and soul/body, in which the prior term is always privileged, a textual hierarchy Jacques Derrida has taught us to scrutinize. *Juliana* asks for such scrutiny, for the literal and figurative violence of the poem is closely bound up with the violent exclusions inherent in these dualities upon which Cynewulf's "unclouded sense of either/or" is erected.[22] As Kenneth Burke pointed out in his study of Greek combat myths, "binary oppositions ordinarily become conflictual when presented in narrative form: the term on one side of the slash is seen as entering into battle with and vanquishing the other, unprivileged term."[23] The directionless polar opposites from which such myths of conflict emerge are necessarily self-implicatory. When translated into narrative, such contrasting pairs serve to account for a system of belief in conflictual terms. Traditional combat myths also provide sanctions for a given social order: by eternalizing the conflict of opposites, they furnish a powerful cultural paradigm for human conduct within time. Such an approach to the social and psychological effects of binary opposites in narrative might be useful in approaching a second series of omissions from Cynewulf's version of the legend. In the *Vita*, for instance, we learn of Juliana's mother as well as her father: "Cujus pater Africanus cognominabatur, qui et ipse erat persecutor Christianorum; uxor vero ejus dum intentione animi sacrilegia Martis [other MSS, Jovis] perhorresceret, neque Christianis neque paganis miscebatur" [Her father, named Africanus, was himself a persecutor of Christians; his wife, who shuddered at the sacrileges committed in worshiping Mars {other MSS, Jupiter}, mingled with neither Christians nor pagans (l.l)]. Why does Cynewulf's version omit the mother? Attention to the clash of contraries in narrative might lead us to view the exclusion of Juliana's

---

22. Calder, *Cynewulf*, 57; subsequent references to this work will be given in parentheses.

23. Kenneth Burke, *Language as Symbolic Action: Essays on Life, Literature, and Method* (Berkeley, 1966), 380–409.

mother as one aspect of a textual strategy for heightening the sense of either/or in the legend. In the traditional legend, the mother alone fails to take up a place on either side of the slash separating opposing principles. Here, as elsewhere, Cynewulf eliminates the possibility of a middle ground between his contending antitheses. Hence, his failure to mention the heroine's mother, who was horrified at pagan sacrifice and the travesties of the sacred such worship entailed. However, she lacked the courage of her convictions, since she resolved her dilemma by associating "with neither Christians nor pagans." Her tactic of psychic and social withdrawal suggests that Cynewulf prefers exaggerating the binary oppositions essential to his schematic technique rather than presenting characters who cannot occupy places on either side of the slash. Juliana needs Eleusius, at least from the vantage point of poetics, and conflict between them must occur if the opposing poles of Christian and pagan are to be reenacted in narrative. If this conflict at the core of the signifying processes of the text should fail to become externalized in a character's actions, a psychic passivity like that of Juliana's mother would be the inevitable result: unable to make up her mind to take an active role in the resolution of her conflict, her psychic and social withdrawal results in a failed psychomachia.

Significantly, Cynewulf's literary strategy erases her failure to choose sides, while simultaneously adding the theme of spiritual warfare. The motifs of spiritual warfare that arrest his attention also index a type of metaphysical violence necessary to maintain the acts of exclusion in the poem's originary oppositions. As Daniel Calder observes: "Except at the highest level, *Juliana* is not a comforting poem . . . . The tale dwells on violent emotions, hatred, cruelty, torture, and death . . . Cynewulf does not permit escape from the violence of this universal collision between good and evil" (156). But we should explore the extent to which this violence informs the most fundamental rhetorical operations of the text. Cynewulf evidently wished to make his *fundamentum divisionis* in the poem a stark one, in order to establish an unambiguous dividing line between good and evil, one even more rigid than that found in the *Vita*. And the conceptual violence of his originary oppositions plays itself out in the violence of the narrative. But is the separation between these opposing terms as clearcut as Cynewulf tries to make it? Is the exclusionary principle successful in its division of reality into a warfare of opposites?

New Critical attention to the texture of language in the poem can supply a starting point for pursuing these questions. Scholars have frequently remarked the contrast between characters in the poem. But to what extent do differences between characters turn out to be differences within?[24] Cynewulf's language, as Daniel Calder has observed, identifies him not with Juliana as one might expect, but with the devil: "Cynewulf and the devil speak in the first person indicative, while Juliana uses the imperative form. Cynewulf thus shares with the devil an inordinate absorption in self. The devil's avowal of his crimes overflows with 'I'; Cynewulf's epilogue does not present so extreme a case, but the sense of an 'I' predominates . . . Cynewulf clearly intends that he himself should fit midway between the poles of the cosmic scheme he has wrought from the bare legend" (102). An astute observation, but is it really "midway" that we find Cynewulf? In the epilogue, he says he will remember the wounds of sins (*synna wunde*, 710) that he worked in the world, and will lament them with tears. Note that this language of "working" the wounds of sin (*ic . . . geworhte*, 710-ll), which is earlier associated with the devil speaking in the first person, is appropriated by Cynewulf here. When the demons are uncertain that they will be able to work Satan's will, the devil says:

> "we beoð hygegeomre,
> forhte on ferðþe.   Ne biþ us frea milde,
> egesful ealdor . . ."
>
> (327b–29a)

["we are miserable in mind and afraid in our spirits. He will not be a mild lord to us, that terrible prince . . ."]

Similarly, Cynewulf is sad (*geomor*, 703) and frightened (*acle*, 706) because his King will be wrathful (*Cyning biþ reþe*, 704). In contrast with the haste of the evil characters, Cynewulf says he was too slow (*Wæs an tid to læt*, 712) in repenting for his sins; his body will tremble (*beofað*,

---

24. "The differences *between* entities . . . are shown to be based on a repression of differences *within* entities, ways in which an entity differs from itself. But the way in which a text thus differs from itself is never simple: it has a certain rigorous, contradictory logic whose effects can, up to a certain point, be read. The 'deconstruction' of a binary opposition is thus not an annihilation of all values or differences; it is an attempt to follow the subtle, powerful effects of differences already at work within the illusion of a binary opposition" (Barbara Johnson, *The Critical Difference: Essays in the Contemporary Rhetoric of Reading* [Baltimore, 1981], x–xi).

708) in the face of the rigors of the judgment, in contrast with the firmness of Juliana. I would suggest that such details index the status of Cynewulf's relationship to the characters of the legend he has elaborated, and that his anxiety springs from a philosophical dilemma as well as a theological one:

> Is me þearf micel
> þæt seo halge me   helpe gefremme,
> þonne me gedælað   deorast ealra,
> sibbe toslitað   sinhiwan tu,
> micle modlufan.   Min sceal of lice
> sawul on siðfæt,   nat ic sylfa hwider . . .
>
> (695b–700)

[There is great need for me that the saint will give me help when those who are dearest depart from me, and the united pair sever their relationship, their great love. My soul will have to leave my body on a journey, I know not where . . .]

Unlike Juliana, Cynewulf fears the division of body and soul. He sees them as *sinhiwan*, a "united pair," in a way that Juliana clearly does not. The textual operations characteristic of the poem organize the basic philosophical constructions that inhabit the soul/body opposition. In the poem, Juliana displays no doubt concerning her soul's destination, but Cynewulf shares only tentatively in his heroine's confidence. He prefers to think in terms of the kinship between body and soul, rather than the separation of the two, and maintains that he does not know where his soul will be destined to dwell.

Juliana ordinarily speaks in the imperative: for this reason, she can be associated with the superego, should one choose to deploy Freudian psychology in dealing with patristic psychology. In such a *translatio studii*, of course, these topological terms will be employed not clinically, but as critical counters. According to Freud's second topology, the superego founds itself upon the exclusion of the impulses of the id. Such excluded impulses, however, constantly threaten to disrupt the psychic economy. In *Juliana*, the promptings of the id are represented figurally, as the devil's attack on the besieged castle of the soul and his combat against the *milites Dei*. Firm resistance against these diabolical assaults can be reinscribed within the Freudian scheme as the suppression of impulses, which the devil tries to "sweeten," one of Cynewulf's descriptive terms influenced by the patristic psychology of sin.[25] Somewhere between the positions of Juliana and the devil, we must locate Cynewulf himself. In Freudian terms, if Juliana belongs with the superego, the devil belongs with the id and Cynewulf with the ego: one sorts out their positions in the schema without much difficulty. But for Freud, the ego is not a point, or even a stable position or layer; it is, rather, the precarious and shifting scene of a conflict between the imperatives of society and the impulses of desire. Cynewulf presents himself as representative of the audience of non-saints, which is also clearly not midway between Juliana's values and those of the devil. A hagiographer and not a saint, he displays his participation in the values on each side of the opposition reconstructed from the *Vita*. He represents the comparatively undifferentiated state which the rhetorical machinery of conflictual opposites configures into narrative form. The complete working through of the conflict found in the legend exceeds Cynewulf's ability, as it does that of any member of the audience: the Christian mythos has other, sacramental means at its disposal for ideal outcomes of this kind. Nor can he be so abstractly imperious as Juliana, since his quite human language reveals a disconcerting kinship with the devil. We are dealing not with midpoints that can be located along some continuum, but with psychical processes within Cynewulf and his audience, who are themselves sites for the conflict of opposing principles. In a manner similar to the founding of the economy of superego and id in the Freudian schema, the saintly is itself founded upon the prior exclusion of the diabolical.[26] A poem like *Juliana* embodies this mode of production of the holy through the rhetorical operations we have been considering, while at the same time displaying all too human uncertainty about those very textual operations.

But these psychological aspects of the poem have wider, sociopolitical implications. After Juliana is beheaded, Sephonia embalms her body and, while sailing to Rome, manages to survive a powerful tempest:

---

25. E.g., *(ge)swetan* (369, 525). Teaching is referred to both *in bono* and *in malo*: *(ge)læran* (149, 281, 297, 307, 501, 574, 638, 647); *lar* (306, 371, 378, 483); and *lareow* (409). One of the richer ironies of the poem occurs in the description of the drowning of Eliseus and his men, where they are referred to as a *geneatscolu* (684), a word derived from the Latin *schola*. Cynewulf has also added many references to journeys (261, 285, 318, 443, 452, 527, 537, 558, 700); he even writes of body and soul as journeying together (*sipedon*, 714) and of the Holy Spirit as Juliana's *gesið* (242) in prison.

26. Samuel Weber, *The Legend of Freud* (Minneapolis, 1982), 13–19, 53–60.

Post paucum autem tempus quaedam mulier Sephonia senatrix transiens
per civitatem Nicomediensem, et veniens ad urbem Romam, tulit corpus
B. Julianae, et condiens cum aromatibus et linteaminibus pretiosis cum
veniret ad urbem, exsurgens tempestas valida, abiit navis usque ad fines
Campaniae. Posita est autem B. Juliana prope territorium Puteolanum,
ubi habet mausoleum uno milliario a mari.

(3.21)

[After a short while, Sephonia, a senator's wife who was traveling through
the city of Nicomedia on her way to Rome, took blessed Juliana's body
and embalmed it with aromatics and precious linens. While she was travel-
ing to Rome, a mighty storm arose and the boat drifted to Campania.
Juliana was buried near Puteoli, in a tomb located one mile from the sea.]

Not only does this material add significant detail to the burial account, it
supplies a neat contrast to the drowning of Eleusius and his men in the
tempestas valida (mighty storm) as well. Its omission by Cynewulf de-
stroys much of the symmetrical design already there in the source and
available for allegorical amplification should he have so desired. Once
again, it appears that typology was not a central thematic concern of the
Old English poem, although typological criticism attempts to read in
precisely the spiritual significance this particular text tends to exclude.
Juliana is a hagiographic allegory of war that works along different lines
than *Elene* or *Judith*. The poem's failure to refer to Sephonia dovetails
with another change often noted by critics, the omission of Juliana's
desire that Eleusius become prefect. It is significant that Sephonia is the
wife of a senator, since Cynewulf has taken pains to emphasize the
unremitting hostility of the state to his heroine. Eleusius sees Juliana's
Christianity as proselytizing for strange gods, forcing him to turn his
back on the powers that have brought earthly success to his people (*þe
þissum folce to freme stondað*, 123).[27] In the Old English poem, earthly
treasure, power, and prestige may be desired only by the characters
arrayed against the heroine. Yet in the *Vita*, Juliana had wanted Eleusius
to attain the prefecture. According to Stanley Greenfield: "In the Latin
Vita . . . Juliana at the beginning is somewhat deceitful, demanding first
that Eleusius become a prefect before she will marry him, and then,

---

27. On the attitude of the pagan characters toward the God of Juliana, see ll.80,
121, 174, 205. In order to highlight the contrast between supernatural and earthly reward,
Cynewulf adds to the *Vita* many references to earthly treasure: *hordgestreon* (22);
maððumgesteald (36); *feohgestreon* (42, 102); *æhtgesteald* (115); *feohgestealde* (685).

when he gains the prefecture, changing her ground to demand conversion as a prerequisite to marriage."[28] Why, then, does she desire her suitor to rise in the world? If we rule out her playing hard to get—as we must, since it is hard to imagine Juliana as anyone's Coy Mistress—evidently she is attempting to secure a safe political environment for her fellow Christians. When Juliana asks that Eleusius receive the Spirit of God before she will marry him, he replies: "Non possum, domina mea, quia si fecero, audiet imperator . . ." ["I can't, my lady, because if I do, the Emperor will hear about it . . ." (1.3)]. Were she to have first asked for his conversion, Eleusius could never have become prefect.

Why does Cynewulf eliminate the reference in the *Vita* to her desire for Eleusius to attain the prefecture, "thus whitening Juliana's character?" An answer, I would suggest, can be sought by examining his textual strategy of heightening the opposition between the otherworldly Church and thisworldly State. Cynewulf's narrative strategies naturalize the opposition by rewriting it cosmically. His technique heightens the opposition in a way that would have been unsuitable at the time of composition of the *Vita*, a biographical account aimed at bolstering the truth claims of the Christian religion and, in so doing, preparing the way for its increasing power in the world. In the ninth century we find a remarkably different political climate, and the contrasting rhetorical strategies of the two works are bound up with such differences in social and historical context. Just as the deletion of the account of Juliana's mother makes sense in terms of her borderline status and psychic withdrawal, both Juliana's wish for Eleusius to become prefect and the presence of Sephonia as a *mulier senatrix* (Senator's wife) display a Church/world interrelationship that the Old English poem excludes.

As Calder has noted, Cynewulf's poem reflects a "closed ideology."[29] Its emphatic textual opposition of the City of God to the City of Man occults claims to worldly power within Christianity. The omission of Sephonia's embalming of the body and of Juliana's wish for Eleusius to become a prefect effectively minimizes the will to power of Christianity while heightening the opposition between Jerusalem and Babylon. Cynewulf's omissions make sense in terms of the constraint, not necessarily conscious, that led him to purge worldly elements from the character of his heroine. Cynewulf's poem removes his heroine from the

---

28. This quotation and the one that follows are from Stanley Greenfield, *A Critical History of Old English Literature* (London, 1966), 111.

29. This term originates with D. C. Muecke; see Calder's *Cynewulf*, 177–78.

claims of the world and even of her family; normal desires for worldly power and familial harmony are represented as dangers for the saint. The poem sanctions the breaking of both family and state bonds. In Freudian terms, the libidinal energies released as a consequence of this severance of ties to the world are then recathected to the Christian religion within the narrative economy of the poem. And the exemplary status of Cynewulf's heroine makes such poetic strategies into powerful social strategies as well.

At the same time that Cynewulf's text heightens the opposition between Church and State, it works toward the legitimization of the Church's power of command. This can best be seen in the way the linguistic and ethical imperatives of the superego are presented in the poem. The question-and-answer method, also found in works like *Adrian and Ritheus*, *Solomon and Saturn*, and the *Joca Monachorum*, assumes great political and social significance. We should look at this commonplace catechetical form in terms of the power of interrogation in the society: Who has the authority to ask questions? Who must answer them?[30] The devil himself initiates the process of questioning in *Juliana* when he asks the heroine why she suffers so needlessly. She seizes control of their conversation by responding with a question of her own. After answering Juliana's series of questions—whence? why? who? how?—the devil will respond to her fifth by asking one of his own: how she became so bold, beyond womankind. But this merely rhetorical

---

30. On discourses of power, see Michel Foucault, *Madness and Civilization: A History of Insanity in the Age of Reason*, trans. Richard Howard (New York, 1973); *Discipline and Punish: The Birth of the Prison*, trans. Alan Sheridan (New York, 1979); and *A History of Sexuality*, vol. I: *An Introduction*, trans. R. Hurley (New York, 1980). See also Allen J. Frantzen, *The Literature of Penance in Anglo-Saxon England* (New Brunswick, N.J., 1983) and Lenore MacGaffey Abraham, "Cynewulf's *Juliana*: A Case at Law," *Allegorica* 3 (1978): 172–89. In our time, the power of command has passed to psychologists and other members of the helping professions who are the secular equivalents of medieval priests. On the power of interrogation in hagiography, Peter Brown writes: "Possession and exorcism . . . contributed to build up a model of the working of the power and presence of the saints in late-antique society. Most important of all for a late-antique man were the heavy judicial overtones of the process of exorcism at a shrine. Exorcism had always taken the form of a dialogue in which the invisible authority behind the human agent of exorcism could be seen to be pitted against the power of the demons who spoke through the possessed human sufferer. What was spelled out with unfailing clarity at a late-Roman shrine was that this dialogue was a judicial inquiry. The horrors of a late-Roman courtroom, which included the application of tortures in the process of interrogation, the *quaestio*, were reenacted with gusto, in invisible form, in the dialogue between the saint and the demons in the possessed" (*The Cult of the Saints: Its Rise and Function in Latin Christianity* [Chicago, 1981], 108).

question is never answered; it has none of the force of authority behind it that can compel an answer. As Michel Foucault has shown in his analysis of discourses of sexuality, the power to command the revelation of another's misdeeds, whether actual or merely mental, is central to the power of the priesthood. And both the *Vita* and the Old English poem sanction ecclesiastical power by the narrative tactic of having the devil himself submit to the questions of Juliana. Such a narrative tactic also serves to support the validity of the discursive practices of the penitentials. And this form of control over behavior had behind it the institutionalized power of the Church, a power which would sometimes be directed to questionable ends when it served the interests of those who wielded it.

In terms of the realities of power in *Juliana*, one final omission remains to be considered. After the demon describes his method of assaulting the souls of the just, he threatens the heroine with Satanic punishment. Juliana will discuss his recalcitrance no further: "Tunc S. Juliana ligavit illi post tergum manus, et posuit eum in terram, et apprehendens unum e vinculis de quibus ipsa fuerat ligata, caedebat ipsum daemonem" [Then Saint Juliana tied his hands behind his back, and placed him down on the ground, and taking one of the bonds/fetters/chains with which she had been bound, she struck the demon (1.10)]. That she uses an iron chain in this inverted passion is made explicit in the textual tradition represented by the Munich manuscript, which reads "unum ligamentum ferreum." Again, differences between turn out to be differences within; significantly, Cynewulf's omission conceals the violence of his heroine and of the Church she represents. The lurid violence so characteristic of his reworking of the *Vita* attaches itself only to the craven representatives of the completely evil state. However, we can look to Cynewulf's historical situation, which was probably late eighth- or early ninth-century England, in order to discover the societal background to the Christian spirituality he seeks to legitimize. Rosemary Woolf has suggested that *Juliana* was originally composed for a group of nuns. This seems probable, just as it seems likely that Cynewulf's concern with "firmness" glances at the monastic vow of *stabilitas*. His reworking of the legend manifests a central concern with the figurally violent onslaughts of libidinal energy—and attempts at their subsequent suppression or repression, whether successful or not—associated with maintenance of the monastic commitment, as well as with the initiation of such a commitment in resistance to familial and cultural bonds. To attempt to exalt Cynewulf for "an abstract comprehension that perceives the figure behind the tale" while simultaneously denigrating the *Vita* for its "credulous attitude towards the historicity of legend"[31] is to fail to interrogate thoroughly the social context for the differing rhetorical strategies of the two works. Cynewulf's are monastic interests, both psychological and political. One advantage of the poem's technique of exaggerating the difference between the Church and the world arises from the paradox that a strategy of resistance to the world is at the same time a strategy for worldly success, enabling the Church to serve the interests of various groups contending for political power. The battle imagery that so interests Cynewulf articulates the psychic and rhetorical energy required for the maintenance of the slash separating the oriinary dualities of Church/state, saint/devil, soul/body that are heightened in *Juliana*. The possibility of the breakdown of the slash—in Freudian terms,the incursions of the id that threaten the ego—is represented by the battle of the *miles Dei* and the devil. This patristic battle imagery parallels suppression and repression in the Freudian psychology, "scientific" concepts which likewise originate in, and can never escape, figurality. Juliana sums up the need for resistance in her death speech, when she urges her people to make their houses firm lest the sudden blasts of the storm destroy them. This biblical image contrasts with the earlier patristic image of the soul as a besieged fortress.[32] In one case, we are given a domestic image, in the other a societal one involving the wider spectrum of inhabitants of a castle, but in both cases the feared deconstruction by the devil is to be resisted. The modern reader can also deconstruct such figures. For these psychological images employed by Cynewulf have both a politics and a rhetoric underlying their construction of firm boundaries between opposing principles and powers. That this rhetoric is founded upon tropes, which deserve thoughtful interrogation rather than critical sympathy, should not be surprising.[33]

---

31. Woolf, ed., *Juliana*, 99.

32. This passage is discussed by Kenneth A. Bleeth, "*Juliana*: 647–52," *Medium Aevum* 38 (1969): 119–22.

33. Daniel Calder's *Cynewulf* is partly designed as an epitome of postwar criticism of Cynewulf, and his remarks concerning *Juliana* will serve to demonstrate the theoretical limitations of traditional critical practice. For example, New Critical pieties such as "We have only just begun to acknowledge the complexities of [Cynewulf's] poetic structures" are modulated rather quickly into pieties of a different sort: "He employs his skill in God's service" (169–70). He can even assert that the reader must share the beliefs of the author in order to appreciate the poem properly: "[Cynewulf's] success will depend on a critic's predisposition toward such projects in the first place" (156); "the triumphant Christian

Cynewulf has made two kinds of alterations to his source. There has been a series of omissions: the allusion to the crossing of the Red Sea, which would have given typological significance to the later drowning of Eleusius and his men in the *tempestas valida*; the account of Sephonia's sea journey with Juliana's corpse and her survival of the *tempestas valida*; the reference to Juliana's mother; Juliana's wish that Eleusius become a prefect; and, finally, Juliana's violence toward the demon. And there has been a corresponding series of additions: most significantly, the various recurrent motifs of spiritual warfare and the ironies that they enable, as well as the notion of Juliana's exemplary firmness. Especially significant is Cynewulf's tactic of placing the language of spiritual warfare in the mouth of the devil himself, causing him to confess to the truth of the tropings of monastic spirituality. Cynewulf's alterations of the legend show his determination to strengthen oppositions, to eliminate whatever might mitigate the violent exclusions upon which the text's dualities are founded. In Cynewulf's poem, the *Vita* is misprised and rewritten, modified not only by patristic psychology but by the Old English alliterative poetic itself. These traditions mesh in a unique manner: the warlike ethos of the Old English poetic offers ideological reinforcement at the site of the slash, in order to serve concerns in some ways quite different from those of the sixth-century source. The graft of traditions within Cynewulf's text is affected by cultural and psychological factors, largely stemming from the internal necessities of monasticism. Such textual operations also serve to define culture and psyche, then as now.

---

irony of the poem" (98–99) which Calder often singles out for praise "elicits a sympathetic response only from those who cleave to Cynewulf's definite and translucent ideology" (82). Able to see light shining through ideology, the sympathetic critic can therefore appreciate the poem's complexity and craftsmanship. These remarks are emblematic of the failure of traditional Old English criticism to question the privileged autonomy of the text: although well qualified to reenact the values of the work, it is unable to interrogate the status of its object or of its own practice.

Chapter 7

Judith

When Judith, recently returned from the decollation of Holofernes, formulates strategy for the upcoming battle with the Assyrians, the day-break sortie she orders is not designed to bring victory in and of itself—not, at least, according to the Vulgate. It is only meant to trigger a predictable chain of events: the enemy watchmen will run off to awaken their slumbering leaders, Holofernes will be discovered wallowing in a pool of blood, and the Assyrian army, demoralized by the death of its general, will break ranks and flee (Liber Iudith 14:2–5). Only then will the Jewish forces be able to triumph. The initial impression of readiness for battle which they give is only a ruse, since they are incapable of resisting the powerful army of Nabuchodonosor by military means alone. Before Judith's successful deployment of feminine wiles to achieve what force of arms could not, her townspeople had begged her to surrender Bethulia to Holofernes, even if it meant they would all die, since their supply of water had been cut off during the siege and they preferred the risks of capitulation to the certainty of slow death by thirst (Liber Iudith 7:2–17). The Jewish people, as they are portrayed in the Vulgate, could not possibly have emerged victorious in battle prior to the panic which arose at the discovery of Holofernes's death, yet that is precisely what happens in the Old English *Judith*. This alteration in the function of the initial charge against the enemy would seem to cast doubt upon the extent of the author's comprehension of his source, if we didn't know that early medieval reinscriptions of biblical narrative are most revealing at just such points.

In the Old English *Judith*, the Bethulians mount a devastating attack upon their enemies, to the anachronistic accompaniment of the wolf, the raven and the eagle, the traditional beasts of battle in Old English poetry. Only after the Assyrian leaders conclude that their forces have been routed do they discover their general's death. The Assyrians lose most of their army in the subsequent battle, as in the Vulgate account; unlike the Vulgate, however, they were already defeated before dissemination of the news of Holofernes's slaying. The Old English poem diminishes Judith's contribution to the Jewish cause while magnifying the military prowess of her townspeople. For the Jews to attack successfully before the discovery of the slain Holofernes transforms this crucial episode in the biblical narrative into a very different story.[1]

The theme of spiritual warfare can be traced in several aspects of characterization and emplotment in *Judith*. And processes of allegoresis promote this theme. The curious battle scene of the Old English poem signals the need for the story of the Assyrian downfall to be understood *sub specie allegoriae* (in an allegorical manner). Knowledge of traditional commentaries on *Judith* can be put to good use in making sense of it. In the preface to the Vulgate translation, Jerome had emphasized the tropological content of the book of Judith:

> Accipite Judith viduam, castitatis exemplum, et triumphali laudi, perpetuis eam praeconiis declarate. Hanc enim non solum feminis, sed et viris imitabilem dedit, qui castitatis ejus remunerator, virtutem ei talem tribuit, ut invictum omnibus hominibus vinceret, et insuperabilem superaret.[2]

> [Accept the widow Judith, an example of chastity, and proclaim her in perpetual commendations and triumphal praise. She offered a model for imitation not only by women, but by men. The one who rewards her chastity allotted such strength to her that, invincible, she conquered one unconquerable by mankind and surpassed the insurpassable.]

Yet in a letter to Salvina, Jerome had given more emphasis to the allegorical significance of the actions of the heroine, who "in typo Ecclesiae, diabolum capite truncavit" [as a type of the Church, cuts off the head of

---

1. I have made use of Jackson J. Campbell's discovery, in "Schematic Technique in *Judith*," *ELH* 38 (1971): 155–72, that Pauline metaphors of spiritual battle are present in Judith's call for battle to the Bethulians. I have also benefited from Bernard F. Huppé's discussion of the poem in *The Web of Words: Structural Analyses of the Old English Poems Vainglory, The Wonder of Creation, The Dream of the Rood, and Judith* (Albany, 1970), 114–88, which argues a thoroughgoing tropological interpretation.

2. Jerome, *Praefatio in Librum Judith, PL* 29:40.

the devil].[3] This tension between the tropolgical and allegorical levels in Jerome prevails throughout the early commentaries. Only rarely does a commentator discuss both levels in the same commentary; one approach is generally emphasized to the virtual exclusion of the other. From the time of Jerome until the seventh century the tropological interpretation was *de rigueur*, as in Fulgentius:

> Denique cum Holofernes innumero Bethuliam obsedisset exercitu, et omnis Israelitarum virtus perturbata languesceret, egreditur castitas oppugnatura lasciviam, et ad interitum superbiae humilitas sancta procedit. Ille pugnabat armis, ista jejuniis; ille ebrietate, ista oratione. Igitur quod omnis Israelitarum populus facere non potuit, sancta vidua castitatis virtute perfecit.[4]

> [Finally, when Holofernes put Bethulia under siege with a huge army and all the troubled strength of the Israelites grew languid, Chastity marched forward to attack Licentiousness, and holy Humility advanced to the destruction of Pride. The one fought with arms, the other with fasts; the one with drunkenness, the other with prayer. Therefore, by the virtue of chastity, the holy widow succeeded in doing what the entire nation of Israel was not able to accomplish.]

Isidore of Seville first reemphasized the allegorical level of exegesis: "Judith et Esther typum Ecclesiae gestant, hostes fidei puniunt, ac populum Dei ab interitu eruunt" [Judith and Esther function as types of the Church; they punish the enemies of the faith and rescue the people of God from destruction].[5]

Aldhelm, in the prose and poetic versions of his *De Virginitate*, commits himself *a priori* to the tropological interpretation since his theme concerns the praise of chastity. The poem discusses only tropological aspects of the Judith story, yet in the prose version Aldhelm construes Judith as a type of the Church before the coming of Christ.[6] Remigius of Auxerre, glossing Prudentius's allusion to the Judith story during the description of *Pudicitia*'s conquest of *Sodomita Libido*, saw

---

3. Jerome, *Epistolae, PL* 22:732.

4. Fulgentius, *Epistolae, PL* 65:319–20. Cf. Pseudo-Augustine, *Sermones, PL* 39:1839; Prudentius, *Psychomachia*, 58–65; and Dracontius, *De Laudibus Dei* 3:480–95.

5. Isidore of Seville, *Allegoriae Quaedam Sacrae Scripturae, PL* 83:116.

6. Rudolf Ehwald, ed., *Aldhelmi Opera, Monumenta Germaniae Historica, Auctores Antiquissimi*, 15 (Berlin, 1919), 317. Cf. the poetic *De Virginitate*, 2560–70.

the conflict of Judith and Holofernes as one between *Ecclesia* and the Devil: "Significat enim aeclesiam, Olofernis vero Diabolum, quem modo veraciter aeclesia interficit" [Judith signifies the Church, Holofernes the Devil, whom the Church truly slays].[7] This eclipsing of the tropological level by the allegorical also characterizes the commentary of Rabanus Maurus of Fulda, whose theological writings deeply influenced the Anglo-Saxons. Rabanus regarded Judith as a type of "sancta Ecclesia" (Holy Church) and Holofernes as a type of Antichrist or Satan: "Holofernem hunc aut gentium principatum, qui persecutus est Ecclesiam Christi, aut ipsum etiam iniquorum omnium caput, et novissimum perditionis filium possumus intelligere. . ." [We can understand Holofernes to be either the leader of those nations who persecuted the Church of Christ, or the source of all evils and most extreme son of perdition].[8] Finally, in Aelfric's Judith homily, written after the probable time of composition of the Old English poem, both the tropological and allegorical levels receive equal attention, representing a return to the balanced treatment of the two levels in Jerome.[9]

The earlier commentaries, then, tended to emphasize the moral level, while those of the seventh through tenth centuries show a shift in importance to the allegorical level, nearly banishing the former locus of interest. Only at the time of Aelfric do both interpretations coexist in the same commentary. This resurgence of the allegorical level coincides with the probable date of composition of the Old English *Judith*. In *Judith*, the obvious moral aspects of the narrative are not elaborated. The poem emphasizes symbolic conflict between *Ecclesia* and *Diabolus*, an approach in keeping with the dominant exegetical approach at that time. Later on, I shall deal once more with the poem's inattentiveness to sexual aspects of the source, but I first want to examine the striking transformation of the battle episode in terms of the emphasis upon the allegorical level in contemporary *Judith* commentaries.

Consider techniques of characterization in the poem. When Holoferenes dies, his spirit departs immediately to hell, where it suffers the binding torments frequently associated poetically and iconographically with Satan and the rebel angels. According to early medieval

---

7. J. M. Burnam, ed., *Commentaire anonyme sur Prudence d'après le manuscrit 413 de Valenciennes* (Paris, 1910), 90.

8. Rabanus Maurus, *Expositio in Librum Judith*, PL 109:558, 546.

9. Bruno Assmann, ed., *Angelsächsische Homilien und Heiligenleben*, Bibliothek der Angelsächsischen Prosa, 3 (Kassel, 1889), 114–15. Cf. ll.407–17 with 434–41.

theology, however, it would be unusual for a sinner, no matter how evil, to be dispatched to hell immediately upon dying; ordinarily condemnation would occur only at the Last Judgment. Such emphasis on the Satanic nature of Holofernes, more satisfying artistically than intellectually, illustrates the difference between poetry and theological commentary. Elsewhere the diabolical reinscription of Holofernes virtually identifies him with the Devil. Explicitly called *se deofolcunda* (the devil-like one, 61), Holofernes is referred to as both *se bealofulla* (the wicked one, 48, 63, 100, 248) and *se inwidda* (the evil one, 28), epithets reminiscent of the designation of Satan as *malus* or *malignus* in the New Testament.[10]

Judith depicts the Assyrian army in similar fashion. In the preliminary battle fabricated out of whole cloth, instead of the thirsty and impotent Bethulians of the Vulgate, we are given a bold warrior troop capable of crushing a diabolical opposition:

> styrmdon hlude
> grame guðfrecan,   garas sendon
> in heardra gemang.   Hæleð wæron yrre,
> landbuende,   laðum cynne,
> stopon styrnmode,   stercedferhðe,
> wrehton unsofte   ealdgeniðlan. . . .
>
> (223b–28)

[The fierce warriors cried out loudly and sent their spears into the troop of brave warriors. The heroes, land-dwellers, were furious at the hateful race, and they advanced, stern of mood and resolute in spirit, and cruelly aroused their ancient enemies . . . .]

The choice of *ealdgeniðla* (old enemy) as antonomasia for the Assyrians is significant. A loan translation of the recurrent motif of the *hostis antiquus*, the word is often used to refer to Satan in Old English poetry. The battle itself is termed a *fyrngeflit* (264), varied by *ealdæfðonca* (265), both recurrent figures for the "ancient strife" between the demons and mankind initiated by Satan's disobedience. And later on, the

---

10. As in Matt. 13.19 and I John 2.13–14; 3.12. In other ways as well Holoferenes is associated with the Devil by the *Judith*-poet. *Se atola* (75) is frequently used in Anglo-Saxon poetry to refer to Satan, as in *Christ and Satan*, 382, 411, 485, 680, 716, 725. Holofernes is called *morðres brytta* (90); the only other use of this formula is in *Andreas*, 1170, where the referent is Satan. Holofernes is called a *wærloga* (71), antonomasia for Satan in *Whale*, 37; *Juliana*, 455; and *Andreas*, 613, 1297.

Assyrians are called *ealdfeondas* (315) and *ealdhettende* (320), also loan translations of the Latin metaphor of Satan as the *hostis antiquus*. These lexical choices make the battle a historical event that is also an allegorical battle against the Devil and his minions by the spiritual warriors of *Ecclesia*, who easily crush their diabolical opponents.

This shift in the characterization of the Jewish townspeople and the conception of their preliminary victory avoids the Vulgate's implication that the Bethulians are capable of only a mop-up operation. Details of the source are altered in a way that suggests that the Bethulian triumph hardly results from the weakness of the powers arrayed against them. They possess sufficient courage and strength to emulate Judith's victory over Holofernes. In the Vulgate, nothing of the sort could possibly have occurred. This departure from the letter of the Vulgate simplifies the story in order to concentrate upon a single triumphant note—the recapitulation of the heroine's victory over the forces of darkness by each of the *membra Christi*. For example, after the description of Judith's slaying of Holofernes and his descent into his native element, Judith's deed is called a *guð* (battle):

> Hæfde ða gefohten   foremærne blæd
> Iudith æt guðe,   swa hyre god uðe,
> swegles ealdor,   þe hyre sigores onleah.

> (122–24)

[Judith gained illustrious fame by fighting in battle, as God granted her, the Lord of heaven, who gave her victory.]

This battle diction looks forward to the victory of the Jewish people over the Assyrian army, just as in the description of that victory the diction hearkens back to Judith's slaying of Holofernes, knitting the two actions together: "*þær on greot gefeoll / se hyhsta dæl heafodgerimes*" (there on the earth fell the greatest part of the head count [307b-8]). A *hapax legomenon*, *heafodgerim* (head count) is an ironic counterpoint to Holofernes's decapitation.[11] A further example of the connection of these two deeds in the text may be found in its two uses of the verb *getacnian* (to symbolize). Judith tells the Bethulians:

---

11. When the Assyrian leaders learn of the death of Holofernes, they are referred to as *heafodweardas* (239).

"Fynd syndon eowere
gedemed to deaðe,   ond ge dom agon,
tir æt tohtan,   swa eow getacnod hafað
mihtig dryhten   þurh mine hand."

(195–98)

["Your enemies have been allotted death, and you will attain honor and
glory in battle, just as the mighty Lord has symbolized to you through my
hand."]

Her decapitation of Holofernes foreshadows the *dom* (honor) and *tir*
(glory) her townspeople will later gain in battle. The Assyrian leader
who found the body of Holofernes also sees the slaying as symbolic:

"Her ys geswutelod   ure sylfra forwyrd,
toweard getacnod   þæt þære tide ys
mid niðum neah geðrungen,   þe we sculon nyde losian,
somod æt sæcce forweorðan."

(285–88a)

["Here is revealed our own destruction, and it symbolizes the time of
tribulations that is approaching, when we must perish, and must all be
destroyed in battle."]

The individual death of Holofernes foreshadows the death of all his
minions while, at the same time, Judith's victory symbolizes the victory
of her townspeople.

This recapitulative principle is designed to operate within the
hearts and minds of the poem's audience, who are encouraged to carry
on their own spiritual warfare. At the conclusion of Judith's prayer
before the beheading of Holofernes, an authorial comment interrupts
the description of her actions:

Hi ða se hehsta dema
ædre mid elne onbryrde,   swa he deð anra gehwylcne
herbuendra   þe hyne him to helpe seceð
mid ræde ond mid rihte geleafan.

(94b–97a)

[Then the highest Judge immediately inspired her with courage, just as he does for each earth-dweller who seeks help from him with wisdom and true faith.]

The audience can recapitulate Judith's action and participate in her triumph, since God inspires all who seek his aid. Members of the audience are also Bethulians, in a manner of speaking, and Judith's story implicates them as well. It is the story of all who have *trum geleafa* (firm faith) at any point in history: Judith's anachronistic invocation of the *ðrynesse ðrym* (power of the Trinity, 86), presupposes Christian revelation. Bethulia and its residents mean more than meets the eye, for their city is described in terms reminiscent of the description of the heavenly Jerusalem in the New Testament. Bethulia was a *haligu burg* (holy city, 203), the conventional epithet for Jerusalem; it was a *beorhtu burg* (bright city, 326), a *wlitigu burg* (beautiful city, 137) whose *weallas blican* (walls shine, 137), not an arid, dusty, water-starved city huddled away in the hills of the Middle East. While listening to the heroic exploits of Judith and her fellow citizens, the audience *Judith* presumes could discover more about that City of God in which it shared membership.

The possibility of the victory of each of the members of *Ecclesia* over the powers of sin and Satan—a victory recapitulating individually that of Judith, who represents *Ecclesia* conceived of as a totality—rests on Judith's instructive example:

> eal þæt ða ðeodguman   þrymme geeodon,
> cene under cumblum   on compwige
> þurh Iudithe   gleawe lare,
> mægð modigre.

(331–34a)

[The warriors gained all that gloriously, bold under their banners in the battle, through the wise teaching of Judith, the courageous maiden.]

This emphasis on Judith's *gleaw lar* (wise teaching) indicates that she exemplifies a particular attribute of *Ecclesia*, the Church as teacher. Such a conception of the magisterial function of the Church had been advanced by Rabanus Maurus in his commentary on the book of Judith: "Judith ergo, quod Ecclesiae typum habeat, magistrorum traditio manifestat; interpretatur *confitens* vel *laudans* . . ." [Judith, therefore, who is a type of the Church, exemplifies the tradition of teachers; her name is to be interpreted as *confessing* or *praising* . . .][12] For Rabanus, who etymologizes her name after the fashion of Isidore of Seville's *Etymologiae*, Judith represents the Church as spiritual *magistra*. She teaches, as she taught the Jews, that true belief and praise of God result in salvation. Judith does not relish the physical emblems of her triumph over the historical Holofernes so much as the true reward she has merited:

> Ealles ðæs Iudith sægde
> wuldor weroda dryhtne,   þe hyre weorðmynde geaf,
> mærðe on moldan rice,   swylce eac mede on heofonum,
> sigorlean in swegles wuldre,   þæs þe heo ahte soðne geleafan
> to ðam ælmihtigan;   huru æt þam ende ne tweode
> þæs leanes þe heo lange gyrnde.
>
> (341b–46a)

[For all of that {treasure}, Judith glorified the Lord of Hosts, who gave her renown and glory on the kingdom of earth as well as a reward in heaven, a victory-reward in the glory of heaven because she always had true faith in the Almighty; indeed at the end she did not doubt the reward for which she had long yearned.]

Judith scarcely values her tokens of victory, referring all praise and glory to God, who rewarded her because she always kept *soð geleafa* (true belief). She looks forward, filled with faith and praise, to the heavenly reward her conquest of evil has merited.

The battle which was recast to communicate more effectively the allegorical core of meaning recapitulates the symbolic act of Judith, and points to the recapitulation of both actions by all members of the Church Militant who profit from the heroine's *gleaw lar*. The conquest of lust by chastity might be involved, but there are broader implications as well: the conquest by the members of *Ecclesia* of all the forces which weaken the living body of the Lord.

I

As we have seen, in allegorical readings like this one, the reader tends to become a member of the implicit audience the text creates for itself. I

---

12. Rabanus Maurus, *Expositio in Librum Judith*, *PL* 109:559.

would again begin the process of resisting such imaginary identification by attending to violent exclusions at the level of the sign in *Judith*. James Doubleday and Carl Berkhout reassert the traditional critical position that "the poet intensifies the contrast between Judith and Holofernes far beyond what he found in his original . . ."[13] The interest of the poem, according to Alvin A. Lee, "lies in the poet's spirited and colorful but highly stylized depiction of a sharply polarized conflict between a woman of God and a creature of Satan."[14] Such intensified oppositions, strengthening the slash separating *Ecclesia* from *Diabolus*, resemble those found in *Elene*. The literal and figurative violence of the poem makes sense in terms of the violent exclusions inherent in such dualities.

By eternalizing the conflict of opposites, narratives predicated upon such contrasting pairs as *Ecclesia* and *Diabolus* reinforce powerful cultural paradigms. Narrative shaped the early medieval Christian subject in his social and psychic dimensions, just as it shapes modern readers. The rhetoricity of *Judith* shows unmistakable signs of the influence of allegorical exegesis which, as I have argued in previous chapters, has multiple affiliations with politics and psychology. But what are we to make of the work's curious inattention to the tropological level, which many critics have read into the poem anyway? According to Rosemary Woolf, the Old English *Judith* is less concerned with the social and political dimensions of the Vulgate account than with the celebration of the heroine's chastity.[15] For Stanley Greenfield, the "poem is . . . almost a hymn to the virtuous maiden who conquered the dissolute Holofernes."[16] David Chamberlain joins me in contesting this tropological reading: "If the poem is limited to celebration mainly of Judith's own virtue, as critics claim, it is quite strange that the heroine is not praised specifically for her chastity or loyal widowhood anywhere in the Old English poem."[17] How are such tropological readings, unsupported by textual evidence, to be accounted for?

---

13. Doubleday and Berkhout, "The Net in *Judith* 46b–54a," *Neuphilologische Mitteilungen* 74 (1973): 633.

14. Lee, *The Guest-Hall of Eden: Four Essays on the Design of Old English Poetry* (New Haven, 1972), 50.

15. Woolf, "The Lost Opening to the *Judith*," *Modern Language Review* 1 (1955): 171.

16. Greenfield, *A Critical History of Old English Literature* (London, 1966), 165.

17. Chamberlain, "*Judith*: A Fragmentary and Political Poem," in *Anglo-Saxon Poetry: Essays in Appreciation*, ed. Lewis E. Nicholson and Dolores Warwick Frese (Notre Dame, Ind., 1975), 154–55. However, he also claims that "an important corollary to this de-emphasizing of chastity is the de-emphasis of allegory" (155).

It might be argued that chastity is deemphasized because it is a narrative given, a textual element so obvious that it goes without saying. While such an answer might be correct, it is not very illuminating. The disproportion between these two exegetical levels might be conceptualized as the problem of the one and the many: while the tropological level concerns the individual (and, in this case, involves undeveloped sexual dimensions of the source), the allegorical concerns society, specifically the battle of *Ecclesia* against *Diabolus*. A strictly tropological reading misses the social encoding of sexuality in the work: *Judith* addresses the conflict of sexual restraint and sexual indulgence only to the extent that a societal discipline of desire marks the ideal reader, or hearer.

In the Liber Iudith, the heroine's prayer for strength to carry out her plot is explicitly concerned with such social encoding of sexuality:

> Domine Deus patris mei Simeon, qui dedisti illi gladium in defensionem alienigenarum, qui violatores exstiterunt in coinquinatione sua, et denudaverunt femur virginis in confusionem, et dedisti mulieres illorum in praedam, et filias illorum in captivitatem . . . subveni, queso te, Domine Deus meus, mihi viduae.[18]

> [O Lord God of my father Simeon, who gave him a sword to execute vengeance against strangers who had defiled and assaulted the virgin in uncleanness and confusion, and who gave their wives away as booty and sent their daughters into capitivity . . . assist, I beseech thee, O Lord God, me a widow.]

Judith alludes to the sword of Simeon in Genesis. After Sichem's rape of Dina, Jacob's sons demanded that the Sichimites be circumcised before reconciliation could take place. Three days after their circumcision, *"quando gravissimus vulnerum dolor est"* (when the pain of the wound was greatest), Dina's brothers Simeon and Levi slew all the Sichimite males with their swords; Jacob's other sons plundered the city in order to revenge the rape.[19] Circumcision was merely the prelude to slaughter, and resulted in the military impotency of the Sichimites—evidently, it is difficult to fight when your foreskin has just been sliced off. The sons of Jacob took full advantage of their weakness, avenging one man's crime with genocide. Judith prays specifically to the God of Simeon, whose

---

18. Liber Iudith 9.2–3. Even those who see *Judith* as a much briefer work agree that this must have been part of the material covered in the original Old English poem.
19. Genesis 34.25–27.

sword of vengeance followed the knife of circumcision, while anticipating her own use of the sword. The Sichimites actually raped Dina, while Holofernes merely intends sexual intercourse with Judith. But the sword will follow his desire nonetheless—literally, the sword of Holofernes himself, symbolically the sword of the patriarch Simeon, who stands in the place of father or husband for Judith.

When Achior, captain of the Ammonites, sees the eventual military success of the Jews against the Assyrians he decides to convert:

> Tunc Achior, videns virtutem, quam fecit Deus Israel, relicto gentilitatis ritu, credidit Deo, et circumcidit carnem praeputii sui, et appositus est ad populum Israel, et omnis successio generis ejus usque in hodiernum diem. Mox autem, ut ortus est dies, suspenderunt super muros caput Holofernis, accepitque unusquisque vir arma sua, et egressi sunt cum grandi strepitu et ululatu.[20]

> [Leaving the religion of the Gentiles, he believed God, and circumcised the flesh of his foreskin, and was joined to the people of Israel with all the succession of his kindred until this present day. And immediately at daybreak, they hung Holofernes's head upon the walls, and every man took his arms, and they went out with a great noise and shouting.]

The Vulgate juxtaposes Achior's circumcision with the ritually displayed head of the decapitated Holofernes.[21] Two distinctive symbolic practices thus merge, marking the power of the Israelites in both religious and political terms. When Achior gives up his religion for a more powerful one, circumcision serves as an emblem for the change. Circumcision inscribes the body itself with the distinguishing mark of absence. Just as cutting off the head of Holofernes functions as a sign of Jewish strength and Assyrian defeat, so does the excision of the foreskin of Achior's penis. It is a ritual of bodily excision enabled by the previous decapitation. Immediately after this metonymic juxtaposition of circumcision and decapitation, the Assyrians visit Holofernes's tent, where *"intolerabilis timor et tremor cecidit super eos, et turbati sunt animi eorum valde"* (14.17) [an intolerable fear and dread fell upon them, and their minds

---

20. Liber Iudith 14.6–7.
21. A ritual practiced in England during the Middle Ages and Renaissance as well. See D. W. Robertson, Jr., *Chaucer's London* (New York, 1968), 147 and Michel Foucault, *Discipline and Punish: The Birth of the Prison*, trans. Alan Sheridan (New York, 1979), 45.

were troubled exceedingly]. They are clearly powerless after coming to understand that their leader is dead.

Textual strands of rape, circumcision, and decapitation are curiously intertwined in the Vulgate account. The circumcision of Achior is juxtaposed with decapitation, a metonymeme mirrored in Judith's allusion to the sword of Simeon, which slaughtered the circumcised Sichimites. Simeon's revenge—genocidal slaughter in response to a sister's rape—is specifically cited by Judith as she prepares to leave for the Assyrian camp, where her beauty will provoke Holofernes's desire.

In the course of establishing a feminist reading that foregrounds sexuality and politics in *Judith*, Alexandra Hennessey Olsen rejects the contributions of allegorical critics:

> Students of the Old English *Judith* . . . usually read the poem in the light of Patristic and early medieval commentaries on its source, the Biblical Liber Iudith, assuming that the poem makes the the same points which the commentators believed that the Liber Iudith made and that it is an allegory about the Church or the triumph of chastity. Stanley B. Greenfield has criticized such interpretations for "pumping external cultural knowledge into a text instead of allowing textual meaning to flow out."[22]

No doubt some critics do what Olsen and Greenfield attack them for doing. But I am more concerned with the Jerusalem of critical practice for Olsen and Greenfield than with their Babylon. The figure of speech which sees textual meaning flowing out of a text without being deflected by the critic naturalizes criticism: Exegetics is represented as filling the text with fluid when all that's needed is turning a shuttlecock so meaning can flow out, along the path of least resistance.

Olsen's response to typological readings of either the tropological or allegorical kind—that is, to those emphasizing the second or third of the four allegorical levels—updates earlier approaches that related alterations of the Vulgate to Anglo-Saxon political history. The critical difference is that Olsen finds a feminist history and politics to the poem:

> I would argue that [the decapitation] presents an ironic inversion of that realistic situation in which men reduce women to objects to be abused and

22. Olsen, "Inversion and Political Purpose in the Old English *Judith*," *English Studies* 63 (1982): 289.

that the decapitation of Holofernes is presented as the symbolic rape of a man by a woman.[23]

Whether this is eisegesis or exegesis, pumping in external cultural knowledge or allowing meaning to flow out, remains an open question. But Olsen puts her finger on an unsettling aspect of the poem, what Burton Raffel called "the sense of disquiet—sometimes reaching rather intense levels—which I experienced while translating *Judith*."[24] This disquiet led Raffel to a curious stylistic break with traditional modes of critical discourse in Old English studies: "I do not propose an elaborate self-analysis; neither do I intend self-advertisement." The notion that the poem might call for a self-analysis—one excluded immediately upon introduction—is a critical feint at the margins of Raffel's nagging personal discomfort: "My basic perception about the poem is precisely that uncomfortable awareness of there being something—not perhaps wrong, but certainly not quite right." My own reaction to the poem is characterized by a similar sense of disquiet.

Like David Chamberlain, Olsen sees the poem serving a practical political purpose. For her, the disturbing sexual violence of the poem was historically motivated:

> Although Judith does indeed kill and not rape Holofernes, the scene is startling, and it seems designed to shock its audience and keep the subject of rape in their conscious minds. It seems, therefore, that *Judith* may have been written for an audience which included women in danger of rape and spiritual abuse by pagans and who had as little real protection as Judith, alone in the Assyrian camp.[25]

As evidence of the oppression that Anglo-Saxon women endured during the late tenth and early eleventh centuries, she cites *Sermo Lupi*: "One common abuse was the gang rape of Englishwomen by the Danes, a situation made worse by the fact that English noblemen were powerless to protect the women . . ." But an authorial design to keep rape in the conscious minds of the audience seems unlikely, and Olsen's use of

---

23. Ibid., 291.
24. Raffel, "*Judith*: Hypermetricity and Rhetoric" in *Anglo-Saxon Poetry*, ed. Nicholson and Frese. All quotations are from p. 124. Raffel deals with his intense discomfort in strict formalist terms, focusing upon problematic instances of hypermetricity in the poem.
25. Olsen, "Inversion," 292.

historical analogues is open to question. Evidently the trick is in seeing to it that only internal meaning flows out, since external cultural knowledge seems to find its way in willy-nilly.

But another theoretical issue arises here as well. The premise underlying Olsen's work, like Chamberlain's, is that *Judith* cannot be political and allegorical at the same time. This kind of false dichotomy shows up often in discussions of allegorical criticism, and not only from those who oppose what they take to be its reductive procedures. Typological critics themselves tend to confuse arguing for an allegorical dimension to an Old English work with arguing that the purpose of the work is allegory. We must recognize that plurivocity of text and subject need not be reduced to univocity by critics. Since allegory is already a form of textual and cultural politics, the move beyond identifying allegory to thinking through its psycho-social implications is a desideratum for Anglo-Saxon studies.

There is no good reason why allegorical dimensions cannot coexist with sexual violence in *Judith*. But I would respond to Olsen's notion of symbolic rape by directing attention to the psychoanalytic process of castration. Doing so means sidestepping the question of immediate historical motivation. Olsen's historical background may or may not be germane; I would focus on the more general historical level of the formation of the Christian subject.

In a mapping of the poem according to Freud's second topology, Judith would be identified with the superego on account of her devotion to duty, Holofernes with the id on the basis of the Old English text's characterization of his uncontrollable desire. Where tropology would see conflict between opposing forces of good and evil within the soul, a psychoanalytic reading would locate them within the psyche. I would modify the work of Huppé and Olsen by situating the theme of the conflict between chastity and lust in the subtext. Attention to diction, characterization, and emplotment leads to concentration on the allegorical level; when attention shifts to the implicit subtext, the tropological level will be emphasized. The thematics of castration bridge explicit allegory and implicit tropology in *Judith*.

Holofernes exemplifies a hypertrophied masculinity. Loud, dominant, and drunk, he is a male parody. But the transcendent male principle of divine patriarchy protects Judith. In the triangle of Judith, Holofernes, and Jehovah, Holofernes is the one blinded by desire: he cannot even conceive of the prior (spiritual) male possession of Judith. Yet

Holofernes, at his worldly apogee, wields a visionary power that leaves others unseeing. He radiates power—and from his bed, of all places. Yet the potency central to Assyrian dominance is veiled in a net that functions like a one-way mirror:

> Þær wæs eallgylden
> fleohnet fæger   ymbe þæs folctogan
> bed ahongen,   þæt se bealofulla
> mihte wlitan þurh,   wigena baldor,
> on æghwylcne   þe ðær inne com
> hæleða bearna,   ond on hyne nænig
> monna cynnes,   nymðe se modiga hwæne
> niðe rofra   him þe near hete
> rinca to rune gegangan.

(46b–54a)

[There was a beautiful golden fly net there, hung around the bed of the leader so the wicked prince of warriors might look upon any of the sons of men who came in there, but no man could look upon him unless, brave man, he bade one of his strong soldiers to come nearer for discussion.]

Carl Berkhout and James Doubleday cite Gregory's *Moralia in Job* to demonstrate that flies represent "carnal desires which intrude upon the soul," and assert that "the figurative use of the net is frequent in the Old Testament."[26] They cite Huppé on the significance of the *fleohnet* in the portrait of Holofernes as a false god:

> In developing his description of Holofernes' bed . . . the poet concentrates on the *fleohnet*, creating for it the function of preventing anyone from gazing through it, but permitting Holofernes to look out. . . . The netting with its suggestion of the mysterious presence of a god-like figure, not seen, but seeing all . . . suggests an analogy to the veil of the holy of holies within the temple . . . The canopy itself may represent, according to Rabanus, "the snares of deceitful thoughts," and the analogy between the canopy and the veil carries with it an ominous implication . . . . Holofernes is a simulacrum of God, but he is false, and the canopy cannot protect him against the daughter of God."[27]

---

26. Doubleday and Berkhout, "The Net in *Judith*," 632, 633.
27. Huppé, *The Web of Words* (Albany, 1970), 163–64.

The poem presents an earthly male ruler, represented as a false God, attempting to conquer a woman devoted to the true Father, Yawheh. In this scene of Holofernes's veiled sexuality and power, both politics and allegory are implicated.[28]

The central Freudian text for understanding the psychoanalytic significance of the decapitation inflicted upon Holofernes is an essay entitled "Medusa's Head." There Freud devotes his interpretive powers to the curiously evocative hair of the Medusa:

> To decapitate = to castrate. The terror of Medusa is thus a terror of castration that is linked to the sight of something. Numerous analyses have made us familiar with the occasion for this: it occurs when a boy, who has hitherto been unwilling to believe the threat of castration, catches sight of the female genitals, probably those of an adult, surrounded by hair, and essentially those of his mother. The hair upon Medusa's head is frequently represented in works of art in the form of snakes, and these once again are derived from the castration complex. It is a remarkable fact that, however frightening they may be in themselves, they nevertheless serve actually as a mitigation of the horror, for they replace the penis, the absence of which is the cause of the horror. This is a confirmation of the technical rule according to which a multiplication of penis symbols signifies castration . . . This symbol of horror is worn upon her dress by the virgin goddess Athene. And rightly so, for thus she becomes a woman who is unapproachable and repels all sexual desires . . .[29]

Within the psychoanalytic model, the decapitation of Holofernes is a castration, as seen in Freud's terse remark "To decapitate = to castrate." Such a linking of castration and decapitation occurs in the Liber

---

28. This violent suppression of sexual desire by the superego was also found in the *Psychomachia*. In a scene which informs a reading of *Judith*'s subtext, *Pudicitia*—the particular manifestation of the superego called into existence by sexual desire—thrusts her sword into *Sodomita Libido*'s throat, giving rise to an exceptionally gruesome description of bloody slaughter explicitly linked to Holofernes's slaying. Prudentius's tropological interpretation of the Judith-Holofernes story provokes a meditation on the power of every Christian to sever the vice's head, since the Incarnation has proven *omnis iam diva caro est* "all flesh is divine now" (76), and the bodies of Christians *purgata suo serventur . . . regi* "must be saved for their own king" (97).

29. Sigmund Freud, "Medusa's Head," trans. James Strachey, in *The Standard Edition of the Complete Psychological Works of Sigmund Freud* (London, 1955), 18:273. See also Hélène Cixous, "Castration or Decapitation?" trans. Annette Kuhn, *Signs* 7 (1981): 41–55.

Iudith when it juxtaposes decapitation with Achior's circumcision, the severed head of Holofernes paralleling the severed head of Achior's penis. The circumcision which functions as a military ruse to incapacitate the Sichimites, leading to the slaughter of the rapists' nation, is invoked by Judith as she summons up the strength to decapitate Holofernes. In her prayer for courage, the sword of decapitation is explicitly linked to the sword of circumcision/castration that wounds the Sichimites' genitals so they can be defeated in battle. Normally, the ritual of circumcision signifies the acceptance of an empowering castration that constitutes membership in society at the same time that it wounds the subject. But the Sichimite circumcision destroys a people under the pretext of incorporating them among the Israelites. Such an ironic circumcision, intended to debilitate and not to empower, is also castration. There are two castrations in psychoanalytic theory, a good one which enables human subjectivity to occur, and a bad one which incapacitates. What links the tropological level of a battle between chastity against lust with the allegorical level of a conflict between *Ecclesia* and *Diabolus* is circumcision, the violent bodily inscription of an empowering castration that renders male desire socially constitutive.

Just before the decapitation of Holofernes, we encounter the following brief, but significant, description of Judith:

> Genam ða wundenlocc,
> scyppendes mægð   scearpne mece
> scurum heardne,   ond of sceaðe abræd
> swiðran folme.

(77b–80a)

[Then the woman with curly hair, the maiden of the Creator, seized a sharp sword, hardened by the storms of battle, and drew it from its sheath with her right hand.]

At the crucial moment of decapitation, the same description recurs:

> Sloh ða wundenlocc
> þone feondsceaðan   fagum mece
> heteþoncolne,   þæt heo healfne forcearf
> þone sweoran him,   þæt he on swiman læg,
> druncen ond dolhwund.

(103b–7a)

[Then the woman with curly hair struck the hateful enemy with her shining sword so that she cut halfway through his neck and he lay swooning, drunk, and wounded.]

In each of these cases, Judith appears as *wundenlocc*, antonomasia which can mean either "with curly hair" or "with braided hair." The first meaning is the preferred one, since the Jews are later referred to as *wundenlocc* when they pillage the Assyrian camp:

Þa seo cneoris eall,
mægða mærost,   anes monðes fyrst,
wlanc, wundenlocc,   wagon ond læddon
to ðære beorhtan byrig,   Bethuliam,
helmas ond hupseax,   hare byrnan,
guðsceorp gumena. . . .

(323a–28a)

[Then, for an entire month, the whole nation, most famous of peoples, proud and curly-haired, carried and transported into the shining city of Bethulia helmets and hip swords, grey coats of mail, the armor of warriors . . . .]

Since there would seem to be no good reason for imagining Jewish soldiers with braids, "with curly hair" is the standard gloss here as elsewhere in the poem. The powerful *wundenlocc* Judith decapitates Holofernes, and later the Bethulians too are *wundenlocc* by antonomasia in their triumphant division of the spoils of war.

The only other use of the word in Old English occurs in *Riddle 25*:

Ic eom wunderlicu wiht,   wifum on hyhte,
neahbuendum nyt;   nængum sceþþe
burgsittendra,   nymþe bonan anum.
Staþol min is steapheah,   stonde ic on bedde,
neoþan ruh nathwær.   Neþeð hwilum
ful cyrtenu   ceorles dohtor,
modwlonc meowle,   þæt heo on mec gripeð,
ræseð mec on reodne,   reafað min heafod,
fegeð mec on fæsten.   Feleþ sona
mines gemotes,   seo þe mec nearwað,
wif wundenlocc.   Wæt bið þæt eage.

[I am a wonderful creature to a hopeful wife, useful for neighbors; I harm none of the city dwellers besides my slayer. My base is erect; I stand up in bed and I am shaggy somewhere beneath. Sometimes the beautiful daughter of a peasant, a courageous girl, will venture to grab hold of me; she assaults my red skin, grasps my head, clamps me in a tight place. Soon she who confines me, the curly-haired woman, feels the effects of my meeting with her. Her eye will get wet.]

On the literal level, the solution is "onion." But, of course, this level screens the other solution, "penis." This talking penis in *Riddle 25* tells how the *modwlonc wif wundenlocc* (courageous curly-haired woman) assaults him, *reafað* (seizes) his head, and clamps him in a *fæsten* (fastness, tight place)—meaning, one can only suppose, that she takes him into her vagina. The sexual intercourse of the riddle's conclusion is initially castration when the penis/onion is plucked from the ground by the courageous, *wundenlocc* woman. The riddle's humor depends upon the anxiety produced when the fates of the riddle's tenors are transposed: if we read "onion," the vegetable is plucked from its bed and its greens chopped off; but if we read "penis," the poem becomes a violent description of castration which segues into a playful description of sexual intercourse.

The penis is *ruh* (shaggy) underneath, a reference to pubic hair. Whether the curly hair of the *wif* grows on her head or on her genitals, the word *wundenlocc* occurs in the context of violent feminine appropriation of the talking penis. This monastic riddle deals with fear of castration by woman's dark place, which monks had reason to fear as individuals and as a group. The screen for this fear is erotic pleasure at the notion of such aggressive feminine desire for the penis, which is seized and thrust into a *fæsten* (fastness)—or "cloister" if the monastic site is acknowledged in translation. As in *Judith*, joy and terror are linked, the riddle's obscene description of sexual intercourse alternating with its frightening description of castration, as the penis is seized and assaulted by the female body. The curly-haired, decapitating/castrating Judith is also a source of pleasure and fear depending, of course, upon one's point of view. The Old English *Judith* elicits ambivalent emotional responses to the *wundenlocc* heroine, who is both object of desire and violent avenger of those who desire unmediated access to her.

We must respect the difference between phallus and penis in order to avoid too literal a reading of castration in psychoanalytic theory.

Castration should not be conceived simply as the male child's fear that his penis will be—or the female child's that it has already been—cut off. The symbolic value of the phallus and castration lies elsewhere. In Lacan's influential version of Freudian castration theory, the phallus plays the role of the signifier *par excellence*: the penis refers to the male organ, while the phallus refers to its symbolic values of potency, authority, and power.[30] For Lacan, if the phallus is the signifier of desire, the Oedipus complex involves the distinction between *being* and *having* the phallus.

The desires of the three participants in the family romance hinge upon this distinction, which is itself the result of a scene of conflict. The child desires the mother, wishing to become what she lacks. Desiring the desire of the mother in this fashion, the child identifies with its ultimate object, the phallus. Before the Oedipus complex is resolved, the child is subjugated to this desire to be the desire of the mother, and to that extent excluded from the status of a full human subjectivity. The child does not yet exist in the symbolic order, but in the imaginary realm of identification with the object of the mother's desire. The Oedipus problematizes this identification for the child, thereby allowing entry into the symbolic order. For this entry to occur, the father must play his cultural role of denial and deprivation: he deprives the mother of the child as the phallus completing her lack, and denies the child's desire to be the phallus for the mother. As a consequence of the father's role as denier (Lacan puns on the *nom du père* and the *non du père*), the child will identify not with the mother, but with the father who has the phallus, but only if the mother acknowledges his authority as representative of the Law:

> The father reinstates the phallus as the object of the mother's desire, and no longer as the child-complement to what is lacking in her. The child's identification with the father announces the passing of the Oedipus by way of "having" (and no longer "being"). He is either he who has the phallus or he who does not have it, or he who can give or receive it in a full sexual relationship. At the same time, a symbolic castration takes place: the father castrates the child by separating it from its mother. This is the debt

---

30. See Jacques Lacan, "The Signification of the Phallus," in *Écrits: A Selection*, trans. Alan Sheridan (New York, 1977), 281–91; John P. Muller and William J. Richardson, *Lacan and Language: A Reader's Guide to Écrits* (New York, 1982), 332–54; J. Laplanche and J.-B. Pontalis, *The Language of Psychoanalysis*, trans. D. N. Smith (New York, 1973), s.v. "phallus."

which must be paid if one is to become completely oneself and have access to the order of the symbol, of culture and of civilization.[31]

The phallus, then, is not so much a physiological as a symbolic term. The child wishes to *be* the phallus for the mother, but the father forbids this. The child is marked, necessarily, with a lack:

> Castrated, that is removed from his mother by the paternal interdiction, the child must renounce the omnipotence of his desire and accept a Law of limitation: he must assume his lack . . . . By assuming the Law of his father, the child passes from the register of being (the all-powerful phallus) to the register of having (having a limited and legitimate desire which can be formulated in an utterance) and enters into a quest for objects which are further and further removed from the initial object of his desire.[32]

Through the Oedipus, we become members of society, real human subjects. The acceptance of castration is constitutive of the subject's identity, translating the originary object of desire to be translated into culturally approved surrogates. Within Christianity, a variety of techniques are employed to displace desire for the mother to desire for what is pleasing to *Ecclesia* as *Mater*. Castration means losing the power to enact one's originary desire but, paradoxically, this powerlessness that results from subjection to authority also produces psychosocial empowerment.

Holofernes's decapitation, a loss of the phallus, is a gain for the Jews, the circumcised people. As an outward emblem of the acceptance of castration necessary to one's identity as a member of the people of God, circumcision marks Jews as separate from heathens.[33] To turn from the psychoanalytic to the exegetical register: if on the allegorical level circumcision is socially constitutive, producing the group as it empowers the individual, on the tropological level it represents the disciplining of desire, particularly sexual desire, within *Ecclesia*, or within the monastic subgroup.

---

31. Anika Lemaire, *Jacques Lacan*, trans. David Macey (London, 1977), 83.

32. Ibid., 87.

33. For Freud, "circumcision is unconsciously equated with castration. If we venture to carry our conjectures back to the primaeval days of the human race we can surmise that originally circumcision must have been a milder substitute, designed to take the place of castration" ("Leonardo da Vinci and a Memory of His Childhood," trans. Alan Tyson, in *The Standard Edition of the Complete Psychological Works of Sigmund Freud* [London, 1957], 11:95–96).

This discipline of the soul initiated by circumcision is a continual process of acceptance of the castrating Law of the Father; and it engenders a compensatory rebellion, as monastic literature has always recognized—I am thinking of traditions of pastoral care and monastic discipline, as well as curiosities like *Riddle 25*. Holofernes represents this rebellion within the soul. He plays the role of the (bad) son in the Oedipus who wants unmediated access to the mother. Holofernes desires Judith without passing through the channeling of desire imposed by Judaism; hence, his sin parallels that of the Sichimites. Rebellious drives in the Christian subject are cathected by the characterization of Holofernes, allowing for powerful investments in the eventual crushing of his raging desire. His rebuke is also a rebuke issued to the ravenous id, which threatens the well-being of the soul, and therefore must be suppressed. His decapitation is a castration which reiterates the process of entry into the symbolic order: those who refuse to accept the castration required by the Church can likewise expect to come to a horrible end. Judith as *mater*, the object of displaced desire, can be possessed only through the frustration of desire by phallic authority. Such an acceptance of the necessity of the Church's prohibitions, which embody the Law of the divine Father, guides desire productively. Castration names this process of psychic formation necessary to the ongoing constitution of the Christian subject.

Judith's imaginative treatment of licit and illicit desire fashions an implicit reader. In Oedipal terms, the audience is encouraged to take up the position of having the phallus rather than being it—that is, taking on authority and power from *Ecclesia* as *mater* only after first surrendering to its authority and power, rather than allowing desire to remain unmediated. Holofernes is denied direct possession of Judith, *Ecclesia* as *mater* on the allegorical level, because possession must be channeled through the sanctions of the heavenly Father. The decapitation of Holofernes represents the threat of castration for those who refuse to acknowledge the authority of the Church in deed, word, or thought.

Burton Raffel's intense sense of disquiet, his uncomfortable awareness that there was something not quite right—but which did *not* require self-analysis or self-advertisement—can be read as his experience of terror and joy at Holofernes's decapitation/castration. The powerful emotions released in the audience, I would argue, reinforce the social and psychological constraints of the symbolic order represented by the

Church.[34] *Judith* recommends having the phallus, acceding to potency and authority through the acceptance of castration. The failure of Holofernes to be the phallus, to work his will upon a Judith who is the symbolic *mater et magistra*, reaffirms the authority of the Father-God. Holofernes's exemplary failure in the role of rebellious son and lover in the Oedipus encourages subject-formation by Church authority. A symbolic castration is ritually enacted in baptism, the sublation of circumcision in the Old Law. Baptism writes a character, the *sphragis*, upon the body and within the soul of one who would become a subject of the Church. Christian identity is constructed upon the acceptance of castration in a spiritual circumcision which, as the allegorical exegetes knew, is not a one-time event, but a lifelong process.[35]

Acceptance of castration on the part of the monastic audience for *Judith* is more complete than for the lay audience: the monastic renunciation of sexual intercourse generates power, including the priestly ability to speak in the name of the arche-Father. *Ecclesia* as *mater* is administered by men who speak for her. The priesthood wielding power is castrated with respect to enjoyment of woman's body, in order to wield authority over the feminine body of the faithful. Clergy are qualified to lead because they have gone further in their renunciation of desire. When the monks took their mixed pleasure in the obscene riddle of the *wundenlocc* plucking the penis, or the decapitation of an Assyrian king looking forward to a night of sexual pleasure, they were also reaffirming their identity as subjects of the discourse of *Ecclesia*. Illicit desire, whether the pleasure of humor or the excitement of dramatic encounter, is opened up by these texts only to be prohibited.

The law of the father, which requires the child to surrender his desire to possess the mother, means that he can no longer be the phallus, although he can have the phallus by submitting to paternal restrictions. Social empowerment follows upon the acceptance of those restrictions. Judith decapitates Holofernes to support the true possessor of authority, God. Holofernes remains a mere pretender, within the veil of his false holy of holies, to the authority of the divine patriarch who is the only

---

34. Castration is threatening and reassuring at the same time: threatening, because the decapitation/castration could be the subject's; reassuring, because it is Holofernes's fate. Castration/beheading in *Judith* is apotropaic, since accepting the good castration of submission to *Ecclesia* wards off the bad castration a character like Holofernes must suffer.

35. On Baptism as circumcision, see Jean Daniélou, *The Bible and the Liturgy* (Notre Dame, Ind., 1961), 63–67.

legitimate husband to the widowed Judith as *Ecclesia*: for *Ecclesia* can be married only to God, in a union that is ultimately apocalyptic. In psychoanalytic terms, Holofernes's attempt to be the phallus when he can only have the phallus is coextensive with his role as pretender to the position only Yawheh can fill. The subject can take possession of Judith only in the name of and under the law of the Father, in this case the patriarchal order with its social and theological components. He is allowed only mediated access to the place of the Father. Holofernes's lust for Judith represents an attempt to enact the childish desire of the id for the mother. Disdaining the prerogatives of the Father God, he is slaughtered for his brazenness. The old enemy, Satan, is the privileged exemplar of such a spirit of rebellion and titanic self-assertion, and Holofernes represents diabolical resistance to the constraints of membership in *Ecclesia*. Punishment of the desire of Holofernes as *Diabolus* is at the same time punishment for unmediated desire. Renunciation of desire for the unmediated possession of the mother and for expression of genital sexuality is constitutive of the monastic subject.

Desire and its violent suppression figured in terms of the false holy of holies that covers up the primal scene: its one-way mirror effect means the copulating king and his consort can always see the Assyrians, intratextual witnesses who cannot return their gaze. As victims of the fantasized primal scene of father and mother in bed, this internal audience is readied for the very slaughter their leader will suffer. Such curiosities of the gaze in *Judith* are made possible by the veiling of Holofernes's bed in its *fleohnet*, which is at the same time the veiling of the power of the phallus.

Psychology is political in *Judith*. While Olsen and Chamberlain follow earlier critics in seeking a *poème à clef*, the politics I argue for is not bound to a specific historical event, unless the very concept of a historical event is taken in an extended sense. A specific historical source for the poem may be agreed upon one day; but that hasn't happened yet, and such a direct opening to history and politics seems unlikely precisely because so many have already been advanced. We have an embarrassment of specific historical parallels, with no accepted criteria for deciding upon one or the other. Rather than argue for a specific historical occasion, I would focus upon broader historical processes. *Judith* demonstrates how a literary text can inculcate the values necessary for the formation of the early medieval subject. Just as Judith is subjected to God as Father, the symbolic mother *Ecclesia* must be served according to the law of the father, which defers satisfaction according to the sexual code of Anglo-Saxon monastic society. The monastic subject sublates sexual desire into the desire for God. Judith is victorious because her desire is not sexual, but political. She longs not for the phallus as penis, but for the phallus itself without an intermediary sexual relationship with a powerful earthly male.

In *De Laudibus Dei*, Dracontius sees Judith as a "manly woman," reinscribing her in terms of the myth of the hermaphrodite.[36] She is manly in multiple ways, chiefly in her possession of the phallus, despite her lack of the penis—or renunciation of the penis in a life of widowhood and continence. Her worldly and political success is achieved through her lack of desire for the actual penis. In much the same way, the female or male monastic subject does not desire the enjoyment of the penis—and here I rely on the ambiguity of the genitive—but translates sexual desire into a religious dimension. This desire for the possession of the phallus becomes reinscribed as war against Holofernes's attempt to *be* the phallus, a war which results in victory for the social body of *Ecclesia*.

Another battle occurs on the level of the politics of poetics. Holofernes's reign is described in terms of conventions handed down from the pagan Germanic past for representing a rapacious *cyning* and small warrior band of terrified soldiers. *Judith* invokes the poetic heritage of the Anglo-Saxons as a warning against the politics of the old world, a historical recontextualization in support of the new reign of Christian authority. Conquest and political power will no longer be achieved in the old fashion. Such poetic displacement of heroism onto the shoulders of a manly woman warrior is not the least of this unsettling poem's charms.

---

36. Dracontius, *De Laudibus Dei*, ed. F. Vollmer, in *Monumenta Germaniae Historica, Auctores Antiquissimi* (Berlin, 1905), 14:105. The importance of this phrase was first noted by Bernard F. Huppé, *The Web of Words*, 167.

Afterword

As flowers turn toward the sun, by dint of a secret heliotropism the past
strives to turn toward that sun which is rising in the sky of history.
Walter Benjamin, "Theses on the
Philosophy of History"

Allegories of War is informed by what has come to be known as critical
theory, a term covering a wide variety of approaches now bobbing in the
wake of the capsized New Criticism. Most Anglo-Saxonists have taken
on Deor's attitude in response to this critical turbulence: *Þæs ofereode,*
þisses swa mæg! There may be some sense in this position, although I
suspect there is also some intellectual timidity—if you have not recently
had your tenure revoked, like Deor, the attitude smacks of complacency
rather than wisdom. I would argue instead that critical theory offers a
remarkably productive vantage point from which to read Old English
literature.

In employing this spatial and visual metaphor, I do not mean to
represent theory as somehow outside the field gazed upon *in figura*;
rather, it is a site that opens within philology itself when traditional
approaches block inquiry. Exegetics and New Criticism are dominated
by philological presuppositions conditioning the kinds of questions that
can be posed, and the kinds of answers that can be rendered. The
theoretical moment in Old English studies occurs when one allows one-
self to encounter such presuppositions, and to recognize them as limits
governing the discipline. I do not mean to suggest that the philological
heritage hasn't produced enormous successes. The problem is that it has
been all too successful; its very dominance keeps Old English studies
from developing in new directions. The moment for critical theory in

Old English studies is not outside but inside philology and its problems, since only the prior existence of philology makes theory possible. The move "beyond" philology takes place within it.[1]

In reading Old English poetic structures as psychically and socially constitutive, *Allegories of War* transgresses the limits of the inherited philological model. Examination of these larger rhetorical structures after Derrida and de Man means posing a different kind of literary question within Anglo-Saxon studies. The value of such different perspectives, as with more conventional approaches, depends on whether or not readers find such lines of argument useful. And that depends upon whether those who evaluate new approaches are able to reflect upon the borders within which Old English studies are normally conducted.

But why, the reader might ask, is such critical reflexivity—or such a tactical intervention as *Allegories of War*—necessary at all? The preceding chapters offer various answers to these questions. But to put these answers into a form that is more succinct, and hence more general and less trustworthy, this kind of book is necessary because the dominant paradigm of Exegetics in league with the old New Criticism has been producing a series of readings which occlude the rhetorical specificity of Old English literature. This series, which has been enabled by its failure to question textual categories, shows no sign of abating, and is leading to the increasing marginalization of Old English studies. To epitomize in a fashion perhaps excusable in an Afterword, the critic of Old English literature typically devotes himself to a mirroring operation which values texts on account of their complex crafstsmanship (New Criticism, as practiced by Old English critics) or their disclosure of a privileged and recherché theological system (Exegetics). When Exegetics and New Criticism work in league with one another they are heroic, even saintlike, in their fidelity to the rhetorical structures of texts, especially if faith is construed as the suspension of critical thinking. The conceptual categories of Old English literature are treated as hypostasized givens, not as textual processes with a conflictual rhetoricity that is necessary to their work in the world. Scholarship and criticism based on this paradigm are oriented toward complicity with rather than critical examination of such textual processes. This often results in a desiccated criticism

---

1. Paul de Man, "The Return to Philology," in *The Resistance to Theory* (Minneapolis, 1986), 21–26.

characterized by the scholarly fallacy (to discover a paraliterary source or analogue is to construct an adequate reading), and by a voluntary or involuntary conservatism. The complexities of Anglo-Saxon literary artifacts are often praised, but seldom put into question. Many of these critics, one comes to discover, are partisans of the values of the Middle Ages who take post-Romantic thought as a regrettable decline.

But even when such values are not applauded by the scholar-critic, one finds a reluctance to interrogate the rhetorical structurations, values, and oppositions which play themselves out in the text. In neither Exegetics nor in New Criticism—*a fortiori* technico-scientific analyses or organic literary histories—is the politics of textuality broached, the social workings of the rhetorical operations of text and critic. Construed as a preexistent given, the text is rendered immune to critical thinking. Such immunity corresponds to the immunity of critical methods from sustained reflection, a pairing of self-assured self-evidentialities that requires training but not education of the practitioner. These methods leave little for reflexive questioning, the interpretation of interpretations which Montaigne found to be more necessary than the interpretation of things, and hence not much room for growth. To execute a program like New Criticism or Exegetics is to put oneself within borders that reward industry more than thought, extension of the dominant paradigm rather than reflection on the nature of the object and method of investigation.

Allegories of War views poems not as sacrosanct unities to be mirrored, but as scenes of conflict to be questioned. I have tried to show how philology itself makes such an intervention crucial, not only by the *dispositio* of the book as a whole, but by the framing of individual chapters as well. At first a quest for the authentically pagan, Germanic origins of an economic and political world power, later an attempt to avoid the resultant blindness to Christian coloring, Old English philology must now learn to renegotiate the confrontation of pagan and Christian in literary texts, as well as in the sedimented history of its own practice. Such negotiations entail a confrontation with the politics of reading, as Lee Patterson and Allen Frantzen have argued.[2] Although Lee Patterson's work focuses on the Middle English period, it has a firm grasp on the politics of medieval studies, particularly the conflict of Exegetics and New Criticism. Allen Frantzen's genealogy of Old English

---

2. Lee Patterson, *Negotiating the Past: The Historical Understanding of Medieval Literature* (Madison, 1987); Allen Frantzen and Charles L. Venegoni, "The Desire for Origins: An Archaeology of Anglo-Saxon Studies," *Style* 20 (1986): 142–56.

studies serves as a useful supplement to it. I offer the following historical sketch of my own as a background to the theoretical questioning in *Allegories of War*.

I

The historical sense dissolves the preconceptions of the present so powerfully that one need only turn to valuable work now being done in the history of Old English scholarship—on the Renaissance deployment of Aelfric in Eucharistic controversy, on the Romantic changes which made Old English studies topical, on the search for Anglo-Saxon paganism, on the politics of Anglo-Saxonism in America—to discover that each historical period comes to Old English with a different framework of understanding. A juxtaposition of Renaissance interests with those of the mid-nineteenth century demonstrates the extent to which such frameworks are also agenda, to use the word in its contemporary, extended sense. And a similar juxtaposition of Romantic and Victorian interpretive frameworks with those of the twentieth century can inform a discussion of the ideological origins of Old English studies. Dissatisfied with cultural transformations at the close of eighteenth century, Romantic poets and scholars turned their attention toward "nature" and toward the ancient roots of modern civilization. Philology itself searched the remote past for sustenance in a time of societal transformation. The research of linguists, etymologists, folklorists, and medievalists opened up dazzling new worlds, which were explored by writers like Coleridge, Scott, Tennyson, and William Morris. Painting and architecture, as well as literature and literary scholarship, were revitalized through contact with philological and historical scholarship. The literary criticism of twentieth-century medievalists like Tolkien and Lewis, which has direct links with these nineteenth-century origins, should be situated within the context of a right-wing anticapitalist ideology adopted by literary Oxbridgeans, who usually took on the values of the landed aristocracy no matter what their origins. To varying degrees, Tolkien and Lewis succeed in modifying a Romantic and Victorian eisegesis that read exotic pagan elements into Christian texts.[3] This particular strain of nineteenth-century neo-paganism, based on a misunderstanding of the relationship between the "Indo-Germanic" language family and some

---

3. If exegesis means taking meaning out, eisegesis means pumping it in.

hypothetical Aryan race that originated it—a misunderstanding attacked by eminent scholars like Max Müller—flourished alongside the pan-Germanicism and neo-Aryanism that preceded the Third Reich. Even in the United States, institutional interest in Anglo-Saxonica was often associated with the use of literature and history to stabilize a cultural tradition disrupted by immigrants from southern and central Europe, or from Ireland—the "teeming refuse" memorialized on the base of the Statue of Liberty.[4]

It is hard for us today to understand the excitement that medieval studies, now considered rather stodgy, once possessed. The critique of ethnocentrism mounted in various forms during the twentieth century has done much to dim the aura that once surrounded the study of the Middle Ages. In modern English departments, an interest in Old English is decidedly unfashionable. When Harvard abolished the Old English requirement in 1954, the field suffered a blow from which it has never fully recovered; as graduate program after graduate program followed Harvard's lead, critical defensiveness mounted. The very place allotted Old English studies within the graduate curriculum was vigorously questioned, much as if Philology's heirs couldn't make up their minds what to do with some big house they had inherited, one that would cost a great deal to maintain and even more to renovate.

Perhaps it can again be made inhabitable for those who, after all, did not build it in the first place. Some architectural history might help with the restoration. Old English scholars at the close of the twentieth century have inherited techniques and standards from a powerful philological enterprise which once commanded the attention of the educated reader, not merely the specialist. The *methode* of philological practice continued even when its *wahrheit* was opposed by those like Tolkien and Stanley, who saw the search for Anglo-Saxon paganism as a barbaric trashing of poems by Christian authors.[5] Contemporary offshoots of philological tradition have produced excellent writing and continue to extend our knowledge of texts. The work of Fred Robinson is exemplary in this regard. On the other hand, contemporary Anglo-Saxon studies

4. Reginald Horsman, *Race and Manifest Destiny: The Origins of American Racial Anglo-Saxonism* (Cambridge, Mass., 1981).

5. J. R. R. Tolkein, *"Beowulf:* The Monsters and the Critics," *Proceedings of the British Academy* 22 (1936), 5–95 remains one of the most sophisticated critical indictments of the old philological approach; see also E. G. Stanley, *The Search for Anglo-Saxon Paganism* (Cambridge, 1975).

are all too often plodding and unimaginative, extending only one's capacity for patience. As evidence for this assertion I would offer my conversations with senior scholars in the field: too many Old English studies seem to be written by novices, they say, too many seem to be papers arising out of graduate seminars. And I agree. Old English critics whose work continues to develop in richness, complexity, and interest are quite rare. Even today, there are scholars working out of the old romantic pan-Aryan premises, although they are encountered more often at medieval conferences than in the pages of scholarly journals. Historical sedimentation is not uniform, and one still finds neo-pagan exegetes, neo-Christian exegetes, and old-style New Critics plying their trade as if such work were capable of rehabilitating interest in Old English studies.

I find the work of the recent historians of Anglo-Saxon literary scholarship promising because one cannot read them without simultaneously reflecting upon one's own historically conditioned practice. It is difficult, of course, to attempt to extend reflection upon the historical situation of Old English scholarship to the present. Attempts to discover the premises molding the approach we take to Old English literature today originate in a sense of crisis rather than in general, unmotivated reflection. Those who find theoretical work urgent—whether beleaguered conservatives like Bruce Mitchell or hemmed-in liberals such as Matthew Marino—reflect upon the premises of their critical practice.[6] Those who do not share this sense of urgency usually find theory uninteresting. As Paul de Man has argued, "the notion of crisis and that of criticism are very closely linked, so much so that one could state that all true criticism occurs in the mode of crisis."[7]

II

Most Anglo-Saxonists trained in the philological tradition have developed critical competency as well. To some extent most of us are scholar-critics, although criticism itself is held suspect by the most conservative wing of the field. The impact of New Criticism in the fifties led those who would practice criticism as well as scholarship to emphasize the craftsmanship of Anglo-Saxon poets. When complexity and craftsman-

---

6. For an illustration of the problems attendant upon the introduction of theory into Anglo-Saxon studies, see Matthew Marino's debate with Bruce Mitchell in "Linguistics, Literary Criticism, and Old English," *Mediaevalia* 5 (1979): 1–14.

7. De Man, *Blindness and Insight*, 8.

ship became the key terms for evaluating literature (and therefore the place of Old English courses and seminars in the curriculum), the Anglo-Saxon literary artifact reconstituted itself. Neglected poems quickly became skillfully crafted little gems. With few exceptions, however, the strict New Criticism of Old English poetry was never practiced, because historical context has always been so important to us. As a result, no radical epistemic break occurred. Philology enlisted close reading to demonstrate the high level of craftsmanship of Old English poems in an attempt to render them worthy of attention after the perspective of English departments shifted. Although the battle over the literary worth of Anglo-Saxon poetry has been going on since the thirties, close readings did not flourish until the sixties. Old English New Criticism, however, was never characterized by a radical interest in theoretical issues, but confined itself to demonstrating artistic skill in poems that impious modernists took to be primitive and rebarbative. Neil Isaacs' *Structural Principles in Old English Poetry* attempted to apply New Criticism to Old English studies, but met with mixed success. He went too far in the direction many of his colleagues were pursuing, according to his reviewers. Nevertheless, among current critics of Old English poetry, there is a New Critical hegemony: typological scholarship is enlisted in order to demonstrate a sometimes implicit, but often explicit, critical point—the intellectual and verbal subtlety of Old English poems. Recent developments in critical theory have provoked widespread hostility, symptoms of strains on the marriage of New Critical Mercury and Old World Philology.

One of the first serious departures from such hostility to theory was Daniel Calder's plea to Anglo-Saxonists at the 1982 MLA meeting.[8] Calder's riposte to the question, "Why should Anglo-Saxonists be interested in critical theory?" was, "Why shouldn't they be?" He took the very resistance to new ideas in the field as a subject worthy of critical interrogation. Calder argued that the suspicion philologists extend toward critics threatens the survival of our field. And it is, after all, disconcerting to realize that Old and Middle English studies were once at the center of literary research, even if one is glad that the ethnocentrism boosting such work has withered away. Would it once again be possible for Old English studies to affect the mainstream of literary

---

8. Daniel Calder, "The Isolation of Old English Studies: Past, Present, and Future," paper presented at the Modern Language Association meeting, Los Angeles, 1982.

studies, as the work of Michel Foucault in seventeenth-century and eighteenth-century frameworks for understanding has captured the attention of the educated layman? Established fields always have workers, but only occasionally do insights important to humanists outside specialized fields occur. Stephen Greenblatt and the New Historicists, for example, are currently drawing the sort of attention to Renaissance studies that writers like Tolkien, Lewis, Curtius, Huizinga, and Panofsky once drew to medieval studies. Perhaps Old English studies could again have something fundamentally important to say to those outside our field.

Since the Second World War—although one can find stirrings of revolt as far back as the twenties and thirties—the movement toward the study of modern literature has entailed questions about the relevance of Old English. And, as I have argued, the abolition of the Old English requirement traumatized defenders of philological tradition. While specialists in other periods moved toward a criticism sophisticated enough to problematize its assumptions, Old English studies stayed in nineteenth-century philological backwaters as far as most English department faculty (and, *a fortiori*, graduate students) were concerned. It is odd that readers attracted to a field so different from the mainstream should have fended off difference in the criticism of texts characterized by radical alterity. Anglo-Saxonists developed defensive formations against the new metacritical discourses almost instantaneously, and Daniel Calder has spoken persuasively on the intellectual aloofness that resulted:

> . . . the theoretical and philosophical inquiries which so animate our profession at large are curiously ignored by those who pursue Anglo-Saxon studies. And I predict that this will not have a salutary effect on our discipline. Some do make sincere attempts to weld the new critical theories and skills to the "old" criticism; however, they are few in number and not welcomed by the field at large.[9]

The trope of welding that Calder employed is one that assumes that the two fields to be joined stand in a relationship of equality and independence. I would argue instead for a necessary leavening, for without some sense of the new questions about text, reader, and method that have been raised in our day, much of what continues to pass for criticism and

---

9. Daniel Calder, "The Isolation of Old English Studies."

scholarship is unleavened dough, suitable perhaps for ritual exchange in journals and conferences, but otherwise unpalatable and unnourishing.

I use this hallowed biblical and patristic metaphor to suggest that an essential transformation of Old English studies by critical theory is a desirable outcome. I hope *Allegories of War* has shown how it can add to our understanding of literature and culture, and perhaps to the number of intellectually adventurous graduate students attracted to our field. For the resistance to theory in Old English studies is in large part an epiphenomenon, the result of our frustration at graduate student flight from once required courses. Alain Renoir, for example, argues that Old English is less popular in the graduate schools because it requires "staggering" amounts of "drudgery" and "ego-shrinking discipline" at a time when "ego-boosting experiences" are available in courses in critical theory. Renoir seems to have no sense of the years of difficult negotiations with Heidegger, Husserl, Derrida, de Man, Lacan, Freud, Marx, and the Frankfurt School that are required before one develops theoretical competence, a regimen which is anything but "ego-boosting." The *Old English Newsletter* finds Renoir's contribution "perhaps the most interesting" of seventeen essays on *Beowulf* pedagogy, and calls it a "battle cry" with no sign of awareness that this is a two-edged epithet.[10] Examples of critical defensiveness can be multiplied easily if one simply jots down remarks about the solidity of philology and insubstantiality of theory that are dourly exchanged at scholarly meetings.

Few Anglo-Saxonists seem troubled that the discipline shows no traces of the best critical thought of the present. The field's New Critical response to a changing literary climate was salutary; but the continuing defense of Old English poems as worthy of the attention of intelligent readers because they are well-crafted has become drone-like. The point has been made, and its reiteration is of doubtful value. The same holds true, I think, for criticism predicated upon typological research, which all too often is enlisted to demonstrate the theological depth and artistic complexity of Old English poets. Old English poetic style and typological practice open up important questions. But instead of a vigorous critical investigation of such questions, we find the continual supplying of exegetical and stylistic evidence for someone else to think about, in

---

10. *Old English Newsletter* 19 (1985): 82; Renoir's remarks are cited by the *OEN* reviewer. The book under review, *Approaches to Teaching "Beowulf,"* ed. Jess B. Bessinger and Robert F. Yeager (New York, 1984), is published under the auspices of The Modern Language Association of America.

another time, another place: some of our more prestigious institutions seem to be teaching graduate students that after enough scholarship has been done, in some utopian future, knowledgeable criticism might occur, but that in the meantime Anglo-Saxonists mustn't rush prematurely into thought.

As an antidote to the retrenchment recommended by Bruce Mitchell, Stanley Greenfield, and Alain Renoir, I would ask Anglo-Saxon scholars to resist the powerful institutional forces of their discipline which would cast them as critical conservatives. I, too, dislike emendation except when absolutely necessary and clearly marked off. I too have had enough of the abacus principle of reading Old English cruces, especially when it yields encrypted homage to Woden. I too spend much of my energy pruning, even weeding, the early critical shoots my students send off, in order to help them develop the linguistic, historical, and methodological skills that might let their term papers become sturdy oaks. But the battle cry calling my students and colleagues to avoid the intellectual discourses of the present if they would seek to truly understand the past strikes me as defeatist and anti-intellectual. We have in Old English studies a version of the problem that preoccupied the thirteenth century, when alien, non-Christian ideas were introduced into Europe through Arabic commentaries on Greek texts. Thomas Aquinas's way of handling this "problem" had much to recommend it. His receptiveness to translations and commentaries coming from the Arab world might serve us well in our response to contemporary theory. All comparisons limp, and this one lists to the left as well. But I agree with Daniel Calder that institutionalized avoidance of contact between hallowed old and unhallowed new ways of reading will result in the continuing marginalization of Old English studies.

Allegories of War is itself a reflection on marginalization. Its attempt at making sense of the concatenation of violence and spirituality in Old English poetry springs from a deep dissatisfaction with answers I came up with over the last decade and a half. It attempts to bring theoretical tools to bear on a crucial problem in Old English poetry, one that illustrates the survival of the antique and pagan in the midst of the modern and Christian. And it has another agendum as well: the historicization of early medieval allegory.

Bibliography

Abbetmeyer, C. *Old English Poetical Motives Derived from the Doctrine of Sin.* Minneapolis, 1903.

Abraham, Lenore MacGaffey. "Cynewulf's *Juliana*: A Case at Law." *Allegorica* 3 (1978): 172–89.

Aelfric. *Aelfric's Catholic Homilies: The Second Series: Text.* Edited by Malcolm Godden. Early English Text Society, Suppl. Ser.: No.5. Oxford, 1979.

Alcuin. *Liber de Virtutibus et Vitiis. Patrologia Latina* 101:613–38.

Aldhelm. *De Octo Principalibus Vitiis. Patrologia Latina* 89:281–90.

———. *Aldhelmi Opera.* Edited by Rudolfus Ehwald. *Monumenta Germaniae Historica: Auctores Antiquissimi,* XV. Berlin, 1919.

———. *Aldhelm: The Poetic Works.* Translated by Michael Lapidge and James L. Rosier. Cambridge, 1985.

———. *Aldhelm: The Prose Works.* Translated by Michael Lapidge and Michael Herren. Cambridge, 1979.

Allen, Michael J. B. and Daniel Calder, trans. *Sources and Analogues of Old English Poetry.* Totowa, N.J., 1976.

Ambrose. *De Cain et Abel. Patrologia Latina* 14:315–60.

Ames, Ruth M. "The Old Testament Christ and the Old English *Exodus.*" *Studies in Medieval Culture* 10 (1977): 33–50.

Anderson, Earl. "Cynewulf's *Elene*: Manuscript Divisions and Structural Symmetry." *Modern Philology* 72 (1974): 111–22.

———. *Cynewulf: Structure, Style, and Theme in His Poetry.* Rutherford, N.J., 1983.

Arens, William. *The Man-Eating Myth: Anthropology and Anthropophagy.* Oxford, 1979.

Assmann, Bruno. "Übersetzung von Alcuin's De Virtutibus et Vitiis Liber. Ad Widonem Comitem." *Anglia* 11 (1889): 371–91.

———, ed. *Angelsächsische Homilien und Heiligenleben. Bibliothek der Angelsächsischen Prosa,* 3. Kassel, 1889.

[Pseudo-Augustine]. *Sermones. Patrologia Latina* 39.

Baker, Peter S. "The Old English Canon of Byrhtferth of Ramsey." *Speculum* 55 (1980): 22–37.

Bede. *De Schematibus et Tropis.* In *Rhetores Latini Minores*, edited by Karl Halm, 607–18. Leipzig, 1863.

——. *Bede's Ecclesiastical History of the English People.* Edited by B. Colgrave and R. A. B. Mynors. Oxford, 1969.

[Pseudo-Bede]. *In Pentateuchum Commentarii. Patrologia Latina* 91:189–394.

——. *Questiones super Exodum. Patrologia Latina* 93:363–88.

Bergman, J. *De Codicibus Prudentianis.* Stockholm, 1910.

Bessinger, Jess B., and Robert F. Yeager, eds. *Approaches to Teaching "Beowulf."* New York, 1984.

Bethurum, Dorothy, ed. *Critical Approaches to Medieval Literature.* New York, 1960.

Biblia Sacra iuxta Vulgatam Clementinam. Edited by R. P. Alberto Colunga and Laurentio Turrado. Madrid, 1953.

Bjork, Robert E. *The Old English Verse Saints' Lives: A Study in Direct Discourse and the Iconography of Style.* Toronto, 1985.

Blackburn, Francis A., ed. *Exodus and Daniel.* Boston, 1907.

Bleeth, Kenneth A. "*Juliana*: 647–52." *Medium Aevum* 38 (1969): 119–22.

Bloomfield, Morton W. "Patristics and Old English Literature: Notes on Some Poems." *Comparative Literature* 14 (1962): 36–43.

——. *The Seven Deadly Sins.* East Lansing, Mich., 1952.

——. "Symbolism in Medieval Literature." *Modern Philology* 56 (1958): 73–81.

Blumenkranz, Bernhard. *Les auteurs chrétiens latins du Moyen Age sur les Juifs et le Judaïsme. Études Juives,* 4. Paris, 1963.

Boenig, Robert. "*Andreas*, the Eucharist, and Vercelli." *Journal of English and Germanic Philology* 79 (1980): 313–31.

Bolton, W. F. *A History of Anglo-Latin Literature, 597–1066.* Princeton, 1967.

Bosworth, Joseph, and T. Northcote Toller. *An Anglo-Saxon Dictionary.* Oxford, 1882–98.

Bosworth, Joseph, ed. *The Gothic and Anglo-Saxon Gospels.* London, 1865.

Bréhier, Louis. *L'art chrétien.* Paris, 1918.

Brooks, Kenneth R., ed. *Andreas and the Fates of the Apostles.* Oxford, 1961.

Brown, Peter. *The Cult of the Saints: Its Rise and Function in Latin Christianity.* Chicago, 1982.

——. "The Saint as Exemplar in Late Antiquity." In *Persons in Groups: Social Behavior as Identity Formation in Medieval and Renaissance Europe,* edited by Richard C. Trexler, 183–94. Binghamton, N.Y., 1985.

Burke, Kenneth. *Language as Symbolic Action: Essays on Life, Literature, and Method.* Berkeley, 1966.

——. *Attitudes Towards History.* 3d ed. Berkeley, 1984.

Burnam, John M., ed. *Commentaire anonyme sur Prudence d'après le manuscrit 413 de Valenciennes.* Paris, 1910.

Byrhtferth's Manual. Edited by S. J. Crawford. London, 1929.

Calder, Daniel G. "Strife, Revelation, and Conversion: The Thematic Structure of *Elene.*" *English Studies* 53 (1972): 201–10.

———. "The Art of Cynewulf's *Juliana.*" *Modern Language Quarterly* 34 (1973): 355–71.

———. *Cynewulf.* Boston, 1981.

———. "The Isolation of Old English Studies: Past, Present, and Future." Paper presented at the Modern Language Association meeting, Los Angeles, 1982.

The Cambridge History of the Bible. Vol. 2: *The West from the Fathers to the Reformation.* Edited by G. W. H. Lampe. Cambridge, 1969.

Campbell, Jackson J. "Learned Rhetoric in Old English Poetry." *Modern Philology* 83 (1966): 189–201.

———. "Knowledge of Rhetorical Figures in Anglo-Saxon England." *Journal of English and Germanic Philology* 68 (1967): 1–20.

———. "Schematic Technique in *Judith.*" *ELH* 38 (1971): 155–72.

———. "Cynewulf's Multiple Revelations." *Medievalia et Humanistica* 3 (1972): 257–77.

Caspary, Gerard E. *Politics and Exegesis: Origen and the Two Swords.* Berkeley, 1979.

Cassian. *Iohannis Cassiani Conlationes XXIIII.* Edited by Michael Petschenig. *Corpus Scriptorum Ecclesiasticorum Latinorum,* 13. Vienna, 1886.

Casteen, John. "*Andreas*: Mermedonian Cannibalism and Figural Narration." *Neuphilologische Mitteilungen* 75 (1974): 74–78.

Chamberlain, David. "*Judith*: A Fragmentary and Political Poem." In *Anglo-Saxon Poetry: Essays in Appreciation,* edited by Lewis E. Nicholson and Dolores Warwick Frese, 135–59. Notre Dame, Ind., 1975.

Chance, Jane. *Woman as Hero in Old English Literature.* Syracuse, 1986.

Cixous, Hélène. "Castration or Decapitation?" Translated by Annette Kuhn. *Signs* 7 (1981): 41–55.

Cohn, Norman. *The Pursuit of the Millennium: Revolutionary Millenarians and Mystical Anarchists of the Middle Ages.* New York, 1970.

Cook, A. S., ed. *Judith.* Boston, 1889.

Crawford, S. J. "Byrhtferth of Ramsey and the Anonymous Life of St. Oswald." In *Speculum Religionis, Being Essays and Studies in Religion and Literature from Plato to Von Hügel,* Presented by the Members of the Staff of University College, Southampton, to Their President, Claude G. Montefiore, 99–111. Oxford, 1929.

Cross, J. E. "The Ethic of War in Old English." *England Before the Conquest: Studies in Primary Sources Presented to Dorothy Whitelock,* edited by Peter Clemoes and Kathleen Hughes, 269–82. Cambridge, 1971.

———, and S. I. Tucker. "Allegorical Tradition and the Old English *Exodus.*" *Neophilologus* 44 (1960): 122–27.

Cunningham, Maurice P. "The Problem of Interpolation in the Textual Tradition of Prudentius." *Transactions and Proceedings of the American Philological Association* 99 (1968): 119–41.

———. "Prudentius." *New Catholic Encyclopedia,* 1967.

Curtius, E. R. *European Literature and the Latin Middle Ages.* Translated by W. R. Trask. Princeton, N.J., 1953.

Cynewulf. *Cynewulfs Elene*, 4th ed. Edited by F. Holthausen. Heidelberg, 1936.

Cyprian. *De mortalitate. Patrologia Latina* 4:581–602.

Daniélou, Jean. *The Bible and the Liturgy*. Notre Dame, Ind., 1961.

Damico, Helen. "The Valkyrie Reflex in Old English Literature." *Allegorica* 5 (1980): 149–67.

Davis, William Stearns. *Life on a Mediaeval Barony*. New York, 1923.

Deferarri, Roy Joseph, and James Marshall Campbell. *A Concordance of Prudentius*. Cambridge, Mass., 1932.

Dekkers, Eligius, and Aemilius Gaar, eds. *Clavis Patrum Latinorum*. Steenbergen, 1961.

de Man, Paul. *Blindness and Insight: Essays in the Rhetoric of Contemporary Criticism*. 2d ed., rev. Minneapolis, 1983.

———. *The Resistance to Theory*. Minneapolis, 1986.

Derrida, Jacques. "The Retrait of Metaphor." *Enclitic* 2 (1978): 14–23.

———. "Différance." *Margins of Philosophy*. Translated by Alan Bass, pp. 3–27. Chicago, 1982.

———. "White Mythology: Metaphor in the Text of Philosophy." *Margins of Philosophy*, pp. 207–71. Chicago, 1982.

———. *Positions*. Translated by Alan Bass. Chicago, 1981.

Dietrich, [Franz]. "Zu Cädmon." *Zeitschrift für deutsches Alterthum* 10 (1856): 310–67.

Dölger, Franz. *Der Exorzismus im altchristlichen Taufritual: Eine religiongeschichtliche Studie. Studien zur Geschichte und Kultur des Altertums*, 3, Pts. 1 and 2. Paderborn, 1909.

Doubleday, James F. "The Allegory of the Soul as Fortress in Old English Poetry." *Anglia* 88 (1970): 503–8.

———, and Carl T. Berkhout. "The Net in *Judith* 46b–54a." *Neuphilologische Mitteilungen* 74 (1973): 630–34.

Dracontius. *De Laudibus Dei*. Edited by F. Vollmer. *Monumenta Germaniae Historica, Auctores Antiquissimi*, 14. Berlin, 1905.

Du Cange, Charles Du Fresne. *Glossarium Mediae et Infimae Latinitatis*. 10 vols. Niort, 1883–87.

Earl, James W. "Christian Tradition in the Old English *Exodus*." *Neuphilologische Mitteilungen* 71 (1970): 541–70.

———. "Typology and Iconographic Style in Early Medieval Hagiography." *Studies in the Literary Imagination* 8 (1975): 15–46.

———. "The Typological Structure of *Andreas*." In *Old English Literature in Context: Ten Essays*, edited by J. D. Niles, 66–89. Cambridge, 1980.

Ehrismann, G. "Religionsgeschichtliche Beiträge zum germanischen Frühchristentum." *Beiträge zur Geschichte der deutschen Sprache und Literatur* 35 (1909): 209–39.

Ferguson, Paul F. "Noah, Abraham, and the Crossing of the Red Sea." *Neophilologus* 65 (1981): 282–87.

Fish, Stanley. "Pragmatism and Literary Theory I: Consequences." *Critical Inquiry* 11 (1985): 433–58.

Fletcher, Angus. *Allegory: The Theory of a Symbolic Mode.* Ithaca, N.Y., 1964.

Förster, M., ed. "Über die Quellen von Aelfrics Homiliae Catholicae." *Anglia* 16 (1894): 1–61.

———. *Die Vercelli-Homilien. Bibliothek der angelsächsischen Prosa,* 12. Hamburg, 1932.

Foster, T. Gregory. *Judith: Studies in Metre, Language and Style. Quellen und Forschungen,* 71. Strassburg, 1892.

Foucault, Michel. *Madness and Civilization: A History of Insanity in the Age of Reason.* Translated by Richard Howard. New York, 1973.

———. *Discipline and Punish: The Birth of the Prison.* Translated by Alan Sheridan. New York, 1979.

———. *A History of Sexuality.* Vol. I: *An Introduction.* Translated by Robert Hurley. New York, 1980.

Frank, R. W. "The Art of Reading Medieval Personification Allegory." *ELH* 20 (1953): 237–50.

Frantzen, Allen. *The Literature of Penance in Anglo-Saxon England.* New Brunswick, N.J., 1983.

———, and Charles L. Venegoni. "The Desire for Origins: An Archaeology of Anglo-Saxon Studies." *Style* 20 (1986): 142–56.

Freud, Sigmund. "Leonardo da Vinci and a Memory of His Childhood." In *The Standard Edition of the Complete Psychological Works of Sigmund Freud,* 11, translated by Alan Tyson, 59–137. London, 1957.

———. "Medusa's Head." In *The Standard Edition of the Complete Psychological Works of Sigmund Freud,* 18, translated by James Strachey, 273–74. London, 1955.

———. "The Taboo of Virginity." In *The Standard Edition of the Complete Psychological Works of Sigmund Freud,* 11, translated by Angela Richards, 191–208. London, 1957.

Fulgentius. *Epistolae. Patrologia Latina* 65:303–498.

Gaudentius. *Sermones. Patrologia Latina* 20:843–1002.

Glunz, H. H. *History of the Vulgate in England from Alcuin to Roger Bacon.* Cambridge, 1933.

Goldsmith, Margaret E. *The Mode and Meaning of "Beowulf."* London, 1970.

Gradon, P. E. O., ed. *Cynewulf's Elene.* London, 1958.

Green, William M. *Initium Omnis Peccati Superbia: Augustine on Pride as the First Sin. University of California Publications in Classical Philology,* 13. Berkeley, 1949.

Greenfield, Stanley. *A Critical History of Old English Literature.* London, 1966.

———. *The Interpretation of Old English Poems.* London, 1972.

Gregory the Great. *Epistolae. Patrologia Latina* 77:431–1327.

———. *Moralia in Job. Patrologia Latina* 75:509–1162; 76:9–782.

Hall, J. R. "Pauline Influence on *Exodus,* 523–48." *English Language Notes* 15 (1977): 84–88.

Hamilton, David. "The Diet and Digestion of Allegory in *Andreas.*" *Anglo-Saxon England* 1 (1972): 147–58.

Harms, Wolfgang. *Homo Viator in Bivio: Studien zur Bildlichkeit des Weges*. Munich, 1970.

Hauer, Stanley R. "The Patriarchal Digression in the Old English *Exodus*, Lines 362–446." In *Eight Anglo-Saxon Studies*, edited by Joseph S. Wittig, 77–90. Chapel Hill, 1981.

——. "Thomas Jefferson and the Anglo-Saxon Language." *Publications of the Modern Language Association* 98 (1983): 879–98.

Hermann, John P. "The Theme of Spiritual Warfare in the Old English *Elene*." *Papers on Language and Literature* 11 (1975): 115–25.

——. "The Green Rod of Moses in the Old English *Exodus*." *English Language Notes* 12 (1975): 241–43.

——. "*The Riming Poem*, 45b to 47a." *Explicator* 34 (1975): 7–9.

——. "The Pater Noster Battle Sequence in *Solomon and Saturn* and the *Psychomachia* of Prudentius." *Neuphilologische Mitteilungen* 77 (1976): 206–10.

——. "The Selection of Warriors in the Old English *Exodus*, Lines 233–240a." *English Language Notes* 14 (1976): 1–5.

——. "The Theme of Spiritual Warfare in the Old English *Judith*." *Philological Quarterly* 55 (1976): 1–9.

——. "*Solomon and Saturn II*, 339a: *niehtes wunde*." *English Language Notes* 14 (1977): 161–64.

——. "*Psychomachia* 423–26 and *Aeneid* 5. 468–70." *Classical Bulletin* 54 (1978): 88–89.

——. "*The Dream of the Rood*, 19a: *earmra ærgewin*." *English Language Notes* 15 (1978): 241–44.

——. "The Recurrent Motifs of Spiritual Warfare in Old English Poetry." *Annuale Mediaevale* 22 (1982): 7–35.

——. "Some Varieties of Psychomachia in Old English." *American Benedictine Review* 34 (1983): pt. 1, 74–86; pt. 2, 188–222.

——. "Language and Spirituality in Cynewulf's *Juliana*." *Texas Studies in Literature and Language* 26 (1984): 263–81.

——. Review of *Cynewulf: Structure, Style, and Theme in His Poetry*, by Earl R. Anderson. *Journal of English and Germanic Philology* 85 (1985): 249–52.

Hertz, Neil. *The End of the Line: Essays on Psychoanalysis and the Sublime*. New York, 1985.

Hieatt, Constance B. "The Harrowing of Mermedonia: Typological Patterns in the Old English *Andreas*." *Neuphilologische Mitteilungen* 77 (1976): 49–62.

Hill, Joyce. "The Soldier of Christ in Old English Prose and Poetry." *Leeds Studies in English* 12 (1981): 57–80.

Hill, Thomas D. "The Tropological Context of Heat and Cold Imagery in Anglo-Saxon Poetry." *Neuphilologische Mitteilungen* 69 (1968): 522–32.

——. "Figural Narrative in *Andreas*: The Conversion of the Mermedonians." *Neuphilologische Mitteilungen* 70 (1969): 261–73.

——. "Sapiential Structure and Figural Narrative in the Old English *Elene*." *Traditio* 27 (1971): 159–77.

————. "Two Notes on *Solomon and Saturn.*" *Medium Aevum* 40 (1971): 218–21.

————. "Hebrews, Israelites, and Wicked Jews: An Onomastic Crux in *Andreas.*" *Traditio* 32 (1976): 361–67.

————. "The *virga* of Moses and the Old English *Exodus.*" In *Old English Literature in Context: Ten Essays*, edited by J. D. Niles, 57–65 and 165–67. Cambridge, 1980.

Holder, Alfred, ed. *Inventio Sanctae Crucis.* Leipzig, 1889.

Holthausen, F. "Die Quelle von Cynewulfs Elene." *Zeitschrift für deutsche Philologie* 37 (1905): 1–19.

————. "Zur Quelle von Cynewulfs Elene." *Archiv für das Studium der neueren Sprachen* 125 (1910): 83–88.

Horsman, Reginald. *Race and Manifest Destiny: The Origins of American Racial Anglo-Saxonism.* Cambridge, Mass., 1981.

Hume, Kathryn. "The Concept of the Hall in Old English Poetry." *Anglo-Saxon England* 3 (1974): 63–74.

Huppé, Bernard F. *Doctrine and Poetry: Augustine's Influence on Old English Poetry.* Albany, 1959.

————. *The Web of Words: Structural Analyses of the Old English Poems Vainglory, The Wonder of Creation, The Dream of the Rood, and Judith.* Albany, 1970.

Irvine, Martin. "Cynewulf's Use of Psychomachia Allegory: The Latin Sources of Some 'Interpolated' Passages." In *Allegory, Myth, and Symbol*, edited by Morton W. Bloomfield, 39–62. Cambridge, Mass., 1981.

Irving, Edward B., ed. *The Old English Exodus. Yale Studies in English*, 122. New Haven, 1953.

————. "New Notes on the Old English *Exodus.*" *Anglia* 90 (1972): 289–324.

Isaacs, Neil D. *Structural Principles in Old English Poetry.* Knoxville, 1968.

Isidore of Seville. *Allegoriae Quaedam Sacrae Scripturae. Patrologia Latina* 83:99–130.

————. *De Ortu et Obitu Patrum. Patrologia Latina* 83:129–56.

————. *Questiones in Vetus Testamentum. Patrologia Latina* 83:207–424.

Jameson, Frederic. *The Political Unconscious: Narrative as a Socially Symbolic Act.* Ithaca, 1981.

Jauss, Hans Robert. "Form und Auffassung der Allegorie in der Tradition der *Psychomachia* (von Prudentius zum ersten *Romanz de la Rose*)." In *Medium Aevum Vivum: Festschrift für Walther Bulst*, edited by Hans Robert Jauss and D. Schaller, 179–206. Heidelberg, 1960.

Jerome. *Epistolae. Patrologia Latina* 22:325–1224.

————. *Praefatio in Librum Judith. Patrologia Latina* 29:37–40.

Johnson, Barbara. *The Critical Difference: Essays in the Contemporary Rhetoric of Reading.* Baltimore, 1981.

Kaske, R. E. "Sapientia et Fortitudo as the Controlling Theme of *Beowulf.*" *Studies in Philology* 55 (1958): 423–56.

————. "A Poem of the Cross in the Exeter Book." *Traditio* 23 (1969): 41–71.

Katzenellenbogen, Adolf. *Allegories of the Virtues and Vices in Mediaeval Art.* New York, 1964,

Keiser, Albert. *The Influence of Christianity on the Vocabulary of Old English Poetry. Illinois Studies in Language and Literature*, 5, nos. 1 and 2. Urbana, 1919.

Keenan, Hugh T. "*Exodus* 312: The Green Street of Paradise." *Neuphilologische Mitteilungen* 71 (1970): 455–60.

———. "*Exodus* 312a: Further Notes on the Eschatological 'Green Ground.'" *Neuphilologische Mitteilungen* 74 (1973): 217–19.

Ker, N. R. *Catalogue of Manuscripts Containing Anglo-Saxon.* Oxford, 1957.

Klaeber, Fr. "Die christlichen Elemente im Beowulf." *Anglia* 35 (1911): 111–36, 249–70, 453–82; 36 (1912): 169–99.

Krapp, George P., and Elliott van Kirk Dobbie, eds. *The Anglo-Saxon Poetic Records: A Collective Edition.* 6 vols. New York, 1931–53.

Lacan, Jacques. *Écrits: A Selection.* Translated by Alan Sheridan. New York, 1977.

Laistner, M. L. W. *Thought and Letters in Western Europe A.D. 500 to 900.* New York, 1931. 2d ed. Ithaca, N.Y., 1966.

Lapide, Cornelius à. *Commentarius in Apocalypsin S. Joannis Apostoli.* 2d ed. Venice, 1717.

Lapidge, Michael. "The Hermeneutic Style in Tenth-Century Anglo-Latin Literature." *Anglo-Saxon England* 4 (1975): 67–111.

Laplanche, J., and J.-B. Pontalis. *The Language of Psychoanalysis.* Translated by Donald Nicholson-Smith. New York, 1973.

Lee, Alvin A. *The Guest-Hall of Eden.* New Haven, 1972.

Lemaire, Anika. *Jacques Lacan.* Translated by David Macey. London, 1977.

Leupin, Alexandre. "The Middle Ages, the Other." Translated by Frances Bartkowski. *Diacritics* 13 (1983): 22–31.

Levison, Wilhelm. *England and the Continent in the Eighth Century.* Oxford, 1946.

Llewelyn, John. *Derrida on the Threshold of Sense.* London, 1986.

Lubac, Henri de. *Exégèse médiévale: Les quatres sens de l' Ecriture.* 2 vols. Paris, 1958.

Lucas, Peter J., ed. *Exodus.* London, 1977.

———. "The Cloud in the Interpretation of the Old English *Exodus.*" *English Studies* 51 (1970): 297–311.

Luria, Maxwell. "Why Moses' Rod Is Green." *English Language Notes* 17 (1980): 161–63.

Mackie, W. S. "The Old English Rhymed Poem." *Journal of English and Germanic Philology* 21 (1922): 507–19.

McNally, Robert E. *The Bible in the Early Middle Ages.* Westminster, Md., 1959.

Macrae-Gibson, O. D., ed. *The Old English Riming Poem.* Cambridge, 1983.

Mahoney, Albertus. *Vergil in the Works of Prudentius.* Washington, 1934.

Mâle, Emile. *L'art religieux du XIIIe siècle en France.* Paris, 1910.

Manitius, Max. *Geschichte der Lateinischen Literatur des Mittelalters*. In *Handbuch der klassischen Altertumswissenschaft*, edited by Iwan von Müller. vol. 9, pt. 2, nos. 1–3. Munich, 1911–31.

Marcus, Jacob R. *The Jew in the Medieval World*. New York, 1938; reprint Westport, Conn., 1975.

Marino, Matthew. "Linguistics, Literary Criticism, and Old English." *Medievalia* 5 (1979): 1–14.

Menner, Robert J., ed. *The Poetical Dialogues of Solomon and Saturn*. New York, 1941.

Migne, J. P., ed. *Patrologiae Cursus Completus. Series Latina*. 221 vols. Paris, 1844–90.

Morrell, M. C. *A Manual of Old English Biblical Materials*. Knoxville, Tenn., 1965.

Morrison, Stephen. "OE *Cempa* in Cynewulf's *Juliana* and the Figure of the *Miles Christi*." *English Language Notes* 17 (1979): 81–84.

Muller, John P., and William J. Richardson. *Lacan and Language: A Reader's Guide to Écrits*. New York, 1982.

Nietzsche, Friedrich. *The Use and Abuse of History*. 2d ed. Translated by Adrian Collins. New York, 1949.

Niles, John D., ed. *Old English Literature in Context: Ten Essays*. Cambridge, 1980.

Ogilvy, J. D. A. *Books Known to the English, 597–1066*. Cambridge, Mass., 1967.

Olsen, Alexandra Hennessey. "Inversion and Political Purpose in the Old English *Judith*." *English Studies* 63 (1982): 289–93.

Palmer, R. Barton. "Characterization in the Old English *Juliana*." *South Atlantic Bulletin* 41 (1976): 10–21.

Parkes, James. *The Conflict of the Church and the Synagogue: A Study in the Origins of Antisemitism*. London, 1934.

Patterson, Lee. *Negotiating the Past: The Historical Understanding of Medieval Literature*. Madison, 1987.

Pepin, Jean. *Mythe et Allégorie*. Paris, 1958.

Pertz, Georgius Heinricus, ed. *Monumenta Germaniae Historica: Scriptores*, 6. Hanover, 1844.

Peters, Leonard J. "The Relationship of the Old English *Andreas* to *Beowulf*." *Publications of the Modern Language Association* 66 (1951): 844–63.

Primasius of Hadrumentum. *In Epistolum ad Hebraeos Commentaria. Patrologia Latina* 68:685–794.

Prudentius Clemens, Aurelius. *Aurelii Prudentii Clementis Carmina*. Edited by Ioannes Bergman. *Corpus Scriptorum Ecclesiasticorum Latinorum* 61. Vienna, 1926.

―――. *Aurelii Prudentii Clementis Carmina*. Edited by Maurice P. Cunningham. *Corpus Christianorum, Series Latina* 126. Turnhout, 1966.

―――. *Psychomachie. Contra Symmaque*. Edited and translated by Maurice Lavarenne. Paris, 1948.

———. *Prudentius*. Edited and translated by H. J. Thomson. 2 vols. Cambridge, Mass., 1949.

Rabanus Maurus. *Commentarium in Exodum*. *Patrologia Latina* 108:9–246.

———. *Enarrationum in Librum Numerorum*. *Patrologia Latina* 108:587–838.

———. *Expositio in Librum Judith*. *Patrologia Latina* 109:539–92.

Raby, F. J. E. *A History of Christian-Latin Poetry from the Beginnings to the Close of the Middle Ages*. 2d ed. Oxford, 1953.

Raffel, Burton. *"Judith*: Hypermetricity and Rhetoric." In *Anglo-Saxon Poetry: Essays in Appreciation for John C. McGalliard*, edited by Lewis Nicholson and Dolores Warwick Frese, 124–34. Notre Dame, Ind., 1975.

Rahner, Hugo. *Griechische Mythen in christlicher Deutung*. Zurich, 1957.

Raine, James, ed. *The Historians of the Church of York and Its Archbishops*. *Rerum Britannicarum Medii Aevi Scriptores*, 71, Pts. 1–3. London, 1879–94.

Ramsey, Lee C. "The Sea Voyages in *Beowulf*." *Neuphilologische Mitteilungen* 72 (1971): 51–59.

Rankin, James Walter. "A Study of the Kennings in Anglo-Saxon Poetry." *Journal of English and Germanic Philology* 8 (1909): 357–422; 9 (1910): 49–84.

Regan, Catharine A. "Patristic Psychology in the Old English *Vainglory*." *Traditio* 26 (1970): 324–35.

———. "Evangelicalism as the Informing Principle of Cynewulf's *Elene*." *Traditio* 29 (1973): 27–52.

Rivière, J. "Muscipula diaboli. Orìgine et sens d'une image augustinienne." *Recherches de Théologie Ancienne et Médiévale* 1 (1929): 484–96.

Robertson, D. W. *Chaucer's London*. New York, 1968.

Robinson, Fred C. "The Significance of Names in Old English Literature." *Anglia* 86 (1968): 14–58.

———. "Anglo-Saxon Onomastics in the Old English *Andreas*." *Names* 21 (1973): 133–36.

———. *Beowulf and the Appositive Style*. Knoxville, 1985.

Rollinson, Philip. "Some Kinds of Meaning in Old English Poetry." *Annuale Mediaevale* 11 (1970): 5–21.

Rosenthal, Elisabeth. "Myth of the Man-Eaters." *Science Digest* 91 (April, 1983): 10–14.

Sabatier, Pierre, ed. *Bibliorum Sacrorum Latinae Versiones Antiquae*. 3 vols. Paris, 1775.

Saint-Jacques, Raymond C. "The Cosmic Dimensions of Cynewulf's *Juliana*." *Neophilologus* 64 (1980): 134–39.

Schaar, Claes. *Critical Studies in the Cynewulf Group*. Lund Studies in English, 17. Lund, 1949.

Schneider, Claude. "Cynewulf's Devaluation of Heroic Tradition in *Juliana*." *Anglo-Saxon England* 7 (1978): 107–18.

Schwen, Christian. *Vergil bei Prudentius*. Bern, 1937.

Seiferth, Wolfgang S. *Synagoge und Kirche im Mittelalter*. Munich, 1964.

Sisam, Kenneth. *Studies in the History of Old English Literature*. Oxford, 1953.

Skemp, Arthur R. "The Transformation of Scriptural Story, Motive and Conception in Anglo-Saxon Poetry." *Modern Philology* 4 (1907): 423–70.

Smalley, Beryl. *The Study of the Bible in the Middle Ages.* Oxford, 1952.

Smith, Macklin. *Prudentius' Psychomachia: A Reexamination.* Princeton, 1976.

Smithers, G.V. "The Meaning of *The Seafarer* and *The Wanderer.*" *Medium Aevum* 26 (1957): 145–53.

Spicq, C. *Esquisse d'une histoire de l' exégèse latine au Moyen Âge. Bibliotheque Thomiste,* vol. 26. Paris, 1944.

Stanley, E. G. "Old English Poetic Diction and the Interpretation of *The Wanderer, The Seafarer* and *The Penitent's Prayer.*" *Anglia* 73 (1956): 413–66.

———. *The Search for Anglo-Saxon Paganism.* Cambridge, 1975.

Stegmüller, F. *Repertorium Biblicum Medii Aevi.* 11 vols. Madrid, 1940–80.

Stettiner, Richard. *Die illustrierten Prudentius-Handschriften.* Berlin, 1895. *Tafelband.* Berlin, 1905.

Stevens, William O. *The Cross in the Life and Literature of the Anglo-Saxons.* New York, 1904.

Strunk, William, ed. *The Juliana of Cynewulf.* Boston, 1904.

Tanenhaus, Gussie Hecht. "Bede's *De Schematibus et Tropis*—A Translation." *Quarterly Journal of Speech* 48 (1962): 237–53.

Thomson, H.J. "The *Psychomachia* of Prudentius." *Classical Review* 44 (1930): 109–112.

Timmer, B. J., ed. *Judith.* 2d ed. London, 1961.

Tischendorf, Constantine von, ed. *Evangelia Apocrypha.* 2d ed. Leipzig, 1876.

Tolkien, J. R. R. "*Beowulf*: The Monsters and the Critics." *Proceedings of the British Academy* 22 (1936), 245–95. Reprinted in *An Anthology of Beowulf Criticism,* edited by Lewis E. Nicholson, 51–103. Notre Dame, Ind., 1963.

Trautmann, Moritz. "Berichtigungen, Erklärungen und Vermutungen zu Cynewulfs Werken." *Bonner Beiträge zur Anglistik* 23 (1907): 85–146.

Trexler, Richard C., ed. *Persons in Groups: Social Behavior as Identity Formation in Medieval and Renaissance Europe.* Binghamton, N.Y., 1985.

Vest, Eugene Bartlett. *Prudentius in the Middle Ages.* Ph.D. diss., Harvard University, 1932.

Vickrey, John F. "*Exodus* and the Battle in the Sea." *Traditio* 28 (1972): 119–40.

Walsh, Marie Michelle. "The Baptismal Flood in the Old English *Andreas*: Liturgical and Typological Depths." *Traditio* 33 (1977): 132–58.

Walther, Hans. *Das Streitgedicht in der lateinischen Literatur des Mittelalters.* Munich, 1914. (Rev. ed. in *Quellen und Untersuchungen zur Lateinisischen Philologie des Mittelalters.* vol. 5, Pt. 2. Munich, 1920.)

Weber, Samuel. *The Legend of Freud.* Minneapolis, 1982.

Wentersdorf, Karl. "The Old English *Rhyming Poem*: A Ruler's Lament." *Studies in Philology* 82 (1985): 265–94.

White, Hayden. *Metahistory: The Historical Imagination in Nineteenth-Century Europe.* Baltimore, 1973.

Wieland, Gernot R. "Aldhelm's *De Octo Vitiis Principalibus* and Prudentius' *Psychomachia.*" *Medium Aevum* 55 (1986): 85–92.

————. "The Anglo-Saxon Manuscripts of Prudentius's *Psychomachia.*" *Anglo-Saxon England* 16 (1987): 213–31.

Willard, Rudolph. *Two Apocrypha in Old English Homilies. Beiträge zur englischen Philologie*, 30. Leipzig, 1935.

Williams, Arnold. "Medieval Allegory: An Operational Approach." *Poetic Theory, Poetic Practice: Papers of the Midwest Modern Language Association*, 1. Iowa City, 1969.

Wittig, Joseph. "Figural Narrative in Cynewulf's *Juliana.*" *Anglo-Saxon England* 4 (1975): 37–55.

Woodruff, Helen. *The Illustrated Manuscripts of Prudentius*. Cambridge, Mass., 1930.

Woolf, Rosemary. "The Devil in Old English Poetry." *Review of English Studies* 4 (1953): 1–12.

————. "The Lost Opening to the *Judith.*" *Modern Language Review* 50 (1955): 168–72.

————, ed. *Juliana*. London, 1955.

————. "Saints' Lives." In *Continuations and Beginnings: Studies in Old English Literature*, edited by E. G. Stanley, 34–66. London, 1966.

Wrenn, C. L. *A Study of Old English Literature*. London, 1967.

Zellinger, Johannes. "Der geköderte Leviathan im Hortus deliciarum der Herrad von Landsperg." *Historisches Jahrbuch* 45 (1925): 161–77.

Zeno. *Tractatus. Patrologia Latina* 11:253–528.

Index